THE NET OF NEMESIS

Studies in Tragic Bond/age

August Nigro

Selinsgrove: Susquehanna University Press
London: Associated University Presses

© 2000 by Associated University Presses, Inc.

All rights reserved. Authorization to photocopy items for internal or personal use, or the internal or personal use of specific clients, is granted by the copyright owner, provided that a base fee of $10.00, plus eight cents per page, per copy is paid directly to the Copyright Clearance Center, 222 Rosewood Drive, Danvers, Massachusetts 01923. [1–57591–036–5/00 $10.00 + 8¢ pp, pc.]

Associated University Presses
440 Forsgate Drive
Cranbury, NJ 08512

Associated University Presses
16 Barter Street
London WC1A 2AH, England

Associated University Presses
P.O. Box 338, Port Credit
Mississauga, Ontario
Canada L5G 4L8

The paper used in this publication meets the requirements of the American National Standard for Permanence of Paper for Printed Library Materials Z39.48–1984.

Library of Congress Cataloging-in-Publication Data

Nigro, August J., 1934–
    The net of nemesis : studies in tragic bond/age / August Nigro.
       p. cm.
    Includes bibliographical references and index.
    ISBN 1–57591–036–5 (alk. paper)
    1. English literature—History and criticism. 2. Tragic, The, in literature. 3. American fiction—History and criticism. 4. English literature—Greek influences. 5. American fiction—Greek influences. I. Title.

PR408.T72 N54 2000
820.9'162—dc21

99–054287

PRINTED IN THE UNITED STATES OF AMERICA

for Amy, Augie, and Jonathan

Contents

1. The Nature of Tragic Bond/age — 11
2. In Greek Tragedy — 25
3. In *Hamlet* — 42
4. In *King Lear* — 55
5. In *Macbeth* — 64
6. In *Paradise Lost* — 73
7. In *The Scarlet Letter* — 83
8. In *Moby Dick* — 91
9. In *The Mayor of Casterbridge* — 101
10. In *Tess of the d'Urbervilles* — 111
11. In *The Portrait of a Lady* — 121
12. In *Heart of Darkness* — 132
13. In *Absalom, Absalom!* — 141
14. The Tragedy of Bond/age — 154

Notes — 173
Bibliography — 181
Index — 187

1
The Nature of Tragic Bond/age

In the *Poetics,* Aristotle refers to the denouement of tragedy as the unraveling of the plot and suggests that some dramatists know well how to tie the knot or develop the exposition and conflict but do not know as well how to untie the knot or develop the denouement.[1] For Aristotle, then, the development of plot is a kind of Penelopean weaving and unweaving of the figure in the tragic carpet. In *The Harvest of Tragedy*, Thomas Henn reappropriates Aristotle's metaphor and describes the two basic plots of tragedy in terms of weaving or net imagery.[2] The first net is the seine, one end of which is connected to the shore and the other end of which is connected to a boat that swings out on the water and makes a horseshoe turn. As the boat is brought closer to the shore, the fish are caught in the narrowing and enveloping net purse. The seine net then is evocative of that outer force of fate or necessity that envelopes the fish/hero in its engulfing arms.

The other snare is the trammel, consisting of three nets, an inner one like the seine, the interstices of which are relatively large or spacious, and two outer, finer ones, the interstices of which are much smaller. According to Henn, in some tragedies the hero contributes significantly to his entrapment by seeking to escape the trammel; he does so by swimming into the fine net and through an opening in the larger net, thereby creating the purse that ensnares him. Thus, the two nets, the seine and the trammel, are images for the two kinds of plots of tragedy: the seine, the image of that tragedy in which the hero is primarily the victim of some external power, and the trammel, the image of that preferred tragedy in which the hero contributes ironically and significantly to his entrapment by his own willed efforts to escape the net of fate.

Aristotle's use of raveling to suggest the form of plot and Henn's use of the woven net to symbolize the entrapping nature of plot explicitly comment on the structure of tragedy and implicitly suggest something about its substance or theme. What it implies has been explained in some detail by Mircea Eliade in his examination of religious symbolism in a chapter entitled "The 'God who Binds' and the Symbolism of Knots." According to Eliade, the recurrence in Eastern as well as Western mythology of the symbol of binding is "that in the Cosmos as well as in human life, everything is connected with everything else in an invisible web; and secondly, that certain divinities are the mistresses of these 'threads,' which constitute, ultimately, vast cosmic 'bondage.'"[3]

Although, in the above summation, Eliade emphasizes that it is the goddesses who are the mistresses of bondage rather than the gods who are the masters, he cites more examples of gods than of goddesses as the manipulators of the threads that ensnare humanity. He points out that Varuna is the god who binds and that his name is a derivative of the Indo-European *uer* (to bind) and *weru* (to thread or embroider). He adds that the Thracian god Darzales derives his name from *darezeit* (to bind) and *darez* (cord or snare) and that the god Odin is often referred to with the epithet, "god of rope."[4] Although he does not provide as many examples of goddesses as he does of gods who bind humanity, Eliade still concludes that it is "mistresses" who control the threads of cosmic bondage.

The latter concept is nowhere more evident than in Greek mythology. Themis, who originates as an earth goddess, an alma mater, and may very well predate Zeus, becomes the second wife of Zeus, and from their union spring two sets of triplets, the Horae and Moirae. Themis herself is associated with the bonds of marriage, family, and society. The Horae, or hours, are associated with the hours or seasons and thereby order in the natural cycle; Dike in particular, like her mother, is associated with justice and is said to sit by Zeus, informing him of and righting all breaks in the natural and social orders. The Moirae or fates are Clotho, she who spins the thread of life, Lachesis, she who measures or directs it, and Atropos, she who severs the irreversible thread.

When humanity—feeling that the orders imposed upon it by nature, society, and fate are a form of bondage—breaks the natural or fatalistic bond, it is Nemesis and the Erinyes who furiously avenge the gods and restore order. Nemesis or Adrasteia (she whom none can escape) is the daughter of night and is often depicted with bridle or yoke. Daughters of the earth goddess Gaia and sprung from the blood of the mutilated Uranus, Allecto (she who rests not), Tisiphone (avenger of murder), and Megaera (the jealous one) are the Erinyes or Furies, who punish violations against filial duty, claims of kinship, and rites of hospitality. In some instances, their revenge is imagistically depicted as a form of thread-like bondage; thus, the Erinyes punish Pirithous, companion of Theseus, by binding him upon a rock in Hades.

That the gods use their power to snare not only human beings but fellow gods as well is demonstrated incisively by Marcel Detienne and Jean-Pierre Vernant in their study of intelligence in Greek culture, in which they explain that one of the primary manifestations in Greek mythology of *metis*, or cunning intelligence, is the bond and the circle. One example of such *metis* is the delicate, light, but inescapable chained net that Hephaestus forges and suspends from the ceiling in a circle around Aphrodite's bed, into which the goddess invites Ares and in which the couple are caught and exhibited to the delight of the other gods on Mount Olympus. Detienne and Vernant point out that the forger's catch is not so much the god of war, but rather the goddess of love, who also hunts down and traps—in her own nets—victims of excessive passion. After citing two more examples of the circular net that binds, those used in hunting and fishing, during which the prey is pushed toward the center to be killed, the authors make this observation about the ironic appropriateness of the net as the instrument of bondage: "The net is a composition of woven or plaited lines and its structure marks it out as the epitome of the bond for it is both bound together and, at the same time, its effect is to bind. It is therefore fully qualified to be called *a-peiron,* without limit, and circular."[5]

The ironic capacity of the circular net is also evident in a different way in the myth of Hephaestus's trap. Hermes, looking on and responding to a taunt by Apollo, says, "Though the bonds that kept me prisoner were three times as many . . . yet would I gladly sleep by golden Aphrodite's side." Detienne and Vernant conclude that Hephaestus's bonds are so compelling that "only a god with the power of binding could possibly wish to be bound by them." They further develop the notion that a circular bond could be both forbidding and enticing by analyzing the Greek word, *peirar*: "Here we find one particular type of path which takes the form of a bond which fetters, and, conversely, the action of binding is sometimes presented as a crossing, a way forward."[6] That the force that binds can be one that connects is also evident in the gods' treatment of humanity.

To the degree that the Erinyes avenge, repair, and reverse what humanity has dared split in the web of existence, the furies secure the well-being of the good, and are therefore also known as the Eumenides or "kindly ones." Eliade, too, recognizes this paradox and points out that the symbol of knots and nets is evocative not only of the bondage of a terrible sovereignty, but also of the knot or weaving or labyrinth that is a protection and defense against enemies and disasters. He suggests that "the religious experiences induced by this same complex among the Hebrews prove that a very pure and profound religious life may find nourishment even in 'bondage' to a God of terrible and binding, appearance" and that "the situation of man in the world, in whatever perspective it may be viewed, is always expressed by key-words conveying the ideas of bondage, shackling, attachment."[7]

It is the very situation of man in the world that gives rise to the symbol of the God who binds. If one were seeking in man's condition in the world the circumstance that generates the symbol of the tragic fall, one need look no further than the law of gravity. In tragic literature, whenever man seeks through hubris or pride to transcend his early chthonic roots, he is reminded humbly of that state by a literal or figurative fall; so in the physical world he is always ultimately the prisoner of the law of gravity. To what universal physical condition of man's situation in the world should one look for the origin of the omnipresent symbol of the force that binds?

The suggestion here is that one need look only to man's ontogenetic origins in the womb to discern the first cord that both bonds and binds, of which woman is the mistress. The umbilical cord is necessary to gestation and evolution, but it also becomes, in time, an impediment to continued growth and individuation. Thus, the umbilical knot must be severed so that man might be freed into existence. One may also look further into the development of the individual to discover other physical connections that serve man through his evolution and that eventually become impediments to individuation. A parent initially holds the hand of an infant trying to take its first steps in order to protect and direct, and the infant welcomes the extended hand, at least until that instant when the supporting hand becomes the restraining hand. Then, the infant seeks to untie or break that constraint. And so it is with whatever tethers or harnesses the infant and the child in the name of support, protection, and guidance. The bond and bondage evident in the physical condition of the infant is paralleled by those manifested in the psychological state.

In his linguistic reappropriation of Freud, and more particularly in his interpolation of Freud's theories of narcissism and the Oedipal complex, Jacques Lacan articulates another source of early infantile binding that has the potential to preclude the evolution of the subject into selfhood. The traditional reading of the myth of Narcissus concludes that the young Greek falls in love with an image of himself and therefore is an archetype of self-love. But in the myth, Narcissus does not know that the figure in the pond is a reflection of himself; for him it is another to whom he is attracted. The implication is that all those to whom we are subsequently attracted are doubles of the ego. For Lacan it is just the opposite: the subjective Narcissus is but a reflection of the objective image in the pond.

In what Lacan calls the mirror stage—six to eighteen months of infancy—the infant literally recognizes itself in the image in the mirror as an entity separate from the flux of existence and consequently as an object out there, but one that is always false: "an odd puppet . . . a baroque doll . . . a trophy made of limbs."[8] In his interpolation of Lacanian theory, Mikkel Borch-Jacobsen, uses a metaphor that is even more evocative of this early source of bondage: "In reality, the only Being, for Lacan, is static Being—coming to a standstill before a 'theoretical' and stabilizing gaze and this is equally true for the Being of the ego, as soon as the ego itself is that world at which it gazes. The 'ego-world' is a statue: as hard as stone, as cold as ice, it is standing in front of the ego that is petrified there—that is, in the ego-world, it both gazes at and petrifies itself."[9] No matter how much the unconscious subject may evolve into a relatively mature self, those uncanny images of that statue self will recurringly haunt him in his dreams and nightmares and in his encounters with the world out there.

In this same arrested mirror stage of petrifaction, which Lacan also calls the *le désir de la mère*, the desire of the mother, the subject desires the mother and imagines itself as the object of what the mother lacks and therefore desires: the universal signifying power of desire, the phallus. In this pre-unconscious state—there is no unconscious because there is as yet no repression—the obvious potential psychotic danger is that, if the infant succeeds in becoming and remaining the object of the mother's desire, it runs the risk of becoming fixed as mere appendage of the mother, or as Jessica Benjamin expresses it in *The Bonds of Love*, of making the "mother an exclusive loved one [who is the] expression of the early narcissistic 'nostalgia for primary fusion, when the infant enjoyed fullness and perfection.'"[10]

Fortunately, this mirror or statue stage is interrupted by the growing intrusion of the third member of the oedipal triad, the father, an interruption that coincides, Lacan suggests, with the introduction of the infant to language. The father thereby becomes associated with both the legal and the symbolic order of the *le nom-du-père*, which in homonymic French translation can mean both the "no" and the "name" of the father: "Thus the oedipal resolution brings about a transition from the imaginary identification with the phallus and the dual relation with the mother to the symbolic identification with the father's name in a pluralized relationship with a place in a structured kin network. This transition is brought about at a price: the child must undergo symbolic castration of the imaginary phallus, which he yields up in payment for entering the symbolic order as a speaking subject."[11]

That place, however, distinguished by being the prohibiting "no," the identifying "name," the signifying discourse of the father, and the liberating site from matriarchal bondage, paradoxically becomes the locus of patriarchal bondage—the social and legal thou-shalt-(k)nots. The subject's attempt to evolve and mature becomes a hazardous rite of passage between the conflicting commands of the unconscious to be like the father, a (dis)embodiment of the signifying phallus, while simultaneously needing to be unlike the father—the object of the mother's desire.

Beyond the physical and psychological worlds of the infant and child, one can find in the social world of the evolving adult more figurative knots and nets. As Eliade suggests, the world is always construed as an invisible web in which everything is tied to everything else. In such a world, connection can be the social bond or safety net that catches the individual thrown into conscious existence. In his archeology of the human sciences, *The Order of Things*, Michel Foucault posits that there have been three major articulations of Eliade's invisible web in Western Civilization: the orders of the Renaissance, the Classical world of the seventeenth and eighteenth centuries, and the Modern world beginning in the nineteenth century. The Renaissance order manifests itself as a great circular and "semantic web of resemblances" based on the contiguity of things, on "adjacencies, of bonds and joints." In a major transformation of epistemes, the Renaissance of resemblance is replaced by the Classical table or grid that maps all things according to both similarity and more importantly difference, the result of which is a "single network of necessities" embedded in the "fabric" of signification. In other words, "the chain of being becomes discourse." At the beginning of the nineteenth century, the Classical table breaks up into "fragments, outlines, pieces, shards"; what reintegrates the order is the narrative of history, in "the thread of which all the discourse of all times, all successions and all simultaneities may be given."

All these unities are but the ontology by which social man attempts to express the eternal, unthought integrity: "Order is, at one and the same time, that which is given in things as their inner law, the hidden network, that determines the way they confront one another, and also that which has no existence except in the grid created by a glance, an examination, a language, and it is only in the blank spaces of this grid that order manifests itself in depth as though already there, waiting in silence for the moment of its expression."[12]

Such epistemes or networks, such ways of understanding and articulating society, the world, and self, such "fabrications" are not only webs that order existence, but also nets that preclude further explorations. Thus, family, community, religious, and peer ties are part of the social network that supports and sustains the evolving self. As that self approaches adolescence, individuation requires that the self cut those figurative cords; it is most appropriate that the word "science" derives from two Latin words, *scire* (to know) and *scindere* (to cut). Every exploration of self into the world out there or the one within requires that the self cut or untie, at least temporarily, the social network of human relationships and the ontology of understanding and expressing what is out there or in here. This ontogenetic condition of the situation of man in the world is recapitulated in man's phylogenetic condition as well.

One of the most influential studies of man's phylogenetic evolution is Freud's *Totem and Taboo*, in which the psychoanalyst explains the origins of social man in terms of the origins of the Oedipal complex.[13] According to Freud, the ancestors of mankind roamed the earth in hordes; the chief of each horde was the strongest male or father. He kept all the women to himself and kept all the young males or sons away from them. Frustrated and rebellious, the sons united to overpower the father and, having accomplished the deed and feeling remorse growing out of their ambivalent feelings of love for him who had protected them and of hate for him who had kept them in sexual bondage, they instituted taboos against parricide and incest, thereby creating society. Thus, in Freud's reading of the origins of social mankind, an uprising against the bondage imposed by the father leads to the establishment of social bonds through the institutionalization of taboo, a primitive form of ordering society through the establishment of difference within the family, between families and clans, and between what is permitted and what is not, the sacred and the profane.

Although he takes exception to Freud's tracing the evolution of such distinction to a single act of murder, the killing of the father, René Girard believes it is the violation of difference that threatens the unity of society and makes necessary the violent, but sacramental, killing of a surrogate victim. The purpose of such sacrifices "is to restore harmony to the community, to reinforce the social fabric," upon which order, peace, and fecundity exist. According to Girard, the sacrificial crisis is one of distinctions because cultural order is primarily a regulated system in which differences among individuals establish their "identity" and "mutual relationships." When the differences and boundaries are violated and chaos breaks out within a society, its members universally and "religiously" seek out a surrogate victim, upon whom to project their own violent propensities. By choosing someone from outside or on the periphery of their space, they distinguish him from themselves, elevate or apotheosize him to the divine, communally kill him in order, paradoxically, to purge themselves and their community of violence and to re-establish a network of unity through difference. Subsequently, Girard reads the myth of Oedipus, who through parricide and incest is the "slayer of distinctions," as a dramatization of the sacrifice of the surrogate victim and a model of the tragic hero.[14] A different, but for the purposes of this study, related reading of the Oedipal mythos is that of the anthropologist, Claude Lévi-Strauss.

In a seminal essay on the myth of Oedipus, in which he demonstrates the structuralist approach to reading and interpreting myth, Lévi-Strauss finds that the myth is an expression of man's futile attempt to liberate himself from his autochthonous roots in the earth and from his blood and tribal connections to kin. Lévi-Strauss discovers two complexes of opposing images in the myth: the first is the opposition of the overemphasis of familial relationships (incest) with the de-emphasis of familial relationships (parricide) and the second, the opposition of man's denial of his autochthonous roots (killing the monster) with the reminder of those roots (lameness).[15] Lévi-Strauss's reading can be interpreted as an expression of man's attempt to liberate himself from dependent connection to the earth and to family; killing kin and earth monsters symbolizes primitive man's becoming civilizing and cultivating man.

Humanity's separation from nature is the rift in the unthought Order of things, and one of its outcomes, according to Hegel, is the transformation of the absolute spirit into two dialectically opposite forms of self-consciousnesses: one "consists in showing itself as a pure negation of its objective form, or in showing that it is fettered to no determinate existence, that it is not bound at all by the particularity everywhere characteristic of existence, as such, and is not tied up with life. . . . The other is a purely existent consciousness and entangled in manifold ways." Both forms of self-consciousness exist dialectically within the individual. The one "is independent, and its essential nature is to be for itself; the other is dependent, and its essence is life or existence for another. The former is the Master, or Lord, the latter the Bondsman."[16]

Master and bondsman exist for Hegel not only within the psyche but also in society, in relationships between pure consciousnesses, and each requires recognition from the other in order to establish a dialectical equilibrium that is the essence of selfhood. As Jessica Benjamin points out, however, in Hegel "the tension between asserting the self and recognizing the other must break down; it is fated to produce an insoluble conflict. The breakdown of this tension is what leads to domination." In this domination of the servant by the master "complementarity has completely eclipsed mutuality, so that the underlying wish to interact with someone truly outside, with an equivalent center of desire, does not emerge."[17] In the absence of such interaction evolves humanity's growing desire to master not only bondsman, but also nature, family, and the familiar.

In order to explore the strange and master nature, humanity must reject the familial and natural, and to do that it must undo the knot that inhibits. In rejecting that bondage, however, man also rejects the bond to earth, family, and others; exploration of the strange, the unfamiliar, can lead to estrangement. Martin Heidegger, alluding to an ode in Sophocles's *Antigone*, concludes that man is the "most strange, uncanny, and unhoused" of creatures "because he is the violent one, who, tending towards the strange in the sense of overpowering, surpasses the limits of the familiar." Evolving mankind's desire to overpower manifests itself as a compulsion to reverse his role and become the one who binds rather than the one who is bound. Thus, Heidegger adds, "A wanderer out of his own housed self, man uproots, constrains, and distorts the delicate cadences, the just precincts of organic life."[18]

According to George Steiner in *Antigones*, the delicate cadences and precincts of organic life that are distorted and constrained are those existing between men and women, youth and age, the individual and the state, the living and the dead, humanity and the gods; consequently, almost all tragedy involves confrontations between the agonists of these five polarized opposites.[19] Like Eliade's primitive religious world and Foucault's civilized one, Steiner's tragic world is one of integrity, in which everything is connected to everything else. Each of these five confrontations engages the other four, and consequently they are almost always found collectively in tragedy. They are the inescapable confrontations of life because they manifest man's ironic and necessary situation in the world—torn between bond and bondage. The leap toward the strange away from the familiar is of necessity accompanied by the pain and angst of separation. He who cuts the familial cord can find himself disinherited, cut off from kin and kind; he who cuts the natural cord can become alienated and deracinated from place. In seeking to assert himself, the tragic hero not only rejects the bondage of the goddess that binds, but also denies the bond that, in a world of integrity, should exist between men and women, youth and age, the individual and the state, the living and the dead, himself and his gods/goddesses.

What Heidegger and Steiner recognize as the unfamiliar and alien, Freud in another context views as the paradoxically familiar. In an essay on the uncanny, Freud notes that in the German language there is often a confusion between *heimlich* (that which is of the home) and *unheimlich* (that which is not), or a confusion between what is familiar and what is strange. After further examination of the dialectical variances of this confusion and of some examples of the uncanny in dreams and literature, he concludes that what often seems uncanny—the unfamiliar that contradicts the laws of nature—is in fact the familiar repressed by guilt and expressed through the symbolism of the unconscious. In a sense, man's preoccupation with the uncanny is really a conscious concern with the surrealistic expressions of the familiar, but repressed, past.[20]

In *Beyond the Pleasure Principle,* Freud expands the boundaries of the familiar and of what binds man. He questions why infants and shell-shocked veterans of war often demonstrate a compulsion to repeat negative and painful external stimuli. His answer is that, through the repetition, both "bind psychically" the external stimuli in a process that enables each to master the situation. By initiating the repetition of the stimulus in dreams or fantasy, each moves from a vulnerable position of passivity—of being acted upon—to a position of mastery or of becoming the one who acts and thereby controls the trauma. Freud adds that there is something instinctual in this compulsion to repeat, some inner "urge in organic life to restore an earlier state of things." Since the inanimate state of the inorganic precedes the animate state of organic life, Freud concludes that the first instinct is to return to the inorganic: "the aim of all life is death." For Freud, thanatos, the death instinct, precedes eros, the pleasure or life instinct; moreover, the function of erotic activity is primarily to "assure that the organism shall follow its own path to death, and to ward off any possible ways of returning to inorganic existence other than those which are immanent in the organism itself."[21]

In *The Will to Power*, Nietzsche suggests that this ontogenetic instinct manifests itself phylogenetically in the erotic rise and thanatotic fall of nations: "A people might just as well designate as a right its need to conquer, its lust for power, whether by means of arms or by trade, commerce or colonization—the right to growth perhaps. A society that definitely and instinctively gives up war and conquest is in decline. It is ripe for democracy and the rule of shopkeepers—in most cases to be sure, assurances of peace are merely narcotics."[22] Thus, Freud and Nietzsche, like Lévi-Strauss, conclude or imply that man's primary and ultimate bond is to the chthonic or inorganic, from which he cannot escape. It is in the very attempt to escape the anonymity of the Dionysian communion or bond, however, that Nietzsche finds the essence of tragedy.

The major thesis of *The Birth of Tragedy* is that the classical drama of Aeschylus and Sophocles is a dialectical engagement of the Dionysian spirit of oneness-in-nature-and-Being and the Apollonian spirit of individuation-from-nature-and-Being. For Nietzsche, "Dionysus appears in a variety of forms, in the mask of a fighting hero, and entangled, as it were, in the net of the individual will." Caught in such a net, Dionysus is dismembered into human individuation, into the many masks of Dionysus who are the heroes of Greek tragedy. This dismemberment implies that "the state of [Apollonian] individuation [is] the origin and primal cause of all [tragic] suffering."[23] Thus, tragedy evokes pity and fear for the suffering—the estrangement and alienation—that accompanies the liberation from the Dionysian cosmic bond into Apollonian individuated bondage. Catharsis, the purgation of pity and fear, is effected by the reintegration of the hero into Dionysian oneness suggested in the recognition and acceptance by both hero and chorus of the other, of the feminine Dike or Themis, that is not only the source of his bondage, but also the source of his reparation-through-bonding.

Silence is part of such deliverance because even language is bondage. Although the Greeks, including Sophocles, believed that language liberated humanity from its prehuman confinement in nature,[24] many contemporary critics have come to agree with Nietzsche's claim that mankind lives suppressed within the "net" or "prison house of language."[25] This transformation of thought has come about primarily through the view that language is not so much a stable, one-to-one reference between the word and the thing or concept-of-the-thing, but rather a complicated, unstable relationship among the word, the thing, and all other (combination of) words.

Humanity is born with the capacity for language built into the brain. This capacity is like a loom: it operates on the principle of interconnecting or weaving combinations of strands, which are the sounds and marks, or words, created by primitive man and learned by socialized infant. The manifestation of the principle of language (as loom) in the experience of man (sounds and marks) creates what might be designated as the carpet of language. Traditionally, this carpet has been regarded as a magic one because it has enabled man through repetition to classify and control phenomena and data, through translation to connect and share with other men in other times and places, and through creation of the work of art to transcend the chthonic, to which all other creatures are bound. Thus, even a phenomenologist like Merleau-Ponty, who recognizes that "speech is a relation to Being through a being, and like it, it is narcissistic, eroticized, endowed with a natural magic that attracts the other significations into its web, as the body feels the world in feeling itself," concludes "that knowledge and the communication with others which it presupposes not only are original formations with respect to the perceptual life but also they preserve and continue our perceptual life even while transforming it."[26] One interpolator of Merleau-Ponty expresses this relationship of life and language in the following way: the "bond of life between the world and language" cannot be severed because "significance is the ground of the ideality that is liberated from things by being snared in language."[27]

The carpet of language, however, occasionally has also been viewed by the disenfranchised not so much as a magic weave, but rather as a fabrication that binds. For example, the carpet within which Cleopatra is delivered to Caesar might be regarded as the language carpet of a patriarchal world that restrains and hands over the female as property to the patronizing male. Of course, there may be many young, disenfranchised males who also view the linguistic carpet as that which imposes upon the innocent and accepting a predetermined way of viewing, articulating, and experiencing the phenomenological world and thereby restricting individuation. As man evolves both ontogenetically and phylogenetically—as his capacity for sensing more phenomena than his language can articulate grows, as his intimation that there are more things in this world than his language allows him to dream of, to perceive or conceive—he may find it necessary not only to cut the psychological and sociological cords, but also to break, or at least reweave or reorchestrate, the linguistic ones. Thus, Mikhal Bakhtin notes: "When thought begins to work in an independent, experimenting and discriminating way, what first occurs is a separation between internally persuasive discourse and authoritarian enforced discourse, along with a rejection of those congeries of discourse that do not matter to us, that do not touch us."[28]

Such is also the case with the canon or the tradition. Just as the capacity for language is a loom, the operation of that capacity within the world of sound and mark an act of language or carpet-making, and the individual work the carpet, so collectively the best carpets of language are stitched together to form a quilt or canon. Critics like T. S. Eliot view that quilt as a benevolent one that inspires and lifts, and some like Virginia Woolf in *A Room of One's Own* and Hèléne Cixous in *The Laugh of the Medusa* see it as a malevolent one that smothers and suffocates.[29] In such cases, both the carpet of language and the quilt of the canon must be abandoned for others, or at least both must be rewoven in order to liberate experience and its evocation. Either a feminine canon or language must replace their masculine counterparts in order to open the windows and doors of the prison house of language.

Even that will not transform the prison, say the deconstructionists, for the fault with language lies not in the weaver but in the loom. The human capacity for language is of such a relative nature that the only linguistic/aesthetic weaves created are labyrinthine ones with no center, no exits, and no ends but loose or dead ends.[30] Because language is not referential in terms of the relationship between signifier and signified, but is only differential in terms of its tendency to express through difference and deferral, all texts are doomed to *aporia* or deconstruction of themselves. In his deconstructive reading of Lévi-Strauss's structuralist reading of the myth of Oedipus, Jacques Derrida uses the metaphor of unraveling to critique structuralism. According to Derrida, Lévi-Strauss focuses upon "one guiding thread among others, the opposition between nature and culture," in order to demonstrate that "what is being unraveled" is Lévi-Strauss's assumption of a center that in fact does not exist, that is only an expression of a nostalgia for a "lost center."[31]

For the deconstructionist, every reading is a misreading because it will not lead to the figure in the carpet but to an infinite number of figures in any carpet. Like the minotaur of Minos, the reader should resign himself from the aesthetics of meaning— successful culmination of his exploration of the labyrinthine carpet in the discovery of the exit or figure or meaning—to the aesthetics of play—repetitions and explorations that culminate only in loose or dead ends. In so doing he will be liberated from the bondage of single meaning into the freedom of infinite meanings.[32]

Implicit in the current dialectic on language is that language both bonds and binds. From the perspective of the structuralist, formalist, phenomenologist, or new historicist, the text is a weave that connects the reader to phenomena, another, society, the tradition—that which has come before and that which will follow. As such it serves the purpose of the mythological talisman, the magic weave or carpet, that enables man to transcend his chthonic roots. It can, however, be misused and allow man to estrange himself from his fellow creatures and fellow man, insofar as he will seek to use it to master, to bind the other. From the perspective of the feminist and deconstructionist, it is also a weave, but one that holds man and woman in the bondage of phallogocentric meaning. Nonetheless, all participants in the dialectic continue to strive to share their findings, meaningful or playful, with the other through the weave of language and text, and thus both artist and critic continue, like Dylan Thomas, "to sing in [their] chains like the sea."[33] That singing, like the song of the bound goat upon the sacrificial altar, is often the stuff of which tragedy is made.

In its situation in the world—both ontogenetically and phylogenetically—and in the myths that evoke that situation and the theories that seek to explain both the situation and its mythic evocation, humanity is the beneficiary and victim of bonds and bondage, an irony that gives rise in tragic literature to a trope that can be designated as "bond/age." (Henceforth in this study, the word "bond" will signify the positive values of supportive ties or connections; the word "bondage," the negative limitations of suppression and entrapment, and the designation "bond/age," the simultaneous and thereby tensively ironic occurrence of both bond and bondage.) Thus, in the complex web of human relationships dramatized in tragic literature, a bond to someone or some power becomes bondage; a single relationship is experienced simultaneously as connection and constraint, and what is a familial tie to one person is foreign entrapment to another. Beyond the personal, one's relationship to nature and, through language, to society also manifests itself as both bond and bondage. It follows that, when the protagonist through hubris rebels against bondage, he must necessarily violate or reject a bond, and he and his community must suffer the consequence of disintegration. Such acts are transgressions of the divine, natural, familial, linguistic, and social order. Appropriately, they are often punished by the gods or the forces of the cosmos through a literal or figurative binding of the protagonist. Punishment and suffering, however, often lead to the recognition, discovery, and acceptance of the necessity of bond/age and thereby to the restoration of bonds and order. Such is the nature of tragic bond/age, a trope evident throughout Greek tragedy.

2
In Greek Tragedy

Prometheus Bound is clearly a tragedy of bond/age. The major action and dominating image of the drama is the enchainment of Prometheus in "unbreakable . . . bonds of indissoluble bronze" on the bare and desolate Caucasian rock.[1] Moreover, Prometheus is bound for his part in liberating humanity from its bondage in nature: "It was mortal man / to whom I gave great privileges and / for that was yoked in this unyielding harness" (69). He has unbound man by giving him fire—knowledge and craft—gifts that enable man to "combine" and "yoke" together letters and numbers in language and counting and thereby ironically to "chain," "harness," and "rein" in the nature to which heretofore he has been subject. With the gift of Promethean fire and by way of language, arithmetic, and husbandry, man has established boundaries in nature and thereby mastered it; in so doing he has also separated himself from nature, from the boundless, and freed himself from chthonic bondage. As the pre-Socratic philosopher Anaximander says, however, "each man does penance for his separation from the boundless"[2] and, we would add, from bondage.

Prometheus, the divine personification of man's situation in the world, is the archetype of tragic bond/age. His identification with mankind causes him to feel the bondage not only of the law of Zeus, which inhibits him and would further inhibit mankind, but also of natural forces, which cripple humanity. Prometheus's defiance of Zeus is both liberation and incarceration. In stealing fire from the gods and disobeying Zeus, Prometheus is disinheriting himself from the gods and bonding himself to man. Like Michelangelo's God who separates man from the dust of the rest of nature by the inspiriting touch of his hand to Adam's—there is no handclasp or handshake or handshaping on the Sistine Chapel—so Prometheus gives humanity the inspiriting gift of liberating fire. The tragic necessity of that act, however, is that Prometheus, like Satan and Adam, and not like Zeus or Jehovah, must suffer for it.

Prometheus's suffering takes the literal form of being bound. In an effective inversion of imagery, Aeschylus fits the punishment to the crime. Early in the play Prometheus sums up his contributions to man's lot with this image: "I yoked the proud horse to the chariot, teaching him obedience to the reins" (21), an image reflective of mankind's early mastery over nature and the chthonic. Towards the end, however, Hermes chides Prometheus for his own hubris: "champing the bit like a new-yoked colt you are restive and struggle against the reins" (40), an image reflective of not only the god's but also man's resistance to restraint. Prometheus's suffering also takes the figurative form of the less evident bondage of self-consciousness, of knowing that he is and must be bound—a punishment that is the result of the very network of consciousness, mastery, and individuation he himself has helped ravel for man. Prometheus is the Greek, divine counterpart of the Hebraic, human Adam; each personifies the individual human condition.

Prometheus Bound effects pity and terror and the purgation of both because the audience responds to what is human rather than to what is divine in Prometheus. His Nietzschean "dismemberment" or separation from the other gods through the stealth of fire is equivalent to man's separation from Eden and nature through the acquisition of knowledge; both Prometheus and Adam's agon is evocative of every man's necessary separation from the boundless through the establishment of boundaries in numbers and letters. Thus, Hermes tells Prometheus toward the end of the play, "don't say that Zeus has brought you to calamity / that you could not foresee . . . your own want of good sense / has tangled you in the net of ruin." (104) In the context outlined here, "want of good sense" is both desire for and absence of good sense and therefore the linguistic counterpart of ironic and tragic bond/age.

The penance that humanity will do for its separation from the boundless is manifested not only in Prometheus's confinement, but also in Io's discontent and deracination. In a tragedy that seeks to dramatize the punishment for Prometheus's crime against the gods on behalf of humanity, it is interesting to note that the only human being in the play is Io, like all other humans the recipient of one god's favor (Io, of Zeus's; humanity, of Prometheus's) and another's disfavor (Io, of Hera's; humanity, of Zeus's). One of the reasons that Aeschylus chooses Io as his representative human is that the myth requires it: it is through the offspring of Io, the heir that will prove to be a threat to Zeus's dominion, that Prometheus will eventually be unbound. Prometheus will use that information as ransom for his redemption; thereby, through the umbilically rooted link with subsequent generations, the great benefactor of humanity will be freed. Another reason for the introduction of Io is that the fate dealt her by a jealous Hera is representative of the necessity that will eventually confront a humanity raised up and separated from the chthonic: like Io, it will become less rooted in time and place and less content with its liberated lot.

Prometheus Bound dramatizes two other themes of the trope of tragic bond/age. One is that hermeneutics—understanding and interpretation—is the means by which man frees himself from the bondage of the experience and awareness of boundaries; knowledge (of who threatens Zeus) ironically is the means by which Prometheus (and man) will cut the Gordian knot of dark bondage. Thus, Themis says to Prometheus: "not by strength nor overmastering force / the fates allowed the conquerors to conquer / but by guile only" (73). The second theme is that such knowledge (and therefore the key to freedom and the future) resides not with the god but rather with the goddess. Aeschylus makes it quite clear that even Zeus is subject to the fates and furies; moreover, he adopts a myth in which Themis, a matriarchal goddess associated with justice and the social unit, has powers beyond those of Zeus. The secret net of fate is known only by woman and shared by her with those to whom she is bound; Prometheus's mother knows who threatens Zeus's power and shares that knowledge only with Prometheus, who uses it for liberation. In *Agamemnon*, Aeschylus repeats and varies the tragic agon of bond/age and reaffirms the affinity between the female and the fatalistic net that binds.

In *Notes Toward a Definition of Culture*, T. S. Eliot writes that family is a "bond which embraces a larger period of time" than the lifetime of the nuclear unit; it is "a piety towards the dead, however obscure, and a solicitude for the unborn, however remote."[3] It is the curse of the House of Atreus to sever such a bond. In his seduction of his sister-in-law and in his preparation of his brother's unholy banquet, Thyestes and Atreus respectively have surpassed the limits of the familiar and engaged the strange in their desire to overpower the other. The family meal or banquet is the sacred center around which families unite: when men eat bread (pan) together (com) they are companions, of the same blood, the same house, the same tribe. To violate the familial bed and board is to violate a bond sacred to man and the gods; this is precisely what Thyestes and Atreus have done. Moreover, as Cassandra's vision suggests, this breaking of the bond results in necessary bondage for the house of Atreus:

> Look there, see what is hovering above the house,
> so small and young, imaged as in the shadow of dreams,
> like children almost, killed by those most dear to them,
> and their hands filled with their own flesh, as food to eat,
> I see them holding out the inward parts, the vitals,
> oh pitiful, that meat their father tasted of.[4]

By linking the crimes of the generations through the repetition of the symbol of the unholy banquet, Aeschylus reminds his audience that Menelaeus and Agamemnon are bound to suffer the curse of their house and therefore compelled to repeat the crimes of their elders. Thus, the chorus says that

> Artemis the undefiled
> is angered with pity
> at the flying hounds of her father
> eating the unborn young in the hare and
>   the shivering mother.
> She is sick at the eagles' feasting.
>
> (9)

Aeschylus's imagery is telling, for the brothers have feasted not only on the living in Troy, but also upon the unborn, and their crimes are violations of family in its most comprehensive sense. Pierre Vidal-Naquet notes that "this hunt-cum-sacrifice is in its turn a repetition of the original murder that took the horrible form of a human sacrifice accompanied by oath swearing, [one] that was worse than a human sacrifice since it was a . . . family feasting, the result of cannibalism in the home." Vidal-Naquet concludes, "there are, precisely, no regular sacrifices in Aeschylus' tragic world; on the contrary, every sacrifice is corrupt."[5]

In overpowering Troy, the brothers have also torn out the polis by its roots and deracinated the city from what has been and what would have been. In sacrificing his daughter, Agamemnon commits a crime against kinship and generation. Like his father and uncle, he has ironically given hostages to fortune. That he has a child makes him vulnerable to necessity; in sacrificing her in order to further his own and his brother's ambition, he literally gives up another hostage and puts his fate in the hands of fortune's agent, Clytemnestra. It is ironically appropriate that Clytemnestra, the "accursed bitch," should initiate her vengeance upon Agamemnon by engaging in another unholy banquet when "she licks his hand" (43), one that has offered up the blood of her daughter as food for the gods.

2 / In Greek Tragedy

The banquets of the brothers are made possible by Zeus who has

> slung above the bastions of Troy
> the binding net, that none, neither great
> nor young, might outleap
> the gigantic toils
> of enslavement and final disaster.
> (16)

and by Artemis who around Argos has "fence[d] high the nets / of ruin beyond overleaping" (17). One of the first variations of the leitmotif of the fatalistic net is Clytemnestra's depiction of the many rumors that she has heard about the death of her husband: "Had Agamemnon taken all / the wounds the tale whereof was carried home to me / he had been cut full of gashes like a fishing net" (31). Clytemnestra then suggests that, had Agamemnon indeed died in Troy, it would have been as though she herself had come within the grip of a malevolent net: "because such tales broke out forever on my rest, / many a time they cut me down and freed my throat / from the noose overslung where I had caught it fast." Both metaphors connect the feared fates of Agamemnon and Clytemnestra in Troy with the image of the net; however, instead of Agamemnon and herself falling within a Trojan mesh, Clytemnestra becomes the very weave that ensnares Agamemnon and avenges Iphigenia and the Trojan unborn.

Clytemnestra tells the populace that it is meet that she should "spread the gates before her husband home from war" (23); those gates spread open by the female are the entrance to Agamemnon's doom. Clytemnestra, in order "to serve necessity," proceeds to entice Agamemnon into walking upon the "silver's worth of webs," the purple tapestries reserved only for the gods; then, once inside their home, to "spread deadly abundance of rich robes" about him, "as fishermen cast their huge circling nets" (50); and finally to stab him ("full of gashes like a fishing net"?). Cassandra, linking the leitmotif of the net of necessity with that of the unholy banquet, envisions the act and likens both to a totemic sacrifice:

> See there, see there! Keep from his mate the bull.
> Caught in the folded web's
> entanglement she pinions him and with the black horn
> strikes. And he crumples in the watered bath.
> Guile, I tell you, and death there in the caldron wrought.
> (40)

Aeschylus confirms the connection between woman and bondage when he has Cassandra observe: "No, no, see there! What is that thing that shows? / Is it some net of death? / Or is the trap the woman there, the murderess?" (40). Indeed, the open gates, the purple woven tapestries, and the spun robes constitute Clytemnestra's as well as Artemis's having "fence[d] high the nets / of ruin beyond overleaping" as Zeus so cast his nets over Troy. Clytemnestra is, however, the agent of Artemis, the goddess who has looked unfavorably upon Agamemnon's feasting upon the unborn of Troy and who is the power behind Clytemnestra's deed. Agamemnon's violation of the familial, political, and divine bond breeds a bondage woven by woman, goddess, and necessity. Vidal-Naquet concurs "Through failing to criticize the oracle, Agamemnon made himself the accomplice of destiny; perhaps, the chorus now admits, the *alastōr* or vengeful spirit was indeed the 'auxiliary' (*sullēptōr*) of Clytemnestra. In this way the designs of the gods and the plans or passions of men are both at work in the tragic decision."[6] Vidal-Naquet also sees a marked contrast between *Agamemnon* and *Oedipus Rex*, for in the latter, he concludes, "it is Oedipus and only Oedipus who pulls the strings."[7] This, however, remains to be seen.

If Oedipus were put to trial as is Orestes in the finale of the *Oresteia*, what might the defense say in his behalf? Surely it would point out that Laius, trying to avoid his fate, has Oedipus fettered before giving him to Jocasta to be put to death and that it is the father and mother who break the familial bond first. In addition, it would also add that Laius repeats the violation later at the crossroads, when once more he initiates the violence by attempting to kill Oedipus. The defense would add that Jocasta participates in the violation by abandoning the child to a herdsman, who in turn is instructed to leave it to die. She too, like her husband, repeats the act of severing the bond with her son when, by hanging herself, she abandons him to the recognition of his accomplished fate. Surely these are circumstances that mitigate Oedipus's crime and that ought to mitigate his punishment.

If such an attorney for the defense of Oedipus had as an aide an interpreter of texts, then the defense might add that Oedipus is also the victim of two alter-fathers. Teiresias, the wise old man who is admittedly provoked by Oedipus himself, accuses him, nevertheless, of the murder of Laius and the pollution of Thebes. Creon, his uncle and therefore even more of a father figure, though equally provoked and commanded by Oedipus's own fiat, exiles Oedipus from Thebes as had Laius and Jocasta earlier. The defense no doubt would turn to the matter of motivation and intention and point out that Oedipus labored in vain to avoid the very crimes of which he is charged: parricide and incest. He even exiled himself from Corinth and suffered expatriation in order not to kill Polybus his father and wed Merope his mother. Finally, the defense would argue, Oedipus saved his homeland twice: once from the mastering and riddling Sphinx and once more in discovering the source of the pollution in Thebes and expiating it through self-exile. In an Athenian court of justice, such would be part of the defense of Oedipus. Why then, with the possible exception of the chorus's recognition of Thebes's debt to Oedipus for liberating the polis from the Sphinx, does no one in the play—not even the chorus or Oedipus—raise any of these mitigating circumstances? The answer is plain: Oedipus's crime is one of defilement, and in defilement intention is of no consequence.

In *Symbolism of Evil*, Paul Ricoeur sees the manifestation of evil in the world evolving from symbols of defilement to those of sin to those of guilt; he then points out that "the inventory of faults under the regime of defilement (as opposed to sin or guilt) is vaster on the side of happenings in the world in the degree to which it is narrower on the side of intention of the agent."[8] He adds that "the division between the pure and the impure ignores any distinction between the physical and the ethical and follows a distribution of the sacred and the profane which has become irrational" for modern man. The original violation in the universe is the defilement of purity; it is impurely physical: what should not be touched has been, and the result is stain.

In *Oedipus Rex*, the symbol of bondage, the net, is coupled with the symbol of defilement, the stain. When Creon returns from Delphi with the news that Apollo has directed Thebes to drive out pollution that is "grown ingrained within the land," Oedipus asks, "Where would a trace / of this old crime be found?" Creon responds, "The clue is in this land."[9] The audience will later discover that the trace or mark or clue of the pollution of Thebes is in the scar upon Oedipus's ankles; it might just as well have been the mark on his belly, his navel, for what the scars on Oedipus's ankles trace is the innateness or the originality of Oedipus's sin, the necessity of tragic bond/age. As we shall see, Oedipus, indeed everyone, has to do what he does; it is not a question of choice—moral, ethical, or otherwise.

When the herdsman removes the fetters from the feet of the abandoned infant, Sophocles's protagonist is Oedipus unbound, and the resonance with Aeschylus's hero is clear. Laius is to Oedipus what Zeus is to Prometheus; both are father figures who would inhibit growth or individuation. That

Jocasta participates in that binding of the hero is a reminder that the threads by which the hero is bound are still woven and cast by women. What the bad father has done, the good father (figure) undoes, and the herdsman loosens the chains from the feet of Oedipus, and he is free to stand erect and walk. The ontogeny of Oedipus recapitulates the phylogeny of race.

What he experiences in infancy is repeated in adolescence. When Oedipus comes of age and hears of the prophecy regarding his parents, he leaves Corinth. In this ambivalent act he separates himself from another good father and kills the bad one at the crossroads that is the intersection of tragic bond/age. Once more, in order to avoid the bondage of birth, the hero must sever a bond; that separation, however, only leads him into another bondage. In order for youth to distinguish and become itself, it must cut the familial connection. Neumann is right when he asserts that man must figuratively kill his parents in order to individuate himself, but so is Lévi-Strauss when he suggests that man necessarily separates himself from his autochthonous roots.[10] Oedipus's use of reason in solving the riddle of the Sphinx and slaying the chimera is symbolic of man's attempt to deny and transcend his autochthonous and matriarchal past. The answer to the riddle of the Sphinx is indeed man.

In marrying Jocasta, Oedipus becomes king, and his uncle does not. That could be read as a variation on the theme of the usurpation of the father's place; it could also be interpreted as an overpowering of the female chimera that has subjected him and the polis. In the one instance, he subdues the autochthonous, female power that holds his people, whom he comes to represent, in bondage; in the other, he subdues the woman who had held him in bondage. Oedipus's solving the riddle of the Sphinx and his marriage to Jocasta momentarily untangle the fatalistic net woven by masters and mistresses, divine and human. Matrimony, however, is paradoxically another bondage: "my fate was to be yoked / in marriage with my mother." (146)

Paul Ricoeur also writes: "there is no taboo in which there does not dwell some reverence, some veneration of order," the implication of which is that taboos are institutions of order. He adds that what is aimed at in expiation, "in this negative act of taking away," is "the act of reaffirming order," and that "suffering is the price for the violation of order; suffering is to 'satisfy' the claim of purity for revenge."[11] What is the purity that is being defiled in *Oedipus Rex*? Is it that of social "wed-lock" and incest the impure violation; is it the purity of patriarchy and parricide the impure violation; is it that of Dionysian oneness and Apollonian individuation the impure violation; or is it rather the purity of Being and the evolution of human being the impure violation? The answer is that it is the latter and, insofar as it is, it is also all the others; that is why in Sophocles the tragedy of bond/age is rooted in defilement.

Antigone also concerns itself with defilement and disorder; however, whereas in *Oedipus Rex* Sophocles links defilement and disorder with the question posed by Teiresias, "Do you know who your parents are?"; in *Antigone*, he connects defilement and disorder to the implied question, "Do you know what your kinship is?" In *King Lear*, Cordelia, when confronted again with the question of how much she loves her father, answers, "according to my bond." Antigone and Creon act according to how each discerns his kinship or his bond. Steiner rightfully suggests that in the confrontation between Antigone and Creon, the five major non-negotiable confrontations of humanity—man and woman, old and young, individual and state, living and dead, humanity and divinity—are dramatized.[12] They are enacted, however, within the enveloping context of the question, "what is my bond." Jean-Pierre Vernant poses the agon of the play in these terms:

> The conflict between Antigone and Creon . . . is not an opposition between pure religion, represented by the girl, and total irreligion, represented by Creon, or between a religious spirit and a political one. Rather, it is between two different types of religious feeling: one is a familiar religion, purely private and confined to the small circle of close relatives, the *philoi* centered around the domestic hearth and the cult of the dead; the other is a public religion in which the tutelary gods of the city eventually become confused with the supreme values of the State for the city . . . its *nomoi* is more venerable, more *sacred*, than a mother, a father, or all one's ancestors put together.[13]

In the foregoing passage, Vernant rearticulates Hegel's summation of the agon: "The chief conflict is that between the state, i.e., ethical life in its universality, and the family, i.e., natural ethical life. These are the clearest powers presented in tragedy, because the full reality of ethical existence consists in harmony between these two spheres. . . . Antigone honors the bond of kinship, the gods of the underworld, while Creon honours Zeus alone, the dominating power over public life and social welfare."[14]

Clearly, Antigone stresses the bond to the blood brother, and Creon, to the societal brotherhood. When questioned by Creon if she is ashamed to have acted alone and broken the law in burying her brother, Antigone responds, "No. I am not ashamed. When was it shame / to serve the children of my mother's womb."¹⁵ Antigone puts blood before scripture, the "gods, unwritten and unfailing law" (196) before the written law of Creon and the state. Creon, on the other hand, puts brotherhood before brother (or son or wife): "he who counts another greater friend / than his own fatherland. I put him nowhere" (187). In his confrontation with his son, Creon goes so far as to aver that the man put in place of governing by the state must have "obedient hearing to his least command / when it is right, and even when it's not . . . There is no greater wrong than disobedience" (204).

The connection Creon establishes between himself and the state is so great that it supersedes the bond to his own family; thus, he says to the chorus of his punishment of Antigone, "She is my sister's child, but were she child / of closer kin than any at my hearth, / she and her sister should not so escape / their death and doom" (197). Not only are Creon's words a foreshadowing of the doom he will heap upon his family and himself, they are also indicative that, in extolling one relationship at the expense of another, Creon has violated the Greek values inscribed on the Temple of Delphi: "know thyself" and "all things in moderation." Antigone in her single-mindedness knows herself well enough, but it is a self that suffers from excessive dedication to the dead and death; she has confused *thanatos* with *eros*. Even before the chorus has claimed that "no fool is fool as far as loving death" (188), Antigone concludes, concerning her intention to bury Polyneices, "For me, the doer, death is best. / Friend shall I lie with him, yes friend with friend, / when I have dared the crime of piety" (183).

In his interpolation of Hegel's commentary on *Antigone*, Derrida observes a dialectic between Hegel and Freud: "When a man binds himself to a woman, even were it in secret (marriage does not depend, according to Hegel, on a formal contract), it is a matter of entrusting her with his death. . . . of maintaining [a marrowless body] in a living, monumental, interminable surrection. In herself, under the earth, but the night of the subterranean world is the woman, Hegel specifies. Freud will also have shown the reverse side of this desire: the fear of being enclosed in the maternal womb is represented in the agony of being interred alive."¹⁶

Both the Hegelian trust and the Freudian fear are manifested in Antigone, who not only knows what her duty is, but also understands that her affinity for the dead comes of having lived a death-in-life, in which she metaphorically has been buried alive as a result of the curse upon the house of Labdacus: "My life died long ago. / And that has made me fit to help the dead" (200). Her uncle recognizes as much when he inters her alive for violation of the law: "Then go down there [Hades] if you must love, and love the dead" (199) and "pray to Death, the only god of [your] respect" (208).

In a variation of the defilement of her father and mother in the act of incest, Antigone is a little too obsessive about burying Polyneices. Having performed the proper ritual and buried her brother's corpse once and having witnessed the wind bury it again, it would appear that the goddess of the underworld would have been satisfied and that Antigone should be. She is not, however, and once again she breaks Creon's law, knowing that the deed means her death and her separation from the nearest living relatives she has, her sister Ismene and her cousin Haemon. She trades a union and life with her cousin for reunion in death with her brother; in so doing she violates her bond with Haemon, with the other. The chorus acknowledges the uniqueness of the latter relationship when it responds to Creon's observation that Haemon will find other furrows to plough, "But where the closeness that has bound these two?" (201).

What the chorus suggests about the "closeness" of Antigone and Haemon is also applicable to that of Antigone and Polyneices and perhaps offers further insight into why Creon fears Antigone's actions. In his study of violence and the sacred, Girard argues that twins in primitive societies threaten the security of the community because, by their very likeness, they violate an order predicated on difference. He adds that fraternal relationship that implies a minimum of difference—for example in the rivalry of brothers for the same crown—exposes a society to the onset of sacrificial crisis necessary for the restoration of difference and unity.[17] The same could be said for a sororal relationship (between cousins as well as brother and sister) so excessive that it would choose death over life. It seems quite possible that underlying his denouncement of Antigone's action on behalf of her brother and his denial of a special bond between his son and niece is Creon's unconscious fear that such like-mindedness within the family undermines the integrity of the city.

Creon's problem is just the opposite of his niece's; whereas Antigone has too great a love and respect for the dead, Creon has not enough. He has allowed his dedication to the state and those who defend it to curtail, indeed, almost eliminate, his observation of the dead, at least all of the dead. Like his niece, he has, as Teiresias points out, "confused the upper and the lower worlds," (217) in that he has allowed Polyneice's body to remain unburied on the upper world while he has buried Antigone alive. He has indeed violated one of the oldest laws that anthropologists say separate humanity from the rest of Being—humanity buries its dead. In leaving his body to rot, Creon has disinherited Polyneices from his ancestors, from the autochthonous earth, and in undoing Antigone's burial of Polyneices, he has killed "the dead a second time" (215). Once again, Sophocles fits the expiation to the defilement. When the messenger begins to tell of what has taken place in the cave, he says of Creon, "Call him a breathing corpse" (220). Afterwards, when he learns of the death of his wife, Creon says, "I was dead and you kill me again" (224). In both instances, he experiences what he has effected in Antigone and Polyneices respectively: death-in-life and death-of-the-dead.

Creon and the house of Menoeceus suffer what Antigone and the house of Labdacus do: the end of their houses, the end of the line, total disinheritance. Just as "the bloody knife / cuts the remaining root" of the family tree of Labdacus when Polyneices and Eteocles die on the sword of the other, so, when he fails to heed the wise advice of his young son to bend with the prevailing wind (of the god that has buried the body of Polyneices), Creon, "the resistant," and his generations "perish root and branch" (205). Sophocles could not have used a more effective image of deracination than this uprooting of the house of being, and that image is but one variation of the leitmotif of binding in tragic bond/age.

As Jocasta had finished "life in the shame of the twisted nets," (183), so does Antigone, "hanging by the neck, caught in a noose / of her own linen veiling" (222). Although man is found uncanny, strange, and awful in controlling the fish and foul of nature "with the twisted mesh of his nets" (192), he is perhaps more strange or estranged in the fact that he himself, in the persons of Antigone and Creon, cannot, like "the horses . . . he holds and harnesses, yoked about the neck," (193), be brought "back to terms" by "small curbs" (197). Thus, Hegel correctly notes that "we find immanent in the life of [Antigone and Creon] that which each respectively combats, and they are seized and broken by the very bond which is rooted in the compass of their social existence."[18] In the final analysis, however, it is Antigone more than Creon who is unyielding in her attempt to escape bondage.

Antigone never wavers in her commitment to brother over brotherhood; Creon does in his to brotherhood over family. One of Creon's fears is that, should he yield, Antigone would be the man and he the woman. If willfulness be the measure of masculinity, then Creon is right to fear emasculation by Antigone. By all other standards, however, Antigone is woman: in her sorority to brother and in her fidelity to blood, to the dead and death, to the autochthonous, and to the unwritten over the written law. If, however, wavering and submission be the standard of the feminine, then Creon is again right to doubt his own masculinity. He is the one whose "mind is torn" (218) and who is "balanced on a razor's edge" (214), the one who discovers that he "can fight necessity no more" (218). To the degree that he is divided within, Creon is the foreshadowing of the Euripidean tragic hero and not the hero of this tragedy; insofar as she is the one who is not so divided, who fights necessity to the bitter end, and whose "sacrificial death only, her union with Dionysus, can restore the mystery of symmetry in moral being," Antigone is the tragic heroine.[19] By this criteria, some, like Racine, would argue that it is Phaedra who is the heroine in *Hippolytus*.

Hippolytus literally means horse (*hippo*), reins (*lytus*); and that could be read to mean he who reins in horses or he who is reined in by horses. In Euripides's play the word ironically bears both meanings. It also reminds the reader of earlier uses of the leitmotif by Aeschylus and Sophocles and prepares him for discerning the design of Euripides's play. In *Prometheus Bound*, the hero's gift frees man from the bondage of darkness and gives him the power to chain, harness, and rein in nature. In *Antigone*, man is the uncanny one who once again snares, tethers, and yokes bird and beast. In both plays, the image of man's harnessing animals suggests man's evolving power to control nature. The image, however, is ironically turned upon man as Prometheus and Antigone resist the curb of the god and goddess's reins. Both reversals from man's reining in to being reined in are necessitated by tragic bond/age. Such is the case in *Hippolytus*; here, however, the leitmotif of the net or yoke is manifested primarily in terms of the bondage of eros.

George Meredith writes in *Modern Love* that in tragic life "no villain need be; passions spin the plot."[20] This is true in all Greek tragedy, but in Euripides, the passion that spins the plot is passion. When the chorus first comments on Phaedra's fever, it foreshadows her fate by pointing out that "she hides her golden head in fine-spun robes."[21] Later, the nurse warns her that "our affections must be breakable chains that we / can cast them off" (243), the implication of which is that Phaedra's obsessive love clearly is, like Prometheus's chains, unbreakable. Still later, the nurse begs Phaedra to "unknit that ugly frown" (244) that has been woven upon her face by unrequited love. Finally, when the nurse sums up Phaedra's agon in these words, "You've fallen into the great sea of love / and with your puny swimming would escape" (253), can there be any doubt that her puny swimming will ensnare her in the trammel net? After she learns that the nurse has betrayed her love to Hippolytus, Phaedra laments, "What trick is there now, what cunning plea / to loose the knot around my neck?" The knot is passion for Hippolytus; the trick that will unveil itself is death and deceit, by which she, by literally "tying the twisted noose around her neck" (265), will loosen the figurative knot of passion there and by which Hippolytus will be "yoked to a cruel fate" (287).

Phaedra is one of tragedy's earliest discontents; the nurse chides her: "There's no content for you in what you have / for you're forever finding something dearer, / some other thing—because you have it not" (240-41). Euripides connects this love for what she has not to her mother's desire for the bull and her sister's for Dionysus: "Mine is an inherited curse. It is not new" (247). In one respect, Phaedra is right: her bondage is her desire for Hippolytus, and that passion for the forbidden is inherited from her mother and therefore indicative of how she is bound by inheritance. In another sense, however, her passion is new, for she wants that which is unattainable. As taboo as the objects of her mother and sister's affections might be, both mother and sister attain what drives them, and it is in the attainment that the suffering occurs. Phaedra, like Echo, loves the unattainable and therein lies her suffering, and, as it does for Narcissus, *eros* becomes *thanatos* for Phaedra. Thus, when she enters the stage, Phaedra has almost starved herself to death for unrequited love of Hippolytus; after her final departure, she hangs herself for that passion, and Hippolytus is subsequently strangled by it.

In what could have been a passage chanted by the chorus of Euripides's play, Emerson writes the following: "Here again, as so often, nature delights to put us between extreme antagonisms, and our safety is in the skill with which we keep the diagonal line. Solitude is impracticable, and society fatal. We must keep our heads in the one and our hands in the other. The conditions are met, if we keep our independence, yet do not lose our sympathy. These wonderful horses need to be driven by fine hands."[22]

Although one may argue that *Hippolytus,* unlike *Antigone*, does not concern itself with the confrontation between the individual and society as much as it does with that between man and woman, one has to recognize that Hippolytus's devotion to Artemis and obliviousness to Aphrodite are indicative of a divided sensibility that renders his hands incapable of conducting the horses along the diagonal line of, and thereby resolving the antagonism between, self-centeredness and involvement with the other. Hippolytus's one-sidedness reminds one of Hegel's explanation of crime in the tragic world: "The ethical act contains the element of wrongdoing, because it does not cancel and transcend the natural allotment of the two laws to the two sexes; but rather, being an undivided attitude towards the law, keeps within the sphere of natural immediacy, and *qua* acting, turns this one-sidedness into guilt, by merely laying hold of one side of the essential reality and taking up a negative relation towards the other, i.e. violating it."[23]

It is interesting to note, for example, that when Hippolytus finds himself unable to convince his father of his innocence, he laments, "If I could only find / another me to look me in the face / and see my tears and all that I am suffering!" (277). The implied allusion to Narcissus is confirmed in Theseus's response to this plea: "Yes, in self-worship you are certainly practiced. / You are more at home there than in the other virtues, / justice, for instance, and duty toward a father."

Theseus's feeling, like his whole reaction to events upon his return home, is clouded by the note from and his devotion to the dead, to Phaedre; nevertheless, he is right in admonishing Hippolytus for self-worship. Insofar as Hippolytus has sworn fidelity to Artemis and has slighted Aphrodite, he has chosen a life that does not require a human other. He suffers what T. S. Eliot would call a dissociation of sensibility that precludes the fineness of hands that allows one to reconcile the antagonism between solitude and society. When he tries to drive his horses along the sea in his banishment from Athens, he is incapable of controlling the team that "heeded neither the driver's hand nor harness / nor the jointed car" and is thereby "tangled in the reins [and] dragged along in an inextricable / knot" (282-83). When one recalls that it is the action of Phaedra as agent of Aphrodite that has impassioned Theseus to curse Hippolytus, one is left with another reminder not only that man is held in bondage, but that the threads of that bondage are controlled by divine and human mistresses. Euripides, however, in his variation of tragic bond/age connects the symbol of the net to that of the root.

Hippolytus believes that in his soul "the seed / of Chastity toward all things alike / nature has deeply rooted" (236) and, later, in response to Phaedra and his father's accusations of rape, he swears "by this deep-rooted fundament of earth" (275) that he is innocent. The rootedness associated with nature and the earth is consistent with his devotion to Artemis, the goddess of chaste nature. It is appropriate that, when he finds himself accused by Phaedra and exiled by Theseus, the chorus comments, "how [Hippolytus's] former happiness lies uprooted" (273). The image of rootedness and uprootedness is an ironic variation on the theme of bond/age: believing himself to be a victim of a violated bond—of father and son—Theseus mistakenly tries to exact poetic or tragic justice; he disinherits Hippolytus, exiles him from Athens, and successfully calls upon his father to murder his son. In so doing, Theseus defiles nature and kinship, and so Artemis says to him, "You have murdered a son, you have broken nature's laws" (284). Medea violates the same taboo out of passion for Jason.

Medea has killed her brother in order to secure Jason's retreat from her homeland with the golden fleece. She has also exiled herself from father and fatherland, a deed that effects a misery, according to the chorus, unsurpassed in the human condition. She has forced the children of Pelias to murder their own father in order to reclaim the throne for Jason. After Jason's marriage to Glauce, she kills the princess and manages her murder so that the daughter becomes the cause of her father's death. Finally, she kills her own sons. And she violates these familiar taboos all for love. The earlier deeds have been done in order to "bind . . . by strong oaths" Jason to herself;[24] the latter, to avenge herself upon Jason when he breaks that bond.

Medea uses oaths not "to join" Jason but rather "to bind" him to herself. Her idea that marriage involves an oath that tethers is reinforced later when Medea alludes to one of the mysteries of marriage—women who "with thoroughness and tact" keep their husbands from "resenting the yoke" of marriage (298). The yoke is indeed central to Medea's seduction of Jason, her leading him to, and successfully away with, the golden fleece. In helping Jason retrieve the bright totem and reclaim the throne of his kingdom, she slays the dragon that guards the golden fleece "with many a wreathed coil" (306). Ironically, once Jason breaks their marriage bond and marries Glauce, Medea feels "penned in" by sorrow (303). Her revenge upon Jason for this humiliation is to break the bonds that he now cherishes.

The first of these crimes to be punished is Jason's tie to a new wife and father. Her gift to the new bride fuses the symbol of the net with that of fire. The finely spun and embroidered robe that enflames its wearer is an ironically appropriate means of revenge for the abandoned Medea; when Creon tries to rescue his daughter, his flesh is made one with Glauce's in an inversion of the crime to which they have been accomplices, the dissevering of the joined-in-marriage flesh of Jason and Medea: "he . . . found himself held fast by the fine-spun robe as ivy that clings to the branches of the bay . . . he strove to rise, but she still held him back" (330). The second punishment of Jason by Medea is to kill their sons.

For Medea, the word of her and Jason's oaths of marriage is made flesh in the issue of that marriage, their sons. Jason believes that he can violate his oath to Medea without violating the incarnation of that word, his children. Medea is there to remind him that, in a world in which everything is connected to everything else, he cannot. As he has severed the oath that binds them in order to perpetuate his own ambition, so she severs literally the flesh that has bound them in order to accomplish her vengeance. Both commit their deeds on behalf of the self and at the expense of the other. Thus, the attendant tells Medea's nurse that Jason's crime is a sign of the times: "every single man cares for himself more than for his neighbor . . .

seeing that to indulge his passion their father has ceased to love these children" (294).

Medea acts out of the same compulsion and thereby becomes a victim of her "own self-will" (325) when she slays her sons, who have become pawns in the conflict of wills between Jason and herself. They will be sacrificed by Jason in order for him to cut the cord that not only connects but inhibits. They will be sacrificed by Medea in order for her to effect for Jason what she was willing to sacrifice for him: deracination, the uprooting of oneself from family and homeland, and the alienation that necessarily attends transplantation to another place. In killing Creon and Glauce and then her own sons, Medea severs Jason—who has already been cut off from all past family, father, and fatherland—from all future generation. As the nurse says, the house of Jason is "a house no more" (295). Medea only does this, however, when she has assured herself of a fatherland once more by assuring herself of a father-figure, Aegeus, and has thereby prepared herself for undoing all that had been done prior to her connection to Jason. Her act of vengeance against Jason not only disinherits Jason but also repatriates herself.

Contrary to the tragedies already discussed here, *Medea* is not so much a matter of necessity as it is a matter of human intention. Although Medea says of her deeds, "For the gods and I with fell intent devised these schemes," (325), it is more difficult to discover the gods' role here than it is to discern Medea's. In previous plays, *Agamemnon* and *Hippolytus* in particular, both Aesychulus and Euripides made it quite clear that the female figures were primarily the agents of goddesses who were pulling the strings that by necessity wove the fates of the protagonists. Themis and Clytemnestra and Aphrodite and Phaedra are the avengers of Agamemnon and Hippolytus. Here, although Medea prays to Themis, Euripides fuses the divine and the human in the figure of Medea, a witch who by her supernatural gifts may be said to participate in the divine and the human. It is she and she alone who is the mistress of the trammel net that engulfs both Jason and herself. Insofar as she is, Medea is the embodiment of what Nietzsche perceives as the precursor of the death of tragedy: the complete separation of the Apollonian spirit from the Dionysian.

3
In *Hamlet*

The shift from emphasis on plot in Greek tragedy to concentration on character in Shakespearean tragedy is accompanied by a change from the prominence of bond/age in the external and fatalistic world to that in the internal and psychological world. This shift is recognized by Hegel as a change from classical tragedy, the essence of which is the conflict between ethical substances as they are embodied in the agonists (the *philoi* in Antigone, the *nomoi* in Creon), to modern tragedy, the essence of which lies in the compelling nature of protagonists, who "in their passion give effect not . . . in the interest of the ethical vindication of the truly substantive claims, but for the simple reason that they are the kind of men they are." Hegel adds that such modern tragic figures are "vacillating characters, more particularly on the ground that they are essentially under the sway of two opposed passions, which make them fluctuate from one resolve or one kind of deed to another."[1]

Despite what is an obvious derision of the modern or romantic hero and what would seem to be a description of Shakespeare's most famous protagonist, Hegel further concludes that "it is precisely Shakespeare who, as a contrast to that exposition of vacillating and essentially self-divided characters, supplies us with the finest examples of essentially stable and consequential characters, who go to their doom precisely in virtue of this tenacious hold upon themselves and their ends." One of those characters is Hamlet. That Hegel could deride the stereotypical internally divided modern tragic hero in one breath and extol the prototypical Hamlet in another is explained by his perception that the creation of such a character requires "a profounder psychological penetration and a greater breadth of particular characterization" and by his observation that "Hamlet is a beautiful and noble heart, not inwardly weak at all," one for whom "the fate of the whole realm and of himself has steadily been developed in his own withdrawn inner life."²

Another explanation for this seeming contradiction or paradox in Hegelian criticism is that, by virtue of that more penetrating psychological development of character, what had been manifested in the external world of ancient tragedy—the conflict of ethical substance in the collision of protagonist and antagonist—is internalized in what Hegel observes as merely the opposition of passions. What collides within the psyche of Hamlet, both consciously and unconsciously, are not only the ethical substances of *philoi* and *nomoi* but also the conflicting demands of what Lacan designates as "*le désir de la mère*" and "*le nom-du-père*," and what is manifested in these collisions thereby is a more internalized, psychological variation of tragic bond/age.

The play begins, however, in the objective world with the breaking of boundaries. The separation of the living and the dead has been broached by the appearance of the Ghost, a phenomenon that bodes for the men on watch a "strange eruption in the state"³ and a collapse of the order of the hours that has made "the night joint-laborer with the day" (1.1.79). As a result of the death of the elder Hamlet and the marriage of Claudius and Gertrude, the "imperial jointress," Claudius observes that young Fortinbras, thinking "our estate to be disjoint and out of frame" (1.2.20), has moved against Denmark in an effort to reclaim those lands "lost by his father, with all the bands of law" (1.2.24) to Hamlet's father. Horatio further likens the condition of Denmark to that of Rome when Caesar fell:

> The graves stood tenantless, and the sheeted dead
> Did squeak and gibber in the Roman streets.
> As stars with trains of fire, and dews of blood,
> Disasters in the sun, and the moist star
> Upon whose influence Neptune's empire stands
> Was sick almost to doomsday with eclipse.
> (1.1.115–20)

Thus, in typical Renaissance fashion, a break in one link of the chain—King Hamlet's death and Gertrude and Claudius's swift marriage—multiplies with breaks throughout the state and the cosmos and, as we shall see, within the hero.

After dispatching his stewards to turn Fortinbras back and responding favorably to Laertes' request to return to Paris, Claudius turns to Hamlet and rebukes him for what he believes are his violations of the boundaries of gender. Hamlet's grief, Claudius reasons, is an "unmanly" one that shows Hamlet in negation of what a prince ought to be: his excessive sorrow reveals "a will incorrect to heaven / A heart unfortified, or mind impatient, an understanding simple and unschooled" (1.2.94–97). Claudius adds that Hamlet's behavior is not only a crime against princeliness, but also a "fault to heaven, / A fault against the dead, a fault to nature, / To reason most absurd, whose common theme / Is death of fathers" (1.2.101–4). That Claudius should believe Hamlet's understanding to be simple and that his charges against his nephew are those of which he himself is culpable—his killing of his brother and his marriage to his sister-in-law are crimes against heaven, the dead, and nature—are an indictment of Claudius and serve perhaps to undermine his argument. Still, what he says about Hamlet's having violated the boundaries of nature will prove true as Hamlet himself will later testify.

The counterpoint to this theme of broken boundaries is that of bondage, in which Hamlet is entangled. This proscription is evident in Laertes' advice to Ophelia, in which the brother points out that Hamlet's "will is not his own / For he himself is subject to his birth" (1.3.17–18), the consequence of which is that "his choice [must] be circumscribed" (1.3.22). Laertes is referring to Hamlet's limitation in his choice of wife, one imposed upon him by the law, custom, and usage of his kingdom and by his position within that law; but his choice is equally restrained by birth and kinship in terms of physical movement and verbal expression.

When Hamlet requests of his king, uncle, and stepfather that he be allowed to return to school in Wittenberg, Claudius denies the petition because "it is most retrograde to our desire" (1.2.114), and Gertrude reinforces Claudius's command by pleading with Hamlet to remain close to her. The physical confinement imposed upon Hamlet at the outset of the action is repeated and reinforced after the Mousetrap and the killing of Polonius. Then, Claudius proclaims that "We will fetters put about this fear [that is Hamlet] / Which now goes too free-footed" (3.3. 25–26). In addition, Hamlet concludes his first soliloquy with the recognition that "I must hold my tongue" (159), a restriction that seriously inhibits the expression of an emerging and most loquacious self and one that likens him to the child who will be seen but not heard. Is it any wonder, then, that Hamlet will indicate to Rosencrantz and Guildenstern that Denmark is for him "a prison"; what will have contributed significantly to its becoming so is his encounter with the ghost.

Hamlet admits at the outset of that meeting that he is "bound" to hear the inspired communication of the dead, and the ghost responds quickly that "so art thou to revenge" (1.4. 6–7). After the ensuing disclosure of the nature of his unnatural death and the queen's infidelity, the ghost withdraws to return to his own "prison house," commanding and beckoning Hamlet to "Remember me," an injunction that conflicts directly with the advice given him by his stepfather: that it is natural in a world in which the death of fathers is a necessity for sons to forget (the death of) fathers. One might add that it is also necessary that sons forget fathers and the law associated with them, both natural and legal, in order to execute their rites of passage into adulthood and kingship. The major leitmotifs of the broken boundaries in the Renaissance great chain of being, of the restraint effected by that chain upon the hero, and of the resentment of the hero in being so constrained are effectively counterpointed in the couplet with which Shakespeare concludes the first act: "The time is out of joint—O cursed spite, / That ever I was born to set it right" (1.5.188–89). The disjointedness and confinement felt here are repeated and varied throughout the remainder of the play.

In the fifth act, Hamlet, speaking to Horatio, refers to himself as being "benetted round with villainies" (5.2. 29). The allusion is to the plot planned by Claudius and carried out unknowingly by Rosencrantz and Guildenstern to usher him out of Denmark to execution in England, but it serves also as a summation of the condition of bondage in which Hamlet finds himself throughout the play. The net that ensnares Hamlet consists of the following knots: one father would bind him to Denmark; another to revenge his foul and unnatural murder, to taint not his mind, and to leave his mother to heaven. Still, another father (figure), Polonius, would spy on Hamlet just as he spies on his own son in Paris; moreover, by exercising parental control over Ophelia, Polonius effects her return of the Prince's letters, no doubt contributing to Hamlet's suspicion that frailty's name is indeed woman and explaining why Hamlet behaves as he does towards Ophelia, a woman whom he will later declare he loved more than scores of brothers could. Polonius also directs Ophelia in staging the first play-within-a-play, one designed to determine the source of the seeming madness of the Prince. Ophelia, by contract with her father, or the elder generation, becomes an agent in the binding of the hero, one of her own generation; so do Rosencrantz, Guildenstern, and Laertes in Shakespeare's variation of a cultural original sin by which the younger generation is made to pay for the crimes of the older. In Shakespeare's play it is clear, however, that the "primal eldest curse" (3.4.37) for which the young are made to pay is not only Adam and Eve's, but also Cain's.

Rosencrantz and Guildenstern, unlike Horatio, switch their allegiance from Hamlet to Claudius. Their motivation is certainly ambiguous; just as Ophelia demonstrates fidelity in one bond, to her father, by betrayal of another, to Hamlet, so do the Prince's companions. Fidelity to the king-that-is means betrayal to the king-that-was, Hamlet's father, and the king-that-should-have-been, Hamlet. Rosencrantz explains their behavior in terms of their recognition of the integrity of king, kingship, and kingdom:

> The cess of majesty
> Dies not alone, but like a gulf doth draw
> What's near it with it, or it is a massy wheel
> Fix'd on the summit of the highest mount,
> To whose huge spokes ten thousand lesser things
> Are mortis'd and adjoined, which when it falls,
> Each small annexment, petty consequence,
> Attends the boisterous ruin.
>   (3.3.14–22)

What Rosencrantz and Guildenstern do not see is that, by aiding and abetting Claudius, they are two of the "mortis'd and adjoined" lesser things that have already been drawn into the gulf of King Hamlet's most foul and unnatural murder and that they are unwitting participants in the binding of the son/prince, who is appointed by necessity to be the avenging scourge and minister of that defilement. Shakespeare effects a subtle touch of justice when he has Hamlet design their demise through the seal of his father's signet ring; thus, the old king, through the agency of his son, avenges himself upon the mortised and adjoined spokes that are Rosencrantz and Guildenstern. Although their culpability is somewhat qualified by their ignorance of Claudius's plan to have Hamlet executed by the English, "they did make love to this employment" (5.2.57) and so must be sacrificed in necessity's restoration of the "massy wheel" that is king, kingship, and kingdom. So must Laertes.

Like Rosencrantz, Guildenstern, and his own sister, Laertes finds himself caught in the conflict between generations. He chooses to honor his father not only in mourning, like Ophelia, but also by avenging his death. Like Rosencrantz and Guildenstern, he chooses to obey his king by joining him in an unholy alliance (no matter what Hamlet may have done to both father and sister, it is ill-becoming of Laertes to seek revenge in such a cunning and ignoble manner) to kill the king's nephew and son, the kingdom's prince and legitimate heir, and his own rival for the favor of the people. In so doing, however, like the others he betrays one of his own, one more kind that kin, in a questionable pact with the elder generation and becomes a part of the net of villainies that binds Hamlet. That net can also be read as a maze of mirrors.

In his article on Hamlet, Lacan focuses on the Prince's line to Osric about Laertes: "I take him to be a soul of great article, and his infusion of such dearth and rareness as, to make true diction of him, his semblable is his mirror, and who else would trace him, his umbrage, nothing more" (5.2.120–25). Concentrating on the connection of "semblable" to "mirror," Lacan concludes that Laertes is for Hamlet the mirror image of the other, "the one you fight" because he is "the one you admire most."[4] Connecting Lacan's usage of mirror here with his suggestion elsewhere that the mirror image, the statue image, is a false one of the ego as seen as an other, the one that inhibits the self that wants to be, we may infer that, in order to complete his rite of passage and attain the signifying phallus and thereby self-identity, Hamlet must overcome the mirror image, the "semblable," that is Laertes. Coupling this observation with the more traditional one that Hamlet has more than one foil, that is, more than one "semblable," one may further infer that, in Elsinore, Hamlet finds himself in a virtual labyrinthine hall of mirrors, through which he must pass in order to discover and liberate his benetted self.

Thus, in addition to participating in the binding and betrayal of Hamlet, Ophelia, Laertes, and others act as mirrors or foils to Hamlet. Ophelia's grief for her dead father, one that drives her mad, reflects the sorrow of Hamlet for his and the relative madness that attends it. Laertes' need to avenge the death of Polonius recalls the need of Hamlet to avenge the death of his father. Although the conflicts that face these young Danes are similar, they also significantly differ. Ophelia's madness is more severe and complete than Hamlet's; he may walk the thin line between sanity and insanity, but, unlike Ophelia, his sojourns into madness are short-lived— he is mad only when the wind blows in one direction—and it also has a method to it that Ophelia's lacks. Laertes' need for revenge is self-generated; unlike Hamlet, no Ghost commands him to remember nor binds him to avenge. His peers serve not only as knots in the net that entangles Hamlet, but also as mirrors of Hamlet's agon; they, together with all the other major characters, suffer a form of bond/age in Shakespeare's domestic tragedy, one attended by moral ambiguity and the reversal of intention.

Polonius and Laertes are well-intentioned when they counsel Ophelia to return Hamlet's letters, to forego his company, and to look with suspicion upon his "sanctified and pious bonds" (1.3.130) that are aimed to beguile her. Hamlet is a prince; Ophelia is not royal; from Polonius and Laertes' points of view, there can be no marriage, and therefore their advice is given to spare Ophelia rejection and pain. In helping effect physical and emotional restraints upon Ophelia, both men help bring about what they believe is destined, Hamlet's break with her. In short, they do the wrong thing for the right reason.

So do they in their relations with Claudius and Gertrude. Polonius will meddle in the affairs of Hamlet not only out of love for his daughter, but also out of fidelity to his king and queen. Just as he would keep a distant tether on Laertes in Paris because he loves his son and seeks to curb whatever self-destructive habits he may develop there, so Polonius stages the play-within-a-play between Ophelia and Hamlet out of the fidelity and service to the royal family. Both good intentions are reversed, and the lovers are only further alienated and Polonius himself eventually killed by Hamlet. Laertes, in his desire to honor the bond between father and son and king and subject, contracts with Claudius to kill Hamlet, the legitimate heir to the throne. Before he accomplishes that deed, he admits that "it is almost against my conscience" (5.2.278).

Caught even more ironically in the bind of divided loyalties is Ophelia, who literally must choose between both father and brother, who admonish her to break with Hamlet, and the prince himself, whom she obviously loves. Ophelia chooses kinship; the choice, coming immediately on the heels of his mother's quick marriage, is read by Hamlet as another manifestation of woman's frailty. The bond between the young lovers is broken, and both begin a courtship with madness. Ophelia's is consummated when she learns that one love, Hamlet, has killed another, Polonius.

Rosencrantz and Guildenstern find themselves in a similar knot, one that is effectively dramatized by Shakespeare when he has Hamlet question them as to whether or not they were sent for, and they are literally caught speechless. With further coaxing from Hamlet, they confide that they were summoned by the king and queen. That confidence will be the last one from Rosencrantz and Guildenstern to Hamlet; for the remainder of the play, they too will choose Claudius. Like Ophelia, the young men, in connecting with the court and their elders, disconnect with Hamlet, and their advancement toward favor and England redounds upon them in death.

Even Claudius, whom the Freudians would hold up as an alter ego for the Oedipal Hamlet, mirrors the tragically bound prince. Like Hamlet, procrastinating between the business of avenging his father and that of redeeming his mother, Claudius finds himself paralyzed by conscience:

> My stronger guilt defeats my strong intent,
> And, like a man to double business bound,
> I stand in pause where I shall first begin,
> And both neglect . . .
> O limed soul, that struggling to be free
>   Art more engag'd!
>   (3.3.41–43, 69–69)

Like Hamlet, Claudius is bound not only by conscience, but also by Gertrude. He confesses to Laertes that "She is so conjunctive to my life and soul / That, as the star moves not but in his sphere, / I could not but by her" (4.7.14–16).

It is tempting to infer from this confession the following scenario of the pre-play history. Claudius, the younger brother, finds himself by birth disinherited from the throne and by nature attracted to his sister-in-law. The bond of illicit sorority proves stronger than the ties of legitimate fraternity and primogeniture. Claudius breaks both boundaries, kills his brother and marries his sister and in so doing manifests not only the general trope of tragic bond/age but also the specific variations spelled out by Lévi-Strauss in his reading of the Oedipal myth—an overemphasis of the familial, incest, culminates in a denial of kinship, fratricide—and by Girard in his reading of the destruction of difference in a society and its consequence—Claudius erases the boundaries between himself and his older brother and thereby undermines social unity. As necessity asserts itself, Claudius is punished in kind. Hamlet, who has won to his shameful moral persuasion, if not his shameful lust, the will of the Queen, pours poison into the mouth of Claudius, who had poured poison literally into the ear of his brother/King and figuratively into the ear of Denmark, while his sins of having effected the murders of his wife/Queen and his nephew/Prince lie fresh upon his "limed soul."

In the case of Gertrude, much of her experience of tragic bond/age must be inferred. If the Ghost can be trusted, and the play and play-within-the-play would seem to indicate that it can, then Gertrude must have known some bond/age between the time she was seduced by Claudius and the instant he killed Hamlet. Marriage to the King must have been bondage if she had found herself drawn to Claudius, and the King's death must have been a liberation, whether she was an accessory or not. Her marriage to and solicitations for Claudius and her sensitivity to Hamlet's condition of melancholy and madness—her intimation that it is both his father's death and her over-hasty marriage that trouble her son—confirm that she is bonded to both son and new husband. Moreover, the absence of any apparent internal conflict within her suggests that, unlike either Claudius or Hamlet, she does not feel bound by this double business. Indeed, Gertrude seems to be the embodiment of wife/mother's capacity to nurture promiscuously. Even after the closet scene, when Hamlet has cleft her soul in twain, Gertrude would seem to have mended the cleavage enough to protect Claudius from a threatening Laertes. Only at the very conclusion of the play does Shakespeare suggest that Gertrude suffers the anguish of being "doubly bound." Before examining that conclusion, however, it will be helpful to explore the significant difference between all the other major characters and Hamlet: they have no mothers and he does.

When he confronts Laertes before the fencing match that will initiate the denouement, Hamlet apologizes for his rude behavior to Laertes and his family by acknowledging, "I am punish'd / with a sore distraction" (5.2.211). The only distractions throughout the entire action of the play to which that comment could apply are Hamlet's brooding over death and his obsession with his mother, with her hasty, incestuous marriage to his uncle, with her infidelity to his father as revealed by the Ghost, with her habit of siding with Claudius rather than with him, as in the decision to keep him in Elsinore, and with what he perceives to be a rank and gross sensuality that has led her to prefer his satyrish uncle to his Hyperion father and his puritan self. In a Shakespearean play that seems to be located in an Anglo-Catholic world, Hamlet's self-distracting obsession with his mother's repulsive sensuality does seem a bit out of Anglo-Catholic character; it is, however, quite in keeping with the sensibility of one whose greatest bondage is not so much what he perceives but rather what he conceives.

When he confesses to his Wittenberg companions that Denmark has become a prison for him and Rosencrantz replies that that is so because it is "too narrow for your mind," (2.2.248), Hamlet retorts, "O God, I could be bounded in a nutshell, and count myself a king of infinite space—were it not I have bad dreams" (249–50). By his own admission, it is Hamlet's "thinking [that] makes [Denmark] so" (246) much a prison. Whereas Claudius's conscience is caught by the Mousetrap, Hamlet himself is caught by his conscience, bound more by his bad dreams than by any villainy around him. Hamlet is the first modern tragic hero who suffers from what Paul Ricoeur describes as the anxiety of the scrupulous soul: "some craven scruple / Of thinking too precisely upon the event" (4.4.40–41).[5] Thus, "conscience does make [a] coward" of Hamlet and for the Prince, "the native

3 / In Hamlet

hue of resolution / Is sicklied o'er with the pale cast of thought" (3.1.81–83). Furthermore, when, in the graveyard scene, Hamlet observes that the dust of an Alexander might stop a bunghole, Horatio admonishes him that "'twere to consider too curiously, to consider so" (5.1.192).

Scruple, conscience, and too curious a consideration concentrate themselves for the most part in Hamlet's being distracted from his bond to his father that he remember him and avenge his most foul and unnatural murder and by his bond to his mother that he make her remember his father and in so doing divorce herself from the enseamed bed of his uncle. In his first soliloquy, Hamlet dwells upon the two subjects that will continue to distract him from the charge given him by his father: death and his mother. Having not the will to effect his own quietus, he begins with the wish that "this too too sallied flesh would melt, / Thaw, and resolve itself into a dew" (1.2.129–30) into a bubble, not unlike the wombish "Round Zion of the water bead" of Dylan Thomas.[6] The soliloquy midway turns to his mother's sudden marriage, her posting with "wicked speed" and "such dexterity to incestuous sheets" (156–57), and the suggestion that not only is Denmark an unweeded garden, but so is Gertrude.[7]

The implication will become more explicit in the closet scene, when Hamlet's oral daggers will point out to Gertrude that she lives "in the rank sweat of an enseamed bed / Stew'd in corruption, honeying and making love / Over the nasty sty!" (3.4.92–94). The conscious intention of Hamlet seems to be to point out to Gertrude the bestial sensuality of her union with Claudius; however, when one recalls that Hamlet earlier had described Gertrude's union with his father as one in which "she would hang on him / As if increase of appetite had grown / By what it fed on" (1.2.143–44), it becomes clear that Gertrude in Hamlet's mind's eyes is a woman who grants her sexual favors somewhat indiscriminately. That clearly identifies her with the only other promiscuous female in the play, fate:

HAMLET: Good lads, how do you both?
GUILDENSTERN: Happy, in that we are not over-happy; on Fortune's cap we
   are not the very button.
HAMLET: Nor the soles of her shoe?
ROSENCRANTZ: Neither, my lord.
HAMLET: Then you live about her waist, or in the middle of her favors?
GUILDENSTERN: Faith, her privates we.
HAMLET: In the secret parts of Fortune? O, most true, she is a strumpet.
                                                              (2.2.223–32)

Traditional psychoanalytical interpretation of the play holds that Hamlet, bound more to his mother than to his father because he desires his mother and the removal of his father as rival, is prohibited by his own neuroses from carrying out the commands of the Ghost. Freud's theory in *Beyond the Pleasure Principle* and Lacan's theory about repression and foreclosure suggest a related, but significantly more complex and richer reading of Hamlet's delay. Hamlet is triply bound: by *eros*—the desire for his mother, for love's body that is tellurian and therefore rank and gross; by *logos*—the symbolic order of the patriarchal world that demands he avenge the death of his father, purify the stained kingdom, leave his mother to heaven, and taint not his mind; and by *thanatos*—the original instinct to return to the inorganic state by way of the dewy zion of the water bead that is the mother's womb.

In his interpolation of Lacan's reading of *Hamlet*, John Muller quotes Anika Leclaire's metaphor for Lacan's distinction between repression and foreclosure, a metaphor that is quite appropriate to the interpretation of tragic bond/age: "If we imagine experience to be a piece of material made up of crisscrossing threads, we could say that repression would figure in it as a rent or a tear which can still be repaired, whereas foreclosure would figure in it as a *béance* due to the weaving itself, in short a primal hole which will never again be able to find its substance, since it has never been anything other than the substance of a hole and can only be filled, and even then imperfectly, by a patch."[8]

Muller suggests that, for Lacan, the absence of the no/name-of-the-father means the subject never achieves primary repression, proper symbolic identification with the father, and integration into the social and symbolic order and that this absence is the basis of psychosis. He then proceeds to read Ophelia's madness as a manifestation of such foreclosure.[9] Although Hamlet's madness is not nearly that of Ophelia's and his problem more one of repression than foreclosure and therefore reparable, there is still the hint of foreclosure within Hamlet that explains both his delay in executing the demands of the father and the symmetry of Shakespeare's ending.

When the reality of the father's world, of the patriarchal requirements of the written and unwritten law, becomes too painful for Hamlet, when he curses his very birth because, being an aggrieved Dane, prince, and son binds him unbearingly, the "consummation devoutly to be wish'd" is deliverance from the world of the father into that of the mother, even if it be the swampish womb associated with her who manipulates the threads of the webbed world, Dame Fortune. All that is necessary for such a consummation is the readiness, and by the fifth act, Hamlet is prepared because he has resigned himself to accept his mother and fortune as they are, to accept what must be.

In the final scene, Gertrude's bond/age is made evident in that she is now more solicitous toward Hamlet than she is towards Claudius; indeed, her concern for Hamlet leads her to defy Claudius. As she wipes the brow of Hamlet, she takes up the cup, rejects the King's command not to drink, and quaffs the poison intended for Hamlet. Furthermore, when she discovers later that she has been poisoned and is dying, she cries out, not to her husband and King, who she has had time enough to conclude is the would-be killer of her son, but to Hamlet himself. Thus, in the moment when she must make a final choice between husband and son, Gertrude chooses her son and by that choice, Hamlet is liberated.

Before he dies, Hamlet acquits himself of the father world honorably and thereby repairs the rent in the fabric of psychological experience. He slays Claudius and is the indirect means of his mother's death. Both deaths rid the patriarchy of the rottenness that taints the kingdom and allow the Ghost of his father to purify his soul more peacefully in purgatory. He accidentally kills Laertes, becoming once more the scourge and minister to those sucked into the moral abyss of Claudius's collapsed and usurped kingship. In his dying breath, he bequeaths his fleeting kingship to another mirrored alter ego, Fortinbras, "a delicate and tender prince" who "with divine ambition puffed" (4.5.48–49) has fulfilled his duties to both father and uncle. He charges still another, Horatio, whose "blood and passion are so well commingled" that he "is not passion's slave," (3.2.74, 77) to forego the devoutly desired felicity and tell his and Denmark's tale in the ensuing silence. In short, Hamlet delivers Denmark from defilement, frees himself from the bondage of his patrimony by honoring "filial obligation," affirms through Horatio and Fortinbras a restorative fraternity over a binding paternity and maternity, and receives a sign of his mother's desire.

It is important to note that, even after Hamlet has murdered the interfering Polonius, has arranged the deaths of Rosencrantz and Guildenstern, who "are not near [his] conscience" (5.2.58) and therefore beyond that which binds him, and has unthinkingly turned Laertes' own springe upon Laertes himself, Hamlet only kills his uncle after Laertes tells him that his uncle has killed his mother. Hamlet's words to Claudius, as he pours the poisonous drink into his mouth, are "Follow my mother" (5.2.309), not "follow my father." It is not only Claudius, however, who follows Gertrude into death; it is also Hamlet, and he does so on the very day, thirty years after his father lost part of his patrimony to Denmark, that Fortinbras marches into Elsinore and reclaims that patrimony. Thus, by virtue of the cry he utters in avenging his father upon his uncle and of the sequence of his own death, coming shortly after his mother's and fortune's reversal of territorial patrimony, Hamlet reveals himself as one still caught in the gap that is the desire of the mother and that has not been fully patched up by his fidelity to the law of the father.

Such is the conclusion of a beautiful orchestration of foreclosure and repression, of the forces of *le désir de la mère* and *le nom-du-père*, of the *philoi* and the *nomoi*, of paternity and fraternity. Such intricate arrangement of dialectically tensive images, metaphors, and symbols is the aesthetic resolution necessitated by a life grown more complex in the boundaries of the external world and divisions in the internal one during the two millennia between Aeschylus and Shakespeare. Both the complexity of Shakespeare's world and the rich orchestration of his art are manifested similarly in *King Lear.*

4
In *King Lear*

King Lear begins with some obvious variations on the trope of tragic bond/age. In his machinations to effect a rift between his father and his brother, Edmund forges a letter in which Edgar is made to write, "I begin to find an idle and fond / Bondage in the oppression of aged tyranny" (1.2.51). Later, in responding to his encounter with Edgar, Edmund tells Gloucester that he tried to remind his brother by "How manifold and strong a bond / The child was bound to the father" (2.1.49). In reversing the true feelings of the brothers' regard for their father, Edmund's speeches manifest the trope of tragic bond/age, whereby what is a bond for one, Edgar, becomes bondage for the other, Edmund, whose "services are bound" to nature's laws (1.2.12). Thus, Shakespeare fashions an agon by which Edgar and Edmund trade places, as Edgar becomes the one with whom Gloucester cracks the parental bond.

What Shakespeare delineates in the subplot, he dramatizes in the primary plot. When asked to express the measure of her love for her father after immediately responding that she can "nothing" say, Cordelia tells Lear that she loves him "according to my bond" (1.1.95). Cordelia, unfortunately, adds "nor more, nor less," a consideration, which, by Horatio's standards, may be to consider too curiously. Indeed, it may very well be that the unnecessary negatives that cancel out the positive of her "according to my bond" constitute her own culpability in the ensuing disaster. Lear, blinded and deafened by his narcissistic needs, does not heed or hear what under ordinary circumstances he himself would understand about love and bondship for a little later he will admonish Regan to "better know'st . . . the bond of childhood" (2.4.181). Of course, Lear not only "hath ever but slenderly known himself" (1.1.296), but also has not known or recognized the requirements of parenthood. Thus, when not satisfied by her answers, Lear, disclaiming all "paternal care/Propinquity, and property of blood"

(1.1.115–16), disinherits Cordelia. Ironically in denying Cordelia and banishing Kent, who has followed his King as would a son a father, Lear effects his own disinheritance and banishment by his other daughters.

The breakdown of the parent/child relationship is but one variation on the intricate theme of tragic bond/age in *Lear*. The King himself initiates the "differences"; he divides up the kingdom by establishing boundaries. As a result of his rejection of his youngest daughter, Burgundy will disengage himself from Cordelia because of her poverty and France wed her for it. Subsequently, Gloucester will renounce Edgar; Edmund denounce Gloucester; Goneril deceive Albany; the sisters, each other, and Edmund everyone. All of these betrayals in the human and social order will resonate with cataclysms in the natural and cosmic ones, and Gloucester will rightly proclaim that "these late eclipses in the sun and moon portend . . . the bond cracked twixt son and father" and "father against child" (1.2.112–17).

As both plot and subplot progress, the image of bondage manifests itself repeatedly. Cordelia tells the court that "Time will unfold what plaited cunning hides" (I, i, 283); and Kent, in commenting to Cornwall upon Oswald's deceit, indicts all those who would break the sacred ties: "Such smiling rogues as these / Like rats, off bite the holy cords a-twain / Which are too intrinsic to loose" (2.2.79). Kent's physical imprisonment in the stock precedes Lear's loss of knightly retinue; Goneril and Regan hold a "hard rein . . . against the old King" (3.1.27); Cornwall orders his men to "pinion [Gloucester] like a thief" (3.7. 24); and Gloucester finds himself "tied to the stake" (3.7.51). Finally, when Edmund does unite himself to someone else, it is a fatal ménage à trois: "I was contracted to [Goneril and Regan] both. All three / now marry in an instant" (5.3.228).

As noted before, it is clear in all of Shakespeare's plays that the world has grown more complex in the two thousand years between Aeschylean and Shakespearean tragedy. Basic to that complexity is the growing intricacy of social and human bonds; the world is a chain of being imprisoning the hero in its complexity. In *King Lear*, Shakespeare suggests that in such a world redemption from tragic bondage needs to take the form of a secular version of what in the medieval religious world was known as the *via negativa*. In *King Lear*, the medieval mystic's quest to experience God through renunciation and the modern existentialist's attempt to discover Being through dread are the parameters of a symbolic pattern of redemption from bondage by way of negation.

In Christendom there have been two basic approaches to an experience and understanding of God: the *via positiva* and the *via negativa*. The former ascribes to the creator the perfect manifestations of those virtues found in creatures and the creation. The difference between God and man is thereby quantitative, not qualitative. God is faith, hope, and charity all made perfect. Such a view is subject to the criticism that it tends to create God in the image of man; its defense is the biblical one that man is after all created in the image of God. The latter view of the *via negativa* denies in God the manifestation of any human or earthly virtue. God is the wholly other who is completely detached from and independent of creation. Moreover, he cannot be known by the finite modes of human intellect or understanding. Because God is like no thing man knows, he can be said to be no thing or nothingness itself. In order for man to experience God in this life, he must strive to become like God—detached from things and nothing himself. He must prepare himself to receive God through the threefold way of purgation, illumination, and union. He must strip away the things and affections of this world, rendering himself "poor" and "naked in intent."[1] Renouncing intelligence and memory, he must enter a mysterious realm of "silence," a "cloud of unknowing," a "darkness beyond light," in which he feelingly sees the wretched self he has been.[2] In this paradoxical state, where "the readiness makes all the difference,"[3] the bitterness of "doubtful dread" is transformed into the "sweetness of grace," and the soul is made ready for a "one-ing with Christ."[4]

What the ontology of the existentialist Martin Heidegger has in common with the theology of the medieval mystic is that both see transcendence of the quotidian world largely in terms of a phenomenological encounter with nothingness. For Heidegger, man is thrown out of nothing into existence, into being-in-the-world. Such existence, however, is not authentic, for man is caught up in the calculation of thingness, and calculation uses up whatever it calculates. In order for man to establish an authentic existence, an essential self, he must experience dread.[5]

In dread, the quotidian, the whatever-is-in-totality, seems to withdraw, and man feels oppressed by the resulting emptiness. Furthermore, as existent, man slips away and has the uncanny feeling that it is another "one" that experiences the anxiety of dread. In the trepidation of this encounter, where the quotidian world and the "I" have slipped away, one is left with nothing to hold on to. That nothing, however, is the ground of Being, because dread, in encountering nothingness or "nothing-ness," encounters pure Being, that which informs all things, but which is itself no thing. Such dread is paradoxically pervaded by an "unintelligible peace and calm," in which the self submits to the "soundless voice" of Being. According to Heidegger, "this projection into Nothing on the basis of hidden dread is . . . transcendence."[6]

The primary difference between the *via negativa* of the mystic and that of the existentialist is that the former leads to a metaphysical God beyond time and history, while the latter leads to a physical Being within all things. Both, however, are a progression towards truth and authenticity, and collectively they imply a symbolic passage acted out by King Lear. Lear initiates his journey down the *via negativa*; the play begins with the King's divesting himself of the bondage of "business," "rule," "interest of territory," and "cares of state" in order that he might "unburdened crawl toward death" (1.1.42). Shortly thereafter, as a result of his narcissistic response to Cordelia's silence and Kent's supplication, Lear renounces "paternal care" towards his daughter and his vassal. He begins to detach himself not only from created things, but also from creatures, and in so doing he begins to break the natural and social bond. Once he begins this journey along the *via negativa*, however, other forces take over, and he is stripped of his kingship against his wishes and beyond his imagination.

One of the most effective dramatizations of the diminution of Lear as both king and man occurs in Act 3, scene 4, when Lear undergoes the torment of having his retinue of knights and thereby his kingship reduced by his ungrateful and impatient daughters. Having fled Goneril, who would cut the number of his unruly knights from 100 to 50, Lear is further shocked to discover that Regan would admit to her castle but 25. Lear turns back to Goneril, still trying to calculate love: "I'll go with thee / Thy fifty yet doth double five and twenty / And thou art twice her love" (262–63). It is too late, however, and Goneril answers, "What need you five and twenty, ten or five?" and Regan, "What need one?" (264–65). The dramatically effective countdown from 100 to 50 to 25 to 10 to 5 to one to none beautifully underscores the lessening of Lear's majesty and the play's inevitable movement towards nothingness.

The diminution of the king is paralleled by the devolution of the kingdom. In his book, *Myth, Religion, and Mother Right,* J. J. Bachofen theorizes that society evolves through three successive stages.[7] The first is a presocial, anarchic, tellurian stage, in which offspring are abandoned and prehuman man lives in bestial and promiscuous chaos. The second is matriarchy, in which women succor and raise children and thereby create and rule an agriculturally based society. The third is patriarchy, a higher form of social life, in which hunting replaces agriculture as the basis of economy, and man assumes control of a society where kinship and inheritance are more spiritual and civil than natural. Although Bachofen's nineteenth-century, armchair anthropology offends both field anthropologists and feminists alike, his theory is a provocative one that has stimulated and inspired mythographers; moreover, it provides a pattern of social evolution that is reversed in Shakespeare's play.

Lear, to the dismay of some of his followers, jettisons the patriarchy by relinquishing his kingdom and his power to his daughters. It may be argued that Lear settles his state upon the Dukes of Albany and Cornwall as well as upon his daughters, but it is in fact Goneril and Regan who command not only their lands and their lords, but also their father, who has become in his dotage an infant to their maternal power. Moreover, in abandoning Cordelia, Lear also abandons the civil and natural "bond" that Cordelia claims is the essence of her love for her father and her king. The result is a devolution to the lesser form of social order, the matriarchy.

From the perspective of the psychoanalyst, this devolution manifests a desire to return to infantile union with the mother. Tired with his rule and role as the no/name-of-the-father figure in the courtly world, Lear is ready for what Freud describes as the instinctive return to an earlier and happier existence or what Lacan calls the object of the desire of the mother. He would do so under the love and protection of the good mother/daughter, Cordelia, but his intention is reversed, and he finds himself not the sole object of Cordelia's desire—she will share her love with any future husband and finds one in France—nor that of his other daughters, who will more boldly and cruelly reject him for others. This slip into traumatic abandonment in second childhood is a necessary station in Lear's pilgrimage down the *via negativa,* one that is torturously intensified when Goneril and Regan, through their infidelities to their husbands and to each other and through their sexual attraction to the natural son of Gloucester, the bastard Edmund, transform the matriarchy into tellurian anarchy.

The tellurian character of the chaos that ensues is evoked primarily and appropriately in terms of animal imagery. Goneril, in forsaking Lear, is described as a "sea monster." Subsequently, Shakespeare inundates the play with bestial images. Goneril and Regan become serpents, wolves, vultures, boars, tigers, centaurs, and fiends; Lear himself becomes a dragon. Edgar describes a world in which man is "hog in sloth, fox in stealth, wolf in greediness, lion in prey" (3.4.95–97) and one in which Edgar himself dines on frog, toad, tadpole, rat, and dog (3.4.134–38). Moreover, the Duke of Albany laments a "humanity [that] must perforce prey upon itself / Like monsters of the deep" (4.2.49–50). Thus, those who have aspired too high are brought, or bring themselves, back down to the chthonic.

The devolution of the state is reinforced by the seeming devolution of the cosmos, as Shakespeare takes the conventional parallel between the king and the kingdom and not only alludes to the "late eclipses in the sun and moon" that forebode the rebellion of child against father, but also has Lear urge the apocalyptic storm to "smite flat the thick rotundity o' the world," to "crack nature's molds," and to "spill out all germens" (3.2.8) and thereby implode nature backwards towards a fluid and unformed mass.

In *King Lear*, ontogeny recapitulates phylogeny for, as the kingdom and the cosmos devolve towards the primordial, so do man and the human mind retrogress towards the more primitive and irrational. Lear's devolution as man takes the form of his becoming a child again, his making his daughters his mother. That he is losing his identity as both king and man becomes clear to Lear himself when he cries, "Doth any here know me? This is not Lear. . . . Who is it that can tell me who I am?" The Fool answers, "Lear's shadow" (1.4.245–50). Later, he adds that Lear has become "an O without a figure." This slipping away of the superfluous self is manifested again on the heath when Lear recognizes in Edgar the *ding an sich*: "Thou art the thing itself. Unaccommodated man is no more but such a poor, bare, forked animal as thou art" (3.4.110–12). Interestingly, this "thing itself" is the same man who, upon his flight from father and court, proclaimed, "Edgar, I nothing am." (2.3.21) Thus, Lear proceeds so far along the *via negativa* that, when he asks immediately after his discovery of unaccommodated man to be unbuttoned, one is tempted to read that as an unbuttoning of the navel as well as of the garment.

Once again, devolution in one sphere is paralleled by retrogression in another, and Lear's loss of self is reinforced by his loss of reason. Justifying his and Cordelia's plain talk, Kent sums up Lear's lapse into foolishness: "To plainness honour's bound / When majesty stoops to folly" (1.1.150–51). Later, the Fool admonishes Lear, "Thou hast pared thy wit o' both sides and left nothing i' the middle" (1.4. 204–5). Lear recognizes his fall into indiscretion and beats at the gate that let folly in and judgment out. Eventually, that fall becomes one into madness, and Gloucester articulates what has happened to both himself and Lear when he acknowledges that "The grief hath crazed my wits" (3.4.175).

This retrogression of the mind from the rational to the irrational—one that Lear tries to forestall—is a transformation not only from wit to madness, but also from light to darkness. Both Lear and Gloucester act out of increasing degrees of intellectual blindness, a motif Shakespeare strikes early when he has Kent beg Lear, "See better, Lear, and let me still remain / The true blank of thine eye" (1.1.160). Unfortunately, Lear's inability to see precludes this, and it is not until later that Kent, together with the Fool and Edgar, puts off the superfluous accoutrements of art and the court and becomes the blank of Lear's eye. The figurative blindness of Lear is made dramatically literal in the gouging out of Gloucester's eyes, which are reduced to tellurian "vile jelly" (3.7.83). The imagery suggests that the literal blinding of Gloucester and the figurative one of Lear are part of the devolution in the play, one, however, by which agenbite makes possible inwit as both smell out what they cannot see.

What all these devolutions and retrogressions have in common is that they all lead towards nothingness, and the essence of Shakespeare's dramatic dialectic is summed up early when Kent responds to one of the Fool's nonsense poems with the words, "This is nothing, fool" (1.4.141). The Fool retorts, "Then 'tis like the breath of an unfed lawyer. You gave me nothing for't. Can you make no use of nothing, nuncle?" (144). Lear responds, "Why no boy, nothing can be made out of nothing" (145). The play abounds with images and repetitions of the idea and phenomenon of nothingness, and the pattern of those images would seem to refute Lear and support the Fool's implication that some use can indeed be made of nothing.

To begin, France tells Cordelia that she has become "most rich in being poor" (1.1.253). Lear himself, as a result of his fall from majesty, comes to recognize that "the art of our necessities is strange / That can make vile things precious" (3.2.70–71)—perhaps even the "vile jelly" of blindness. In addition, when mad Lear and blind Gloucester meet at Dover, the king is able, as a result of his encounter with and transformation into unaccommodated man, to share with Gloucester the truths he has learned about justice. Edgar's response that Lear's argument is "reason in madness" (4.6.179) recapitulates the theme in the play that much madness is divinest sense, an idea also manifested in the truths implicit in the Fool and Tom's nonsense.

In depriving himself of kingdom and kin and in being disinherited as king and father, Lear becomes literally poverty-stricken, unhoused, silent ("I will say nothing"), and naked in intent. He enters a cloud of unknowing or forgetting, where he is disoriented in the world of things and even fails to recognize those closest to him. Through one alter-ego, Gloucester, he experiences the dark night of the soul and ascends the steps of Mount Carmel in the form of the cliffs of Dover. Through another alter-ego, Edgar, he experiences the loss of public self and becomes a "houseless poverty" (3.4.26).

Like Gloucester, he sees "feelingly" the wretched self that he has been; he also realizes that the hand Gloucester would kiss "smells of "mortality" (4.4. 136). He has been propelled into this state by the "climbing sorrow" he calls the *hysterica passio*, a condition, it might be well to recall, that attends his sense of the loss of self and one that is therefore not unlike dread. In this state, he comes to learn with Edgar, that "ripeness is all" (5.2.11), that one need only ready oneself for the "going hence" (10), for transcendence.

Clearly, Lear is driven down a symbolic *via negativa* that dialectically combines medieval mysticism and modern existentialism, but does he find either Christ or Being? The general pattern of the play suggests that he does, that his reconciliation with Cordelia—with the child who goes about her father's business, whose kiss brings restoration and reparation for the wrongs he has done and have been done against him, whose simple reply of "nothing" to her father's query of how much she loves him can be read to mean like no thing in the quotidian world—is a reconciliation with the other, with Christ. Moreover, this same Cordelia, we are told, "redeems nature from the general curse" (4.6. 210), a redemption that is not only nature's, but also Christ's. In her love and in his confrontation with the uncanny and strange elements, Lear recovers the familiar and draws near to Being.

In this light, then, the wheel of fire upon which Lear is "bound" and the bleeding O's that were Gloucester's eyes are paradoxically images of zero, the sign of nothingness, and circles, the sign of wholeness or allthingness. They are symbols of a nothingness that is purgative, truth-revealing, and redemptive. Lear, "by the art of known and feeling sorrows" is made "pregnant to good pity" (4.6.226–27), and Cordelia and he experience a sweetness and grace, a peace and calm, that transform Apollonian bondage into Dionysian bond/age: "We two alone will sing like birds i' the cage" (5.3.9). Shakespeare thereby suggests that woman is both the source of the hero's bondage, Goneril and Reagan, as well as his liberation, Cordelia.

Cordelia, however, is hanged, and Lear is made to suffer a further deprivation that is unbearable not only to him, but also to many readers as well:

> And my poor fool is hanged. No, no, no life.
> Why should a dog, a horse, a rat have life
> And thou no breath at all? Thou'lt come no more,
> Never, never, never, never, never!
> Pray you undo this button.
>
> (5.3.304–9)

The repetition of eleven negatives in these five lines seems to shift the dialectic away from a nothingness that is redemptive and truth-revealing to one that is empty and apocalyptic. It is as though the playwright, having completed his orchestration of the symbolic *via negativa*, adds a coda that is an ironic counterpoint to his main theme. Shakespeare seems to imply that, although the pilgrim may have been properly prepared through renunciation and illumination to receive a "one-ing" with the wholly other, he may ultimately be abandoned, disinherited once again. One is tempted to conclude that Shakespeare in the end accepts the pessimistic and nihilistic implications of Lear's logic—that nothing can be made of nothing. The entire dialectic of the play, however, suggests that Shakespeare was sensitive to the need and promise of the symbolic *via negativa*, but also uncertain as to its possibility. It is the evocation of this uncertainty, just one manifestation of the growing doubt of an age undergoing a cultural transformation from tradition to modernity, one in which tradition seemed bondage and all bonds were in question, that is at the heart of the dramatic achievement of tragic bond/age in *King Lear*.

5
In *Macbeth*

One common theme in Greek and Shakespearean tragedy is that of the crime against kinship. In *Hamlet*, it is experienced primarily in the person of the Prince, who feels disinherited of kingship and love by his uncle and his mother. In *King Lear*, a father disinherits one daughter and in turn is cut off by the others. Although Macbeth has neither parents nor children, his crimes against kinship surpass even more terribly the limits of the familiar. In *Macbeth*, crime against kinship is orchestrated through repetitions and variations of the leitmotifs of vegetation, the banquet, and the babe, and such scoring evokes the point/counterpoint of rootedness and deracination, *nomoi* and *philoi*, magic and religion.

Early in the play, just after the weird sisters have told Macbeth of his fate, Banquo questions them about his own:

> If you can look into the seeds of time,
> And say which grain will grow and which will not,
> Speak then to me, who neither beg nor fear
> Your favors or your hate.
>   (1.3. 58–61)

The metaphor establishes a connection between fate and vegetation, generation, and royal lineage. The witches' response, that Banquo will be paradoxically lesser than Macbeth insofar as he will not be a king and greater insofar as he will beget kings, identifies greatness and nobility with vegetative fertility and generation. That identification is continued and extended later when Duncan describes his relationship with his two great warriors and kinsmen, Macbeth and Banquo, whom he has lately honored and elevated, in the following manner: "I have begun to plant thee, and will labor / To make thee full of growing" (1.4.28–29). Banquo's response, "There if

I grow / The harvest is your own" (1.4.32–33), suggests that the fruit of such royal husbandry is the flowering of an obedient and faithful thane. Furthermore, Shakespeare extends the metaphor of royal lineage and vegetation when he has Banquo recall the witches' prophecy that he "should be the root and father of many kings" (3.1.5–6). Finally, at the conclusion of the play Malcolm refers to the "calling home our exiled friends abroad / That fled the snares of watchful tyranny" as a deed to "be newly planted in time" (5.8.65–67).

This motif of the royal house as a growing plant is repeated and varied when Macbeth laments the fact that, according to the witches, he shall not be succeeded by one of his own immediate house:

> They hailed him father to a line of kings.
> Upon my head they placed a fruitless crown
> And put a barren scepter in my gripe,
> Thence to be wrenched with an unlineal hand,
> No son of my succeeding.
>
> (3.1.60–64)

For Macbeth, who has himself wrenched from Duncan and Malcolm the throne with an unlineal hand, there can be no succession and no flowering, no rooting and fathering of kings, for, in murdering Duncan, he has deracinated himself. Moreover, the fruitless crown and barren scepter are suggestive respectively of the unsexed and therefore fruitless Lady Macbeth and the equally unsexed—he is more than once chided by Lady Macbeth for failing to act as a potent and virile man—and therefore impotent Macbeth. Furthermore, in cutting themselves off from their root (that is, from Duncan, who is figuratively father both to Macbeth—"our duties are to your throne and state children and servants" [4.4.24–25]—and to Lady Macbeth—"Had he not resembled / My father as he slept, I had done't" [2.2. 13–14]), they cut themselves off from the future.

Shakespeare again repeats and varies this leitmotif of the rooted lineage in the second prophecy of the witches when Macbeth learns the conditions of his kingdom and mortality. The second and third apparitions that appear to him are a bloody child and one with a tree in its hand, and the accompanying prophecies are that "none of woman born / Shall harm Macbeth" (4.1.80–81) and "Macbeth shall never vanquished be until / Great Birnam Wood to high Dunsinane Hill / Shall come against him" (4.1.92–93). Macbeth's response to the latter is "That will never be. / Who can impress the forest, bid the tree / Unfix his earth-bound root?" (4.1.94–96). In a sense, Macbeth's fall is a failure of hermeneutics, an inability to interpret imaginatively the "double" meaning of the witches' visions and words.

Macbeth cannot see that his nemesis is one "from his mother's womb / Untimely ripped" (5.8.5–16) or more appropriately one uprooted, nor that a forest can be figuratively uprooted if an army disguises itself with branches from that forest and seems to be the very wood moving towards Dunsinane. More importantly, Macbeth cannot understand that, in killing Duncan and in ordering the deaths of Banquo, Fleance, and Macduff's family and servants, he is the one who has severed the family tree or the family flower from its root. Before parting from him to go out riding with his son, Banquo pledges to Macbeth that his duties are to his king "with a most indissoluble tie / Forever knit" (3.1.16–18). The pledge will have ironic meaning; as soon as Banquo departs, Macbeth will seek to sever that tie:

> Come, seeing night
> Scarf up the tender eye of pitiful day,
> And with thy bloody and invisible hand
> Cancel and tear to pieces that great bond
> Which keeps me pale.
> (3.2.46–50)

Is that great bond the one that Banquo earlier pledged to Duncan, which, if honored, threatens Macbeth's newfound kingship? Or is it the one that links Banquo in bondage to Macbeth himself, one that the newly-crowned King would tear to pieces so that he not be judged unfavorably in the eyes of the kingdom and his fate of imperial impotence not resolve itself in favor of Banquo's issue? Or is it the one among Banquo, Fleance, and their royal progeny; in having Banquo and his son killed, Macbeth would have unraveled what the Weird sisters prophesy fate has plotted. The great bond is of course all these, and on the one hand it will be canceled insofar as Banquo will be killed; on the other hand, Macbeth will be forever knit to, in the bondage of, Banquo as his ghost will haunt the banquet and his children supplant Macbeth on the throne. In a futile attempt to realize through Macduff what he has failed to accomplish through Banquo—the deracination of the familial that stands between him and maintenance of the throne—Macbeth will seek the end of Macduff by killing all those "that trace him in his line" (4.1.153). He will succeed in erasing the traces of the line—Macduff's family—but in contrast to his success with Banquo and Duncan, he will miss the head, Macduff himself, who will avenge himself and Scotland upon the usurper.

That such revenge should be achieved through a son, who has been from his mother's womb and whose children have been from him untimely ripped, when a wood is from its roots unfixed, fits the punishment to the crime. The irony of such justice is further evident in the fact that Macbeth suffers from an avarice that "grows with more pernicious root / Than summer-seeming lust" (4.3.85) and that both Macbeth and his Lady suffer from a mind diseased by a "rooted sorrow" (5.3.41), one that derives from having "eaten on the insane root / that takes the reason prisoner" (1.3.84–85). In contrast to the benevolent planting evident in the reciprocity between Duncan and his loyal thanes is the malevolent rooting manifested in that which feeds the avarice and madness of King and Lady Macbeth.

This last image indicates that, just as there are two kinds of rootedness in the play, so there are two kinds of banquets: fair and foul. The benevolent banquet appears both at the beginning and middle of the play. When Shakespeare has Duncan indicate that Macbeth "is so full valiant / And in his commendations I am fed. / It is a banquet to me" (1.4.53–56), he reiterates the idea that the worthy thane is not only flower but also fruit for the king that has planted him. At the conclusion of Act 3, the anonymous Lord suggests that when the forces gathering in England turn their strength against Macbeth and dislodge him from his unlineal throne,

> we may again
> Give to our tables meat, sleep to our nights,
> Free from our feasts and banquets bloody knives,
> Do faithful homage and receive free honors:
> All which we pine for now.
> (3.6.33–37)

What the Scots long for now and what has been missing from their tables since Duncan's murder is the generous banquet at which the king feeds upon the deeds of his loyal thanes, and they also thrive on the honors generously bestowed upon them by him. What has also been missing is true companionship, ceremony by which those who break bread together are knit together. That Duncan's death means the end of such banquets is evident when Macbeth metaphorically describes that murder in these terms: "The wine of life is drawn. . . . The spring, the head, the fountain of your blood / Is stopped; the very source of it is stopped" (2.3.95–98). In this particular corruption of the sacrificial killing of the king/god, Shakespeare suggests that Duncan's murder denies the Scots their communal banquet. How can there be a communion without the blood/wine of the host/Host?

In place of that fair banquet and communion is the foul one served up by both Macbeth and Lady Macbeth. Having successfully implored the ministering spirits to "take my milk for gall" (1.5.49), Lady Macbeth obviously must serve up to those babes that have sucked at her breast that which nourishes not. Also, whatever she pours into the ear of her husband upon his return home at the beginning of the play is anything but the "milk of human kindness." Moreover, the wine she serves the king's guards is evidently not that of life; it is a vintage that makes them drunk and her bold in their treason to their king.

Macbeth does not literally serve up anything as malevolent as Lady Macbeth's gall or wine; nevertheless, he is associated with the malevolent banquet. He himself declares that sleep is the "chief nourisher in life's feast . . . that knits up the raveled sleave of care" (2.2.39). In murdering sleep by murdering Duncan, Macbeth thereby destroys that which nourishes life's feast, allows "wicked dreams [to] abuse / The curtained sleep" (2.1.50), and tears up the bonding effect of slumber. Moreover, Macbeth is not the host that Duncan is; initially, he betrays his guests by leaving the banquet before Duncan has supped. Subsequently, just after learning from his hired assassins that Fleance has escaped and lamenting that "now I am cabined, cribbed, confined, bound in / To saucy doubts and fears" (3.3.23–24), his Lady must once more remind Macbeth that his rude withdrawal from the banquet with his thanes robs it of its generosity, ceremony, and benevolence:

> The feast is sold
> That is not often vouched, while 'tis a-making,
> 'Tis given with welcome. To feed were best at home;
> From thence, the sauce to meat is ceremony;
> Meeting were bare without it.
>   (3.4.33–37)

This is the same banquet about which Lady Macbeth says that, if Banquo "had been forgotten, / It had been as a gap in our great feast" (3.1.11–12) and Macbeth urges Banquo, "Fail not our feast" (3.1.27). It would appear that both are anxious that Banquo attend a dinner at which Macbeth will prove a bad host. The audience, of course, learns that Macbeth intends that Banquo shall be the meat upon which he feeds rather than the guest whom he serves. Moreover, Banquo ironically and hauntingly attends the banquet, driving Macbeth to greater distraction and rude behavior as a host and reiterating once more that Macbeth, like Hamlet, is bound not only by "the dagger of the mind" (2.1.37), but also by the mind's "horrible shadow" (3.4.106) that is the mocking spirit of Banquo.

Later, when the heir to the throne confronts Macduff in England, Malcolm, pretending to be the worst possible leader in order to test Macduff, describes himself in terms that are more suited to Macbeth, who is both the voracious devourer of Scotland— "And my more-having would be as a sauce / To make me hunger more" (4.3.81–82)—and the host who would once again deprive Scotland of its human kindness:

> Nay, had I power, I should
> Poor the sweet milk of concord into hell
> Uproar the universal peace, confound
> All unity on earth.
> (4.3.97–100)

In addition, Malcolm also refers to himself as the "weak, poor, innocent lamb" that others would offer up to appease the "angry God" that is Macbeth.

As he himself later proclaims, Macbeth has so "supped full with horrors" (5.5.13) that he has "almost forgot the taste of fears" (5.5.9). Macbeth is the one whose deeds cause Duncan's horses unnaturally to "eat each other" (3.4.18) and who hopes that "famine and the ague eat [Malcolm's army] up" (5.5.3-4). He also has fed to satiety on the words of the witches and Lady Macbeth, and, consequently, once more in tragic bond/age it is the female who through her word helps weave the line that ensnares the protagonist. This participation in the malevolent banquet—the feeding upon the witches' prophecy, Lady Macbeth's verbal incitement, the innocent lamb, and the blood of his king and country—and the failure to participate wholly in the ceremonial meal either by absence or distraction preclude Macbeth's participation in the communal banquet and, as in the drama of Aeschylus, corrupt all rites. This failure to engage in the communal banquet, together with his tendency to uproot, effect the only fear that Macbeth tastes throughout the tragedy: that he shall not be succeeded upon the throne of Scotland by his own sons.

After learning from Macbeth of the prophecy of the witches and having invoked the spirits that tend upon mortal thoughts to unsex her, Lady Macbeth proclaims upon Macbeth's arrival home, "I feel now / The future in the instant" (1.5.58–59). What she thinks she senses is the accomplishment of the murder of Duncan and the crowning of Macbeth; what the lines ironically foreshadow is the realization of Macbeth's lone fear that he shall not be succeeded by generation of his own. Because she has unsexed herself and because, in killing Duncan, Banquo, and Macduff's family, Macbeth has dared more than becomes a man, because he has ceased to be the very man Lady Macbeth feels he may not become in failing to kill Duncan—has indeed become impotent—there can be no children for both. What seems fair at the moment to Lady Macbeth, feeling the future in the instant, is foul for, in the very moment she and Macbeth contemplate cutting the root of the family tree of Scotland, they cut themselves off from the future, and their suffering is their childlessness. One can easily imagine, for example, that, when Lady Macbeth cannot wash the blood from her hands, it is not only Duncan's that Shakespeare would have us see in our mind's eye, but also the blood of those babes whom she has metaphorically aborted.

Perhaps that is why Macbeth fears that pity for Duncan will take the form of a naked, newborn babe and trumpet his crime throughout the kingdom: that infant is but one variation of the same one that Shakespeare repeats throughout his play. It is the babe whose brains Lady Macbeth would dash out, the one that appears in the last prophecies of the witches representing Macduff, the one who is from its mother's womb untimely ripped, and Banquo's issue, replacing on the throne the sons of Macbeth who might have been had Macbeth and Lady Macbeth continued their participation in rootedness and the benevolent banquet. Macduff, in learning of the execution of his family, laments the fact that he cannot avenge himself totally upon Macbeth for Macbeth "has no children" (4.3.216); what Macduff cannot see is that such is precisely the vengeance Macbeth most fears. Moreover, in severing Macbeth's head from its body, just as Macbeth himself had severed the head of Scotland, Duncan, from the body politic, Macduff acts as the scourge for fate and for all those who have been from their mothers' wombs untimely ripped by Macbeth: Macduff's children and Macbeth's sons.

In *Macbeth*, Shakespeare embraces the same devotion, the same bond, to the unborn and the dead that T. S. Eliot does; indeed, one might argue that Macduff, in leaving his family vulnerable to the will of Macbeth, does not so much abandon his nuclear family, the *philoi*, as much as he seeks to cure what ails the tribal family, the *nomoi*. Steiner's interpolation of Hegel provides us with a more detailed framework within which to contrast the actions of Macbeth and Macduff. In an early essay, Hegel discerns a creative conflict between the *Kriegstaat,* a war-state, and the *Privatrecht*, the private right, whose primary impulses are not those of civic sacrifice in battle but rather the preservation of the family. Steiner adds that, according to Hegel, "the family is the highest totality 'of which nature is capable,' that the generation of children within the family is the modus of reproduction of 'totality' itself, a modus constantly and legitimately challenged by the bellicose ideals of the state."[1]

Such a conflict is dialectically evident in *Macbeth*. Macduff illustrates the difficulty of maintaining a balance between the conflicting demands of the *Kreigstaat* and the *Privatrecht*, and he pays dearly in the one realm for fulfilling his duties in the other. Banquo, in protecting Fleance's escape from the assassins, fulfills paternal obligation while he himself becomes the victim of Macbeth's bellicose ambitions. Macbeth on the other hand violates all familial obligation, both the filial owed to Duncan and the paternal due his descendants.

J. Douglas Canfield in *Word as Bond* suggests that Macbeth's killing of Duncan "destroys the traces and harnesses of patriarchal order" and that, because it is a act of symbolic castration which allows Macbeth to seize the power of the father, "recapitulates the archetypal killing of the primal father Freud discusses in *Totem and Taboo*."[2] Although we agree with the first of these observations and although we have noted that the murder of Duncan suggests parricide, we do not concur that it is a recapitulation of what Freud describes in *Totem and Taboo*, but is rather a manifestation of the Oedipal complex. The difference is implied in Freud's own theory and confirmed in Girard's: the original deed of the killing of the father is a communal one, out of which grows religious sacrifice and tribal unity. Subsequent individual psychological manifestations of that deed can and more often do occur within the confines of either the family circle or the individual psyche. One is acted out on behalf of the community; the other on behalf of the ego.

Such is the nature of Macbeth's act of regicide: it is a manifestation of what Durkheim designates as magic—the manipulation of the natural or supernatural to promote personal ends—rather than religion—the incantation of both to generate communal ends and thereby bond the community.[3] The word religion literally derives from *legare*, to bind or fasten. Macbeth, in his egomaniacal pursuit of power, not only scatters the community to various parts of the island, literally cuts off kin from each other, and divides members of the *nomoi*, but also violates the communion of the demonic. Thus, Hecate chides the three witches: "all you have done / Hath been but for a wayward son, / Spiteful and wrathful, who, as others do, / Loves for his own ends, not for you" (4.3.10–13). In separating themselves from all communion, Macbeth and Lady Macbeth conspire in the greatest of domestic tragedies: a self-centeredness that effects deracination and disinheritance. Thus, the small circle of the nuclear family of both is made even smaller in the course of the drama, as Lady Macbeth, unsexed and barren, and Macbeth, unmanned and impotent, turn even from each other.

In this uncanniest of Shakespeare's tragedies, one cannot help but infer that, when Macbeth beholds the supernatural ghost of Banquo at the unholy banquet and comes face to face with the unnatural Macduff, untimely ripped from his mother's womb, he is looking into a Lacanian mirror of the image of not only the other, but of himself as he once was and might have been. His intent to destroy what he sees is reversed as those personifications of the forsaken self avenge themselves upon the alienated ego. Here, Hegel, foreshadowing Nietzsche on the Apollonian, sums up the tragic in Macbeth's bond/age: "This 'lord and master of world' takes himself in this way to be the absolute person, comprising at the same time all existence within himself, for whom there exists no higher type of spirit. He is the person: but the solitary single person who has taken his stand confronting all. These all constitute and establish the triumphant universality of the one person; for the single being, as such, is truly what it is only *qua* universal plurality of single units: cut off from this plurality, the solitary and single self is, in fact, a powerless and unreal self."[4]

6
In *Paradise Lost*

In John Milton's *Paradise Lost*, the god who binds becomes the god who bounds. Divinity in the person of the Father or Son is the God of boundary or what C. S. Lewis in his preface calls hierarchy. According to the hierarchical concept, "everything except God has some natural superior; everything except unformed matter has some natural inferior. The goodness, happiness, and dignity of every being consists in obeying its natural superior and ruling its natural inferior. When a being fails in either part of this twofold task . . . by stepping out of its place in the system (whether it step up like a rebellious angel or down like an uxorious husband) it has made the very nature of things its enemy. It cannot succeed."[1] In stepping out of place, or, as Milton suggests, out of "bounds," Adam, Eve, and Satan break God's boundary, become the enemy of the nature of things, and find themselves thereby ironically enthralled.

In the beginning of Milton's epic world are God and the void; each is boundless. Thus, after sin unlocks the gates of hell, Satan stands on the threshold of "a dark / Illimitable Ocean without bound / Without dimension, where length, breadth, & highth, / And time and place are lost" and "Night and Chaos . . . hold eternal Anarchie."[2] That ocean is also female: "The Womb of nature and perhaps her grave," where the elements war in anarchy and confusion, "Unless th' Almighty Maker them ordain / His dark materials to create more worlds" (2:911–16). Milton's "more worlds" implies what Abdiel later indicates to Satan, that the Father through his Word, his Son, has already created at least two worlds: the empyrean of the angelic host, where the Son "formed the Pow'rs of Heav'n . . . and circumscribed thir being" (5:824–25), and the hell of the rebel band of angels, wherein the Father the "powers of darkness bound" (3:256). That creation is a matter of a boundless God ordering boundless chaos through the prescription of boundary is more graphically evident in the Son's creation of the world of man.

The Son, who is "Love without end, and without measure Grace" (3:142) and therefore boundless himself, takes the golden compasses prepared by the Father "to circumscribe / This Universe," and, placing the fixed foot in the center and turning the other through the "vast profunditie obscure," ordains the world of man: "thus farr extend, thus farr thy bounds / This be Thy just Circumference, O World" (7: 226–31). That the Father's Word draws more than one circle is evident in Raphael's teaching to Adam the great chain of being or scale of nature: "all / Such to perfection . . . indu'd with various forms various degrees . . . Each in thir several active Sphears assignd, / Till body up to spirit work, in bounds / Proportiond to each kind" (5:473–79). Within this circle of existence all creatures are bound only, or as Milton writes it, "one-ly," by obedience; thus, Raphael says in one of the most terse expressions of tragic bond/age in English literature, "Our voluntarie service he requires" (5:529).

The key word is "requires." Etymologically the word means to call again; it is not a requirement in the same sense that necessity and fate are; as God says, where his creatures do "onely what they needs must do [they] had served necessitie / Not mee" (3:105–11). Requirement is rather a call, a vocation, from God to man, freely to obey and serve: "I made him just and right, / Sufficient to have stood, though free to fall, / Such I created all th' Ethereal Powers / And Spirits, both them who stood and them who faild" (3:98–101). Raphael, in his lesson to Adam, connects service with love: "freely we serve / Because wee freely love, as in our will / To love or not; in this we stand or fall" (5:538–40). In Milton's version of tragic bond/age, angel and man are bonded to God when bound by God's gift of the freedom to love and obey; that bond becomes bondage only when each is seduced, "led away," from the bounds and thereby each introduces, "leads into," the world sin and evil. Moreover, the major trope in *Paradise Lost* for such bond/age is standing or falling, transcendence of chthonic origins or the fall into a chthonic end. Satan is the first of God's creatures to break boundary, to suffer bondage, and to be reduced, led downwards, to a chthonic state.

For Satan, the degree and proportion of heaven, in which he stands more equal than all the other angels, is arbitrarily altered when, in a scene reminiscent of Duncan's elevation of Malcolm, the Father ordains the election of his Son:

> This day I have begot whom I declare
> My onely Son . . . Under his great Vice-regent Reign abide
> United as one individual Soule
> For ever happie: him who disobeyes
> Mee disobeyes, breaks union."
>
> (5:602–12)

Again, the freedom of angels is bounded by God's requirement that they obey him by obeying his Son. The problem for Satan and for some readers is that God seems to have changed the law, the rules, the boundaries: even if one reads "begot" as "exalt" and not as "created," accepting that the Son has always been, but only this day has been exalted and ordained, the exaltation and direction to obey is change, and that change is a test that Satan and a third of the heavenly host fail.

God not only names his Son begotten, but also names him sole "Heir of all my might" in the hierarchy. The result is that Satan, failing to see that the Son's elevation is his and every other angel's because all are united as one soul in the Son and anticipating the response of Cain to God's elevation of Abel, feels himself diminished and disinherited: "Satan . . . fraught / With envie against the Son of God . . . could not beare / Through pride that sight, & thought himself impair'd" (5:661–65). Milton makes it clear that Satan is not the victim of bondage by the Father when he has Abdiel admonish Satan in the following words:

> Unjustly thou deprav'st it with the name
> Of Servitude to serve whom God ordains . . .
>   This is servitude,
> To serve th' unwise or him who hath rebelld
> Against his worthier, as thine now serve thee,
> Thyself not free, but to thy self enthralled.
>
> (6:174–80)

Paul Ricoeur's observation in *Symbolism of Evil* that "seduction from the outside is ultimately an affection of the self by the self, an auto-infection, by which the act of binding oneself is transformed into the state of being bound"[3] is applicable to Satan. God only binds him after Satan has enthralled himself with his own pride and envy. The Son, responding to the Father's command to "pursue these sons of Darkness, drive them out / From all Heav'ns bounds into the utter Deep" (6:715–16), says he will "Armd with thy might, rid heav'n of these rebell'd, / To thir prepar'd ill

Mansion driven down / To chains of darkness, and th' undying Worm" (6:736–40); thus, self-enthrallment becomes god-enthrallment. Such bondage is manifested through the agency of fate, a power withheld from God's creatures prior to Satan's fall: when personified hell sees the rout of heaven, it tries to run away from the falling angels, but "strict fate had cast too deep / Her dark foundations and too fast had bound . . Hell at last / Yawning receavd them whole, and on them clos'd" (6:869–75). In hell, the fallen angels' punishment for their sin of self-enthrallment is not only to be bound in adamantine chains, but, like Prometheus, to be conscious of their bondage.

Essentially, the war council in hell is, among other things, a debate on what to do about bondage. Moloch, who dreads being "The Vassals of [God's] anger" (2:90) and having self-enthrallment punished by self-flagellation—"when the Scourge / Inexorably, and the torturing hour / Calls us to Penance" (2:90–93)—declares for open war. Belial, fearing that, in a second war with the almighty, loss and punishment may take the form of greater restriction in hell—"Caught in a fierie Tempest . . . each on his rock transfixt . . . or forever sunk / Under yon boyling ocean wrapped in Chains" (2:180–83)—recommends accommodation to their fallen condition in hope that the father will forgive. Mammon, pointing out that restoration of heaven would require new "Subjection" and "Strict Laws impos'd" (2:239–41), argues for trying to make a heaven of hell by mining what is around them, "preferring / Hard liberty before the easie yoke / Of servile Pomp" (2:255–57). Finally, Beelzebub, in order to turn the angels from opting for Mammon's solution, points out that God has doomed them not to safe retreat in hell, but rather "to remaine / In strictest bondage, though thus far remov'd / Under th' inevitable curb" (2:320–22).

Beelzebub is convincing, and the band of angels opts for revenge against God through guile against his new creature, man. In order to do that, however, they must break through the boundaries of hell, and Satan becomes he "whom no bounds / Prescrib'd, no barrs of Hell, nor all the chains / Heapt on him there, nor yet the main Abyss / Wide interrupt can hold" (3:80–86), one who, "through all restraint broke loose," wings his way towards paradise. There, however, Satan's troubled thoughts stir "the Hell within him" (4:19) so much, that he ironically decides to lower himself to toad and serpent in order to accomplish the seduction of Adam and Eve: "This essence to incarnate and imbrute / That to the hight of Deitie aspir'd" (9:166–67). Satan's self-enthrallment becomes entrapment within the chthonic, which he heretofore has not known: for Adam and Eve, it becomes bondage within the chthonic, from which they have stood up.

Adam and Eve have been created by the Word that "rais'd [them] from the dust" (4:416); they too are also created bound: "Not equal, as thir sex not equal seemd; / For contemplation hee and valour formed, / For softness shee and sweet attractive Grace, / Hee for God only, shee for God in him" (4:296–99). The primary image of their bond and their obedience to boundary is their passing through paradise "hand in hand," for their resistance of boundary and bondage, their withdrawing of hands. Thus, when Eve, caught by the image of herself in the lake, turns away from Adam to return to that narcissistic image, Adam stops her, and she learns an early lesson about God's hierarchical world. Eve describes the event, beginning with Adam's words to her as he arrests her movement:

> Part of my Soul I seek thee, and thee claim
> My other half: with that thy gentle hand
> Seisd mine, I yielded, and from that time see
> How beauty is excelld by manly grace
> And wisdom, which alone is truly fair.
> (4:487–91)

Eve learns that in the scale of nature manly grace and wisdom excel female beauty and charm and that happiness and love exist in her yielding to the gentle hand of Adam. Adam learns that the incomplete self that he had described to God is made whole through his bond with the separated part of himself who is Eve and that it is the nature of things for him to exercise wise control over her. The reader learns that, although Milton makes it clear God will extend his grace to Adam and Eve and not to Satan because the latter has been seduced by the self and the former by the other, Eve by Satan and Adam by Eve, the innocent couple's fall and consequent punishment are brought about also by self-enthrallment.

That Eve is so disposed is foreshadowed in the very scene in which she is attracted to her image in the lake. Both God, by speaking to her and directing her to Adam, and Adam, by gently seizing her hand, lead her away from that temptation of the self. Subsequently, when Eve seeks separation from Adam in order to cultivate another part of the garden and thereby resists Adam's argument that "our joynt hands / Will keep from Wilderness with ease" (9:244–45), Milton extends and varies the hand leitmotif: "from her Husbands hand her hand / Soft she withdrew" (9:384–85). Milton uses what has been previously described as one of the most universal symbols of the tragic bond/age of man's situation in the world: the hand that holds, directs, and protects becomes the hand that restrains. In withdrawing her hand, even softly, from Adam's, Eve is breaking boundary, resisting bond/age, and preparing the way for her fall.

Her withdrawal from Adam is but one step in Eve's growing resistance to boundary. In trying to convince Adam to allow her to go her own way in the garden, Eve says, "If this be our condition, thus to dwell / In narrow circuit strait'nd by a Foe / Suttle or violent... how are we happie?" (9:322–25) Her discontentment with her narrow circuit of space is extended to include the narrower circuit of mind. After Satan tempts Eve with the suggestion that she "freely" taste the fruit of the forbidden tree, she convinces herself with her desire for more knowledge: "For good unknown, sure is not had, or had / And yet unknown, is as not had at all. / In plain then, what forbids us to be wise? / Such prohibitions binde not" (9:756–60). Self-deceived as well as Satan-deceived, Eve commits the deed: "So saying, her rash hand in evil hour / Forth reaching to the Fruit, she pluck'd, she eat" (9:780–81). The hand that had yielded to Adam's gentle hand and subsequently softly withdrew now rashly reaches beyond boundary and, in seizing the apple, places itself in Satan's grip. Like Satan, she reaches upward in the hierarchy and falls.

Adam exhibits the same pre-disposition to break boundary as does Eve. In describing his and Eve's creation to Raphael, Adam indicates that, upon awakening to the becoming of Eve, he exclaimed,

>   now see
> Bone of my Bone, Flesh of my Flesh, my Self
> Before me; Woman is her Name, of Man
> Extracted; for this cause he shall forgoe
> Father and Mother, and to his Wife adhere;
>   And they shall be one Flesh, one Heart, one Soule.
>   (8:494–98)

In what is a variation of a Platonic definition of love, reunion with the other half of one's divided body, Adam, and it is important to note not God, describes bondedness. In so doing, Adam implicitly denies boundary. Forgoing one's mother and father is of course a projection of what Adam's ancestry will do in the boundary-affirming rite of marriage; in his case, it can only be a foreshadowing of what Adam will do in choosing Eve over God the Father, creature over creator, earth over heaven, mortal over immortal, the chthonic over the transcendent. That he will so choose is also evident in his overpraising of Eve to Raphael: "so absolute she seems / And in her self compleat... All higher knowledge in her presence falls /

Degraded" (8:547–51). Dismayed, the angel contracts his brow and chides Adam for "attributing overmuch to things / Less excellent," things worth "thy cherishing, thy honouring, and thy love, / [but] Not thy subjection" (8:565–70). Raphael's admonishment, however, is in vain for what is foreshadowed here, Adam's rejection of boundary and God, is accomplished after Eve's fall. When informed by Eve of her deed, Adam does not hesitate in his commitment; feeling the "Bond of Nature" drawing him to Eve, he says, "Our State cannot be severd, we are one, / One Flesh; to loose thee were to loose myself" (9:955–59).

Instead of having stood erect in obedience as he might have and instead of aspiring to soar in disobedience like Satan and Eve, Adam breaks boundary by moving downward in the great chain of being. For Adam the bond of nature is greater than the bond of God, and, as in Greek tragedy, the female is the source of human bondage. Unable to resist the first of "female snares" that will disturb the earth (10:897), Adam reaches for the apple "with liberal hand" and knowingly eats. The immediate result is that this time he passionately seizes Eve's hand, and both, "as with new Wine intoxicated . . . swim in mirth, and fancie that they feel / Divinitie within them breeding wings / Wherewith to scorne the Earth" (9:1007–11).

The swimming in mirth anticipates the trope Milton will use later to depict the sons of Seth, who "let thir eyes / Rove without rein till in the amorous Net / Fast caught" (11:585–87) they generate offspring beautiful, but without love. Of course, the amorous net is the trammel bequeathed to their posterity by Adam and Eve, and the dream of winged transcendence is a variation of both Satan and Eve's dream, one that will be transformed into a nightmare when the couple learn the punishment for their crime against the Word's boundary:

> In the sweat of thy Face shalt thou eat Bread,
> Till thou return unto the ground, for thou
> Out of the ground wast taken; know thy Birth,
> For dust thou art, and shalt to dust return.
> (10:205–8)

Like Oedipus, Adam is reminded of his chthonic beginning. and both Eve and he are exiled from the garden, deracinated from the ground of their being.

Exile and the return to dust, however, shall be only temporary for Adam's choice is the Son's—incarnation—and by Christ's election Adam will pass from bondage by God into union with God, from the chthonic to the transcendent. In reappropriating his biblical materials, Milton develops some ironic variations on his theme of tragic bond/age. In offering himself as sacrifice and atonement for man's transgression, the Son reverses his own decree and ironically breaks boundaries and thereby union with God. He leaves God's bosom to become Adam's "bondsman": he gives surety to the Father and becomes the "ransom paid" for Adam; he links himself to Adam in weal and woe and thereby becomes the covenant or tie between man and God; he does so by suffering the bondage of the chthonic flesh and of being "naild to the Cross" in "cursed death" (12:406). Having suffered the descent and bondage of incarnation, Christ will then "ascend / The Throne hereditarie, and bound his Reign / With earths wide bounds, his glory with the Heav'ns" (12:369–71) and become once more the God of boundary.

The final irony, however, will be that boundary shall be short-lived too for, after the Son accomplishes his resurrection and judgment and punishment of Satan and his hellish host, he will lay aside his imperial staff "For regal Scepter then no more shall [he] need / God shall be All in All" (3:340–41), and, as the Father declares to the Son, redeemed man shall be "made one with me as I with thee am one" (11:44). Thus, the resolution of Adam's tragic bond/age is boundlessness, oneness with God in eternity, an end so much to be desired that, after hearing Michael's account of that outcome, Adam wonders "Whether I should repent me now of sin / By mee done and occasiond, or rejoyce" (12:473–74). The boundless God of boundary will un-create bounds and all loving creatures will become one God and thereby soaringly divine.

All that is except Satan and those who enthrall themselves to him; they shall be condemned, and "Hell her numbers full, / Thenceforth shall be for ever shut" (3:331–32). In that infinite hell, no doubt, the other fallen angels will experience the same chthonic transformation that Satan undergoes when, after his last speech before the fallen angels, he experiences corporeal self-enthrallment as "His Visage drawn he felt to sharp and spare, / His Armes clung to his Ribs, his Leggs entwining / Each, till supplanted down he fell / A monstrous Serpent on his Belly prone" (10:511–14). He will also be made to eat ashes and unable to speak the word, and thus infinite bondage—chthonic, mute, and hellbound—shall be the resolution of tragic bond/age for Satan.

Whereas Adam's tragic bond/age ends in eternal bondedness, Satan's ends in eternal bondage. Because he suffers bond/age more completely than does Adam, because his ambivalent hate/love relationship with God is more dynamic (nothing or no one comes between Satan and God except Satan), because the violation of boundary is greater in his striving upward than it is in Adam's bending downward, because his punishment is more terrible in its enormity, because he experiences a greater, personal, more searing recognition and has to bear a more self-redounding reversal of intention, and because he dramatically personifies the tension between the Dionysian impulse towards boundlessness and the Apollonian tendency towards individuation, Satan is the hero of tragic bond/age in *Paradise Lost*.

Upon his arrival on the earth, Satan's "conscience . . . wakes the bitter memories / Of what he was, what is, and what must be / Worse" (4: 23–25). That awakening leads to the recognition that his rebellion against God was uncalled for, was "unrequited," for God "deservd no such return / From me" (4: 41–42). Moved by memory of paradise lost and the realization of his violation of the bond and boundary between God and himself, Satan momentarily contemplates, but finally dismisses, reconciliation:

> O then at last relent; is there no place
> Left for Repentance, none for pardon left?
> None left but by submission; and that word
> Disdain forbids me.
> (4: 79–82)

In this scene, Milton develops an heroic character who manifests the kind of ambivalence Freud finds at the root of filial relationship—Satan both loves and hates the Father—and that ambivalence transforms freedom from heavenly bond/age into infernal bondage. Such irony is repeated in a series of reversals of Satan's intentions: instead of soaring upward in the scale of nature, Satan falls downward to chthonic proneness; instead of effecting a "league" with Adam and Eve in "mutual amitie so streight" (4: 375–76), he separates himself from both and all the redeemed; instead of breaking the boundary between himself and God, he only brings about the multiplication of boundaries in the cosmos and effects the only eternal boundary of a closed hell in the otherwise open and boundless Dionysian integration of creator and creation.

Norman O. Brown in *Love's Body* writes sympathetically about Dionysus: "the mad god breaks down the boundaries, releases the prisoners; abolishes repression, and abolishes the *principium individuationis*, substituting for it the unity of man and the unity of man with nature."[4] From Milton's more critical point of view, Satan is the mad angel who breaks down boundaries and releases, albeit only temporarily, those who feel themselves prisoners of God's bondage: the rebel angels, sin, death, and Eve. He is also the one who helps effect, through the agency of Adam and Eve, the substitution of the unity of man (and woman) and the unity of man with nature for the unity of man with God. He does all of this, however, in the name of his own individuation, conscious that, in so doing, he has forsaken all bonds with the other. He, more than Adam, Eve, or the Son, is the heroic personification of the Dionysian/Apollonian tension that informs tragic bond/age.

7
In *The Scarlet Letter*

In the interview that takes place between Hester Prynne and Roger Chillingworth shortly after Hester, Pearl, and the scarlet letter have been revealed upon the scaffold, Hawthorne has Chillingworth make this observation about the four principal characters of the novel: "I find here a woman, a man, a child, amongst whom and myself there exist the closest ligaments."[1] The key and curious word is "ligaments," which is but one of Hawthorne's variations on the universal trope of tragic bond/age. Ligaments is appropriate to the speaker, a man of medicine; it is also appropriate to a man of letters like Hawthorne because its etymology incorporates the paradoxical elements of tragic bond/age. It derives from the Latin *ligamentum* (bond or bandage), which in turn derives from *ligare* (to bind), which is also the root of the word "religion." Ligament serves, consequently, as an introduction to the image and theme of bond/age, and the sentence alerts the reader to the fact that among the principal four characters exists such bond/age.

One of the first manifestations of the trope of tragic bond/age is an important prop in the setting of the first revelation of the scarlet letter. As he introduces Hester and her severe punishment to the reader, Hawthorne pays particular attention to a significant part of the penal machine: "It was, in short, the platform of the pillory; and above it rose the framework of that instrument of discipline, so fashioned as to confine the human head in its tight grasp, and thus hold it up to the public gaze. The very ideal of ignominy was embodied and made manifest in this contrivance of wood and iron" (41).

What Hawthorne focuses on and ignores about the instrument sheds light on his particular manifestation of the agon of tragic bond/age. The pillory inhibits physical movement and is thereby a rather basic, primitive example of penal bondage. Although Hawthorne does not mention the fact that this instrument ordinarily also restrains the hands, probably because of his own concentration on the confinement of the head, it is important to note such restraint because it implicitly resonates with what will later be in *The Scarlet Letter,* as it is in *Paradise Lost,* the primary physical manifestation of the human bond—the handclasp. Here, however, Hawthorne is concerned with the yoke-like imprisonment of the head, which prevents the condemned from hiding from the public gaze his own eyes, the windows to his soul. Although Hester (and Dimmesdale) is not made to suffer literally the physical anguish of confinement in the pillory, she does undergo by association the figurative, as well as the psychological, pain of the scaffold and the scarlet letter.

Hester, the narrator tells us, is "the people's victim and life-long bond-slave" (153); as such she suffers a punishment not unlike that of Prometheus shackled or Eve earthbound: "Her sin, her ignominy, were the roots which she had struck into the soil. The chain that bound her here was of iron links, and galling to her inmost soul, but never could be broken" (56). Hester exchanges the customary bonds of community for what Milton might have called the adamantine chain of mutual sin: "The links that united her to the rest of human kind—links of flowers, or silk, or gold, or whatever the material—had all been broken. Here was the iron link of mutual crime, which neither [Dimmesdale] nor she could break. Like all other ties, it brought along with it its obligations" (109).

One of those obligations is that she feels compelled to give Chillingworth her word that she will not reveal his true identity and their marital relationship. When she gives him her pledge, she also gives Chillingworth her bond; unfortunately it is transformed from connection to confinement: "Hast thou enticed me into a bond that will prove the ruin of my soul" (55), she asks Chillingworth. He responds, "Not thy soul. . . . No, not thine!" (55). Her husband's response clearly indicates that what both he and Hester are helping to weave is the net that will bind her lover. Although Hester intimates that this is so, it does not become clear to her until seven years later that she has indeed participated in the psychological punishment of Dimmesdale. Before coming to that recognition, however, Hester must travel further through the "moral maze" under the weight of the scarlet letter.

How much of a restriction the scarlet letter has been upon her body as well as her spirit is not realized by Hester until she takes off the tribal totem in her reunion with Dimmesdale in the forest: "'Let us not look back,' answered Hester Prynne. 'The past is gone! Wherefore should we linger upon it now? See! With this symbol, I undo it all, and make it as it had never been!' So speaking she undid the clasp that fastened the scarlet letter.

... The stigma gone, Hester heaved a long, deep sigh, in which the burden of shame and anguish departed from her spirit. O exquisite relief! She had not known the weight, until she felt the freedom!" (137–38).

It is a somewhat curious observation of the narrator, provoking the reader into wondering whether or not Hester had ever taken off the stigma, whether indeed upon retiring for the evening she had merely replaced it from her blouse to her nightgown. It is a tempting inference, especially since it strikes a most tantalizing resonance with what we learn from Chillingworth's voyeurism is her lover's own misfortune to carry to sleep upon his breast his own evolving scarlet letter. Even if it is only now, upon renewing her intimacy with Dimmesdale in the sympathetic forest that she feels the exquisite relief of this particular removal of the scarlet letter, it is plain that the wearing of the scarlet letter involves a clasping which is a variation on the leitmotif of bondage. It also suggests that the stitching or needlework that creates the letter suggests the weaving of the net of nemesis, and who is it that fashions such a net? Well, it is society that orders it, a society which, through a puritanical reading of scripture, accents the commandment against adultery and ignores the directive to let her who is without sin sew the first stitch. It is Hester, however, who designs the symbol of bondage, reiterating that in tragic bond/age the protagonist participates in the weaving of her own fate and also that it is often the female that is the mistress of the threads of a terrible divine sovereignty.

It is most ironic, then, when one reads that, "At the head of the social system as the clergymen of that day stood, [Dimmesdale] was only the more trammelled by its regulations, its principles, and even its prejudices. As a priest, the framework of his order inevitably hemmed him in" (136). Clearly, the trammel net that captures Dimmesdale is ordered by society; just as apparent, however, is the fact that it is one fashioned partly by Hester and sought after by Dimmesdale himself. That such is the case is further reinforced by Hawthorne's observation about Hester's judges: "who should be less capable of sitting in judgment on an erring woman's heart, and disentangling its mesh of good and evil?" (46). It is that morally ambiguous "mesh of good and evil" that leads Hester thrice to do the wrong thing for the right reason and cast the mesh of tragic bond/age about Dimmesdale.

Can there be any doubt that it was Hester who originally seduced Dimmesdale? It is entirely inconsistent with Hawthorne's development of both characters to conclude otherwise. The only person that Dimmesdale has the strength to seduce is himself, and this, as we shall shortly see, is what Hawthorne implicitly suggests he does. Hester again does the wrong thing for the right reason when she gives Chillingworth her word that she will not betray his identity; she intuits as much when she gives that word and acknowledges it when she sees the result that her silence has had upon her lover's sanity. Finally, tending to oversimplify the ambiguity of tragic bond/age and place the cause of Dimmesdale's bondage at the doorstep of the Puritan patriarch—"and what hast thou to do with all these iron men, and their opinions? They have kept thy better part in bondage too long already" (134)—Hester repeats her crime of seduction when in the forest she would lead (*duce*) Dimmesdale away (*se*) from purgation by admonishing him to forget the past, leave Boston, and be thereby twice born. Moreover, she does so while ironically restraining him in a love embrace: "With sudden and desperate tenderness, she threw her arms around him, and pressed his head against her bosom; little caring though his cheek rested on the scarlet letter. He would have released himself, but strove in vain to do so. Hester would not set him free, lest he should look her sternly in the face" (133).

Not only does Hester act as an agent of the sovereign power that confines humanity within its grip, but she does so in order to avoid what she has had to endure so long and what Dimmesdale seeks in vain to avoid himself: the condemning eye of the public. Dimmesdale suffers from an act of Hester's, which ironically proceeds from the impulse of charity; moreover, his suffering is described in the image of the knot of tragic bond/age: "Crime is for the iron-nerved [like Hester], who have their choice either to endure it, or, if it press too hard, to exert their fierce and savage strength for a good purpose, and fling it off at once! This feeble and most sensitive of spirits could do neither, yet continually did one thing or another, which intertwined, in the same inextricable knot, the agony of heaven-defying guilt and vain repentance" (102).

Paul Ricoeur posits several insightful theses about the evolution of the symbols of evil that are most illuminating about Dimmesdale and the "inextricable knot" in which he finds himself bound. The first is that the major distinction between the primordial sense of defilement and society's more advanced notion of sin is that the latter is "the violation of a personal bond."[2] Not only has Dimmesdale violated his bond with God by breaking one of his commandments, but also, by the same act, he has broken his bond with his lover. He confesses to Hester, "we forgot our God, when we violated our reverence for the other's soul" (173). Thus, Hester's words to Chillingworth—"Hast thou enticed me into a bond that will prove the ruin of my soul?"—could have been directed between Hester and Dimmesdale and are, in fact, an apt summary of the tragic bond/age in which both find themselves linked.

Ricoeur also suggests that, in the evolution of sin into guilt, the individual seeks to replace the community with himself as the tribunal of his moral conduct, and the result is alienation: "The guilty conscience is shut in first of all because it is an isolated conscience that breaks the communion of sinners."[3] By her very nature, by the very visibility of her sin—initially a bulging belly and subsequently Pearl herself—Hester, in a more primitive and communal manifestation of defilement and sin, must suffer the stain and purification of her sin. Hawthorne writes: "Hester had often fancied that Providence had a design of justice and retribution, in endowing the child with this marked propensity [to draw attention to the scarlet letter], but never until now had she bethought herself to ask, whether, linked with that design, there might not likewise be a purpose of mercy and beneficence" (123). For Hester, Pearl is the scarlet letter personified and thereby one of the furies that binds; however, she is also becoming one of the Eumenides or kindly ones, who purge and thereby liberate. Such, however is not the case for Dimmesdale, whose tendency towards Puritan self-examination, or what Sacvan Bercovitch calls Puritan auto-machia,[4] compels him to examine himself repeatedly and thereby transform sin into what Ricoeur calls the "servile will" of guilt, one of whose manifestations is the Babylonian notion of bondage.[5]

Ricoeur posits that there are three conditions of the servile will: evil is not the absence of good, but rather the manifestation of the "power of darkness"; man's wickedness is always secondary, the result of the seduction of the evil that is out there; the physical contact that stains in defilement becomes in guilt the seduction that infects and thereby binds. Ricoeur, as we have seen, however, notes that seduction from the outside is but a transference of seduction from within.[6] Dimmesdale's auto-infection or Puritan auto-machia is a binding of oneself, one which is projected externally as bondage to Hester and Chillingworth and the marks of which are the stigmata upon his breast.

It is apparent that Dimmesdale, even more than Hester, participates in the weaving of the inextricable knot, in which he finds himself bound. He does so because, as Hawthorne tells the reader, he is too weak for the more heroic action to endure stoically his tribulation or to fling it off defiantly, as does Hester when "she cast[s] away the fragments of [the] broken chain" (112) of the law. A significant part of the net in which Dimmesdale finds himself bound is his compulsion to repeat Puritan auto-machia or what

Freud would have analyzed as a compulsion to repeat trauma in order to master it and the uncontrollable passion that brought it about. By intensely examining his own guilty condition, Dimmesdale moves from the passive object of the eye of the observer, be it God or society, to the active subject, who sees and thereby seemingly controls. It will take him seven years to discover that the price of such mastery is not only his soul, but his sanity as well; and, when he finds this out, he also discovers that he has been unwittingly and most ironically the object of the "evil eye" of the man he cuckolded, a fate, Hester suggests, "far worse than death!" (134).

Not only does Chillingworth bind Dimmesdale through the machinations of the malevolent gaze, but also he figuratively lives off the minister as the leech does the host, the alienist the alienated, the hater the hated, and the sadist the masochist. Thus, Hawthorne writes in the concluding chapter, "[Hatred or love], each in its utmost development, supposes a high degree of intimacy and heart-knowledge; each renders one individual dependent for the good of his affections and spiritual life upon another; each leaves the passionate lover, or no less passionate hater, forlorn and desolate by the withdrawal of his object" (175). This passage explains the withering up, "like an uprooted weed," that Chillingworth experiences upon the death of Dimmesdale; moreover, in this passage, Hawthorne anticipates the sadomasochistic theory of Jessica Benjamin, who posits that even the master (the leech) is dependent upon the slave (the minister) for recognition and identity.[7]

Chillingworth is also bound by his need for revenge: "as he proceeded, a terrible fascination, a kind of fierce, though still calm, necessity seized the old man within its gripe, and never set him free again, until he had done all its bidding" (89). In his conversation with Hester, when she would have her husband release her from her word, her bond, Chillingworth varies the trope of the ligament that binds the major principal characters with the tragic flower of fate: "By thy first step awry, thou didst plant the germ of evil; but, since that moment, it has all been a dark necessity. Ye that have wronged me are not sinful, save in a kind of typical illusion; neither am I fiend-like, who have snatched a fiend's office from his hands. It is our fate. Let the black flower blossom as it may!" (119).

It may be fate that has nurtured the black flower whose seed was planted by Chillingworth, Hester, and Dimmesdale, but it is "Providence" who has decreed that from that "rank luxuriance of a guilty passion" shall also blossom the "lovely and immortal flower" (62) that is Pearl. As the bastard child of fate and providence and the natural child of Hester and Dimmesdale,

Pearl is "a law unto herself" (93) and thereby relatively unbound. Her freedom is most evident when Hawthorne describes her as more "airy sprite" than "human child," one who, "hovering in the air" as though "she might vanish," forced Hester "to pursue the little elf in the flight which she invariably began,—to snatch her to her bosom, with a close pressure and earnest kisses,—not so much from overflowing love, as to assure herself that Pearl was flesh and blood" (64). Implicitly, Hawthorne suggests that Pearl transcends even the chthonic in her extraordinary independence from the law and society; ironically, such transcendence precludes her humanity.

Not having known what it is to suffer, Pearl knows not human bond/age. It is this spell of inhuman transcendence that is broken when Dimmesdale finally embraces his daughter on the dreaded scaffold within sight of the sun, God, and the community. Twice before, during the midnight vigil and the meeting in the forest, Dimmesdale had joined hands with Hester and/or Pearl in a short-lived regeneration of life. Upon the scaffold at midnight, while Pearl held hands with Hester, "The minister felt for the child's other hand, and took it. The moment that he did so, there came what seemed a tumultuous rush of new life, other life than his own, pouring like a torrent into his heart, and hurrying through all his veins, as if the mother and the child were communicating their vital warmth to his half-torpid system. The three formed an electric chain" (105).

This connection contrasts sharply with the chain of communal sin and dramatically demonstrates the dialectical nature of tragic bond/age. In the forest the clasp of chilled hands between Hester and Dimmesdale, although lacking in the dynamic energy that Pearl's hands enjoin, nevertheless is a consolation for their seven-year separation and the initiation of another momentary revitalization: "It was with fear, and tremulously, and, as it were, by a slow, reluctant necessity, that Arthur Dimmesdale put forth his hand, chill as death, and touched the chill hand of Hester Prynne. The grasp, cold as it was, took away what was dreariest in the interview. They now felt themselves, at least, inhabitants of the same sphere." (129)

Unfortunately, what he would do in the darkness of midnight or the forest, Dimmesdale, fearing public humiliation, refuses to do in the light of day, and the rebirth upon the midnight scaffold and in the forest is aborted. Indeed, the reunion of Hester and Dimmesdale in the forest and the subsequent revitalization of the minister is so short-lived that, upon next seeing Dimmesdale on his way to deliver his Election Day sermon, Hester dreads that "there could be no real bond between the clergyman and herself" (162).

After the Election Day sermon, however, Dimmesdale calls Pearl to him, is embraced about his knees by the spritish child, persuades Hester to "twine thy strength about me" (171), and advances towards the scaffold, supported by the arms of Hester and still clasping Pearl's hand. With the strength of the "ligaments" that are Hester and Pearl, Dimmesdale ascends the scaffold, Pearl kisses him, the spell is broken, and Pearl's tears, falling upon her father's cheeks, become "the pledge that she would grow up amid human joy and sorrow, nor for ever do battle with the world, but be a woman in it."

Whatever matriarchal bond Hester and Pearl have known as outcasts of society is not sufficient to humanize Pearl; it takes patriarchal kinship as well. Pearl has experienced in the fabric of her experience that Lacanian absence which manifests itself as a tear, a gap, a hole. She has literally not known the name-of-the-father and consequently has been uninhibited by the law of the father. All of it that she has encountered is what Lacan designates as the *objet petit a*, the object that takes the place of the missing signifying phallus, of which the mother is deprived and which the father provides, a substitute object that carries with it a relationship to the *Autre*—the law and discourse of the Other—but that can never take its place completely.[8] In *The Scarlet Letter*, that *objet petit a* is the signifying scarlet letter A, which not only is an obvious sign(ifier) of the severe puritanical patriarchal society, but also could be read to designate the French *Autre*, or other, and its discourse.

Benjamin explains the danger in a young girl's psychological development when having to make do with a substitute for the absent father: "this lack or gap left in a little girl's subjectivity by the missing father precludes her identificatory love of the father that is the basis for later heterosexual love."[9] Dimmesdale's revelation of his true identity on the scaffold repairs the tear in Pearl's psychological development and indeed makes it possible for her to become a woman in the world. Pearl is not only humanized by Dimmesdale's embrace and her own tears, but also legitimated by Chillingworth, who gives her his name and declares her his heir. It is evident that Pearl cannot become human in society without both mother and father. It is equally clear that the patriarch, dialectically manifested in this gothic novel in the split master/slave figure of Chillingworth and Dimmesdale, cannot exist without woman; nor can the matriarchal Hester, who leaves Boston only after Chillingworth's death and returns to be interred alongside the remains of Dimmesdale, both of whose graves are marked by a single headstone, exist without man. To try to do so were to try to live without a vital ligament (or rib).

8
In *Moby Dick*

Late in Melville's *Moby Dick*, Ishmael contemplates the serenity and calm of the Japanese waters that bring reminders of the tall grass of rolling plains, a land-like feeling towards the sea, and an intimation of wholeness: "And all this mixes with your most mystic mood; so that fact and fancy, half-way meeting, interpenetrate, and form one seamless whole."[1] The interpenetration of fact and fancy in a "seamless whole" is one of many images of weaving that Melville varies shortly thereafter as Ishmael remembers that "the mingled, mingling threads of life are woven by warp and woof; calms crossed by storms, a storm for every calm." He then contemplates the lack of an "unretracing progress in life," the fact that there does not seem to be a pattern in this carpet of existence that reveals to man any final harbor in the passage of life: "Where is the foundling's father? Our souls are like those orphans whose unwedded mothers die in bearing them: the secret of our paternity lies in their grave, and we must there to learn it." As these passages so concisely demonstrate, the manifestation of tragic bond/age in *Moby Dick* is informed by what seems to be an exploration for and redefinition of kinship. The universal symbol of that bond/age, the threads that both connect and tether, is expanded and made more meaningful in Melville's fictive variation of the archetypal trope.

As one might expect in a narrative that takes place almost entirely upon a nineteenth-century American whaler, women are almost nonexistent and consequently so is the traditional form of family. Ishmael is both an orphan and a bachelor, and Queequeg, like so many of the ship's crew, is one uprooted from his native soil and bound to a life upon the sea. Starbuck seems to be the only family man aboard the *Pequod*, and his commitment to family is seriously undermined by his newfound, albeit not always willed, commitment to his captain. Ahab, the reader discovers very late in the narrative, is also an orphan, one who married after fifty years of bachelorhood and, according to his own testimony, one who, because he subsequently abandoned both wife and child in his monomaniacal hunt of Moby Dick, "widowed that poor girl when [he] married her" (408). In addition, the crew of the *Pequod* is a collection of "Islanders ... each Isolato living on a separate continent of his own" (108), all of whom, Starbuck fears, "have small touch of human mothers in them" (143). The members of the crew, however, do not remain separate, and from Ishmael's meeting with Queequeg in New Bedford through much of the voyage of the *Pequod*, they are periodically transformed from a collection of exiles into communities of saints, and by those transformations Melville redefines kinship and points towards the resolution of tragic bond/age.

The first of these new communities occurs between Ishmael and Queequeg when the former finds himself "spliced" to the latter through the "bridegroom" clasp in the huge marital bed of Peter Coffin. Leslie Fiedler calls that figurative union an *heirogamous*, an innocent homosexual union between the white American protagonist, who is wary of the female, and a colored man, who takes the place of woman as the significant "other," through whom the hero achieves identity.[2] Such relationships, according to Fiedler, are celebrations of brotherhood as the primary manifestation of kinship in democratic America. In *Moby Dick* that relationship is reinforced later when Ishmael finds himself tethered by the monkey-rope to Queequeg, dangling below deck on the partly submerged whale. For Ishmael, it is as though "my own individuality was now merged in a joint stock company of two; that my free will had received a mortal wound; and that another's mistake or misfortune might plunge innocent me into unmerited disaster and death" (273). What Ishmael does not see as yet is that the reverse could, and in fact will, be true in the course of his voyage: from that bond he will experience salvation from disaster and death because of another's virtue and sacrifice.

Melville develops the trope of bond/age and the experience of the bond through the image of the line that splices and binds. Not only are Ishmael and Queequeg literally and figuratively tied to each other through the monkey-rope and the bridegroom clasp, but the latter encounter reminds Ishmael of an uncanny experience of childhood when, having been caught trying to climb up a chimney and put to bed early by his stepmother, he, in a half-conscious state in the dead of night, felt "a supernatural hand" placed in his (41). Whatever else that dream image signifies, it introduces for the first time in the narrative a leitmotif of bond/age that Melville will vary with growing meaning.

The first variation is Queequeg's bridegroom clasp: "Now, take away the awful fear, and my sensations at feeling the supernatural hand in mine were very similar, in their strangeness, to those which I experienced on waking up and seeing Queequeg's pagan arm thrown round me" (41). Although the immediate impression made upon Ishmael is that of a similar strangeness sans the awful fear, by the time Ishmael orients himself the uncanny has been attenuated and what was strange is made more familiar as the grasp that merely restrains: "I then rolled over, my neck feeling as if it were in a horsecollar" (41). The implication is that part of the original dread felt by Ishmael in the oneiric experience is the fear of containment, of bondage; but like the handclasp of any child by any adult it is but part of the awful fear, and in this case more a part of the fear than the awe. The fear of restriction is attenuated by his growing relationship to Queequeg, and the source of the awe he feels is clarified in the next variation of the handclasp image in "A Squeeze of the Hand."

There, a "strange kind of insanity" overtakes Ishmael in his squeezing of the whale's sperm, and he finds himself "unwittingly squeezing my colabourers' hands in it, mistaking their hands for the gentle globules," and desiring to "squeeze hands all around . . . to squeeze ourselves into each other . . . into the very milk and sperm of kindness" (323). Thus, the handclasp becomes a very important element in a mystical experience of the oneness of a brotherhood—a community of saints—that had been heretofore a collection of isolated, enisled, independent whalers. The repetition of the leitmotif explains another part of the meaning of the original mystical grasp of hand: the awfulness of the fear of the young Ishmael comes from the intimation of both mortality and immortality. The strange hand can be read as both the hand of death that binds and separates Ishmael from his stepmother as well as the hand of the other, who, across the threshold or "counterpane" of death, guides and bonds Ishmael to his blood family. As a child, Ishmael intuits what he will discover in his great whaling voyage—that only through the strange other and through death or death-in-life experiences do orphans discover their true kinship.

In another variation the leitmotif also bonds a stepson to a stepfather. When the line holding the log breaks and the Manxman castigates Pip as a "crazy loon" loose on the quarterdeck, Ahab intercedes on Pip's behalf in a passage that offers several variations on the symbol of the thread that bonds or binds:

> "Here, boy; Ahab's cabin shall be Pip's home henceforth, while Ahab lives. Thou touchest my inmost centre, boy, thou art tied to me by cords woven of my heart-strings. Come, let's down."

"What's this? here's velvet shark-skin," intently gazing at Ahab's hand, and feeling it, "Ah, now, had poor Pip but felt so kind a thing as this, perhaps he had ne'er been lost! This seems to me, sir, as a man-rope; something that weak souls may hold by. Oh, sir, let old Perth now come and rivet these two hands together; the black one with the white, for I will not let this go." (394)

Ahab succumbs to the same desire for union with the other that Ishmael does and offers Pip his hand to lead him to his cabin, that sanctum sanctorum of the isolated captain. Pip notes that, had such a hand been proffered to him as it had to the young Ishmael, he might not have become the estranged child he is. In having Pip see the handclasp thusly, Melville reinforces it as the image of the soul-saving bond of human solidarity and brotherhood, and, by having Ahab accept Pip's hand and lead him to his cabin, he suggests that Ahab has repented of his abandonment of his own child and his denial of the familial relationship and that once more he welcomes human connection. This choice, however, like the first one manifested in Ahab's marriage, is short-lived, and later Ahab abandons Pip as he has his own child and as he will abandon the lost child of *Rachel*.

The images of weaving—the tie to Pip woven of the heartstrings of Ahab and the riveting of the black hand to the white—are two more variations on the trope of the thread that bonds in tragic bond/age. Clearly, the image of weaving is central to *Moby Dick* and to the idea of tragic necessity in the novel. In a typical conversion of a classical symbol into a romantic one, Melville transforms the relatively static image of the net-as-fate into the more dynamic one of weaving-as-fate and in his orchestrated fiction repeats and varies the leitmotif. In "Matmaker," time is a loom, in which the existing warp is necessity; the ball of marline that Ishmael weaves between the lines of the warp is free will; and Queequeg's "impulsive, indifferent" sword that slides in and out of the warp and woof is chance. Ishmael comes to the conclusion that, in the making of the mat upon the loom of time, one discovers "chance, free will, and necessity—no wise incompatible—all interweavingly working together" (177). Here, the woven net momentarily is not so much necessity as it is the coexistence of necessity, free will, and chance.

The cry of "There she blows!" from Tashtego, who, in making the first sighting of a whale on the voyage, confuses what he beholds with "the shadows of fate" (178), however, causes Ishmael to drop the ball of free will. This dramatic reversal implies that, in the real world of ocean and sperm whale, free will is but an illusion. If Ishmael or man's free will does not wield the woof of the mat, then what does? The answer is implicit: it is the whale that plies the woof insofar as it is the sighting of the whale that effects the loss of free will; the idea is developed more fully in the total pattern of all repetitions and variations of the weaving leitmotif.

In "A Bower in the Arsacides," Melville further develops the rich texture of the symbolic weave in a metaphysical conceit by which the oxymoronic "industrious earth" is a weaver's loom; the great sun, the flying shuttle; and vegetation, in the form of the leaves and tendrils lacing themselves in and out of the skeleton of a beached whale, the rich fabric woven. Again the weaving leaves man in ignorance, facing the prospect that metaphysical communication and communion lie beyond life: "The weaver-god, he weaves; and by that weaving is he deafened, that he hears no mortal voice; and by that humming, we, too, who look on the loom are deafened; and only when we escape it shall we hear the thousand voices that speak through it" (346).

Melville intensifies his reappropriation of the classical symbol of the net as fate and makes it more dynamic and organic by identifying it with the natural elements that effect vegetative growth. By having tendril, leaf, and flower—warp and woof—lace themselves in and out of the skeleton of the whale, Melville also suggests that the whale itself may be the victim of tragic necessity, an implication in keeping with one theme developed in *Moby Dick*, that whales are doomed by technology. It is not, however, consistent with another: that at least one whale, Moby Dick, is more agent, rather than victim, of the bond/age of tragic necessity. Reading the image of the laced skeleton of the whale in the latter context, one may conclude that the ribs of the skeleton constitute the warp through which the woof of vegetation is plied. Melville repeats this paradox of whale as both victim and agent in another variation of the leitmotif in "The Chart."

This chapter depicts Ahab in his cabin trying to encompass Moby Dick's circumnavigation of the globe by tracing the longitudinal and latitudinal lines, the warp and woof, on the blank maps before him: "While thus employed, the heavy pewter lamp suspended in chains over his head, continually rocked with the motion of the ship, and forever threw shifting gleams and shadows of lines upon his wrinkled brow, till it almost seemed that, while he himself was marking out lines and courses on the wrinkled charts, some invisible pencil was also tracing lines and courses upon the deeply marked chart of his forehead" (164–65).

The table on which Ahab seeks to trace or square the circumnavigation of Moby Dick is Foucault's table on which eighteenth-century classical man seeks to order all things through the discourse of taxonomy: "I use the word 'table' in two superimposed senses: the nickel-plated, rubbery tale swathed in white, glittering beneath a glass sun devouring all shadow— the table where, for an instant, perhaps forever, the umbrella encounters the sewing-machine; and also a table, a *tabula*, that enables thought to operate upon the entities of our world, to put them in order, to divide them into classes, to group them according to names that designate their similarities and their differences— the table upon which since the beginning of time, language has intersected space."[3]

That table exists, however, aboard a nineteenth-century, and by Foucault's demarcations, modern whaler, and its viability as instrument of control and order is undermined by the very forces it seeks to master. Melville ironically implies that the whale may be the victim of the tragic necessity of science and technology that will square its circle and will successfully hunt it down and extinguish it, while simultaneously he suggests that the undulation of the sea conspires with the fire in the lamp to throw upon the brow of the protagonist the same pattern of woven bondage. Manifested in this single variation of the weaving leitmotif and in the pattern of variations throughout the narrative is the dialectical conflict between the tragic hero, who would be weaver of his and the White Whale's fate, and the net of tragic necessity— woven by sea, fire, and White Whale—that will bind the protagonist.

Ahab would not only cast lines on a map to catch Moby Dick, but also "weld his own iron" to accomplish the deed. After ordering Perth to forge twelve rods of horseshoe nails, he grabs the rods and fuses them into what will be the shank of the harpoon he hopes will snag the white whale. As Perth dips the newly crafted shank into the water, the resulting steam almost scorches Ahab's face, and in his retort Ahab foreshadows one result of tragic bond/age, "Would'st thou brand me, Perth? . . . have I been but forging my own branding iron?" (373) Ahab proceeds to order Perth to weld the barbs from the best steel of his own razors. After tempering the barbs in the blood of his harpooners while deliriously invoking the name of the devil, Ahab has the end of a new towline unstranded in order that "the separate spread yarns [be] all braided and woven round the socket of the harpoon" and pole, iron and rope be made one. The juxtaposition of the weaving of the rope round the socket of the harpoon with the forging of the shank and the garbs suggests that the joining of separate iron strands is but a variation of the weaving of separate strands of yarn, a c[h]ord reinforced by Pip's desire to have his black hand riveted to Ahab's white.

Whatever it is that weaves Ahab's heartstrings into cords that tie him to poor Pip, it is something recessive in Ahab, and that image of the weaving of a string that would connect is the exception that proves the rule that most of Ahab's weaving would bind, not bond. Ahab would be his own weaver of a fate that controls not only Moby Dick, but also the crew. In this manner is Starbuck bound to Ahab without a knife to cut that fatal tie, and, by virtue of his demonic rituals on the quarterdeck and his monomaniacal, but charismatic, quest for revenge, are "all varieties [of crew members] welded into oneness" (418) by their captain. That Ahab would be the weaver of Moby Dick's fate is also suggested by the manner in which Melville documents the preparation of the tow line before the lowering of the whale boat.

Ishmael describes in graphic detail how that line, prior to the lowering, is taken from the tub containing it and run back and forth and in and out of the boat, "resting crosswise upon the loom or handle of every man's oar, so that it jogs against his wrist in rowing" (225) before coming to rest in the shank of the harpoon over the bow. Ishmael concludes that "thus the whale-line folds the whole boat in its complicated coils, twisting and writhing around it in almost every direction" and "thus hung in hangman's nooses . . . like the six burghers of Calais before King Edward, the six men composing the crew pull into the jaws of death, with a halter around every neck." It also leads Ishmael in one of his more pessimistic utterances to extend the metaphor to all human bondage: "All men live enveloped in whale-lines. All are born with halters round their necks; but it is only when caught in the swift, sudden turn of death, that mortals realize the silent, subtle, ever-present perils of life." In another variation and foreshadowing of the leitmotif of tragic weaving, Melville extends his image of the raveling rope as symbol of tragic bond/age and suggests that the halter in which all men find themselves bound is one coexistent with birth itself—the umbilical cord by which all whalemen are bound to the whale and all men to tragic necessity.

More terrible than the actual chase and experience of the racing line in the boat during the hunt is the anticipation of that experience: "the graceful repose of the line, as it silently serpentines about the oarsmen before being brought into actual play—this is a thing which carries more of true terror than any other aspect of this dangerous affair" (226). The intimation that behind every calm (the line in repose) is a storm (the line brought into play) is one of the more dreadful "loomings" in a tale filled with literal and figurative foreshadowings and intimations of doom and disaster. When the actual play of line is experienced, however, it effects a terror-in-actuality commensurate to the terror-in-anticipation because it manifests what is only implied in Ishmael's account—that the dreadful shuttling of line into halter is caused by Ahab.

Although Ahab sets the lines to shuttling, Moby Dick completes the nautical weaving, and in that completion Ahab finds not only himself but also his crew literally, as well as figuratively, "bound" to the White Whale. On the second day of the chase, after all three harpooners have hurled their lances into the flesh of the White Whale, Moby Dick, "in his untraceable evolutions . . . so crossed and recrossed, and in a thousand ways entangled the slack of the three lines now fast to him, that they foreshortened, and, of themselves, warped the devoted boats towards the planted irons in him" (420). His intention to forge the harpoon that would bind Moby Dick to his boat is reversed, and Ahab finds himself bound to the white whale and on the threshold of being impaled upon the irons imbedded in it. Ahab, however, quickly and deftly reaches through the tangle and twice cuts the lines, and momentarily himself, away from Moby Dick and his fate.

His respite is temporary for, immediately after this act, Ahab and his crew are "drawn up towards Heaven by invisible wires" as the White Whale dashes "his broad forehead against its bottom" and upends the boat. Soon afterwards, Ahab learns that Fedallah, his dark alter ego, has been pulled overboard and beneath the surface of sea, "caught among the tangles of [Ahab's] lines" (422). Ahab, in disbelief, responds, "*My* line! *My* line?" What is becoming clear to Ahab is what has been evident to the reader: Ahab's intention to ensnare the elusive creature has been tragically reversed, and he joins Moby Dick in the fatal weaving that binds each to the other. Thus, on the third day of the chase, when Moby Dick surfaces from one of his many dives, Ahab bears witness to his own death as he discovers "lashed round and round to the fish's back; pinioned in the turns upon turns in which, during the past night, the whale had reeled the involutions of the lines around him, the half torn body of [his alter ego] the Parsee . . . his sable raiment frayed to shreds; his distended eyes turned full upon old Ahab" (427). With that sighting, Ahab repeats the experience of Ishmael when Tashtego first sights a whale: "the harpoon [of free will] drops from his hands."

Recovering from the shock of recognition, Ahab picks up the harpoon and casts it defyingly at Moby Dick. He then stoops to clear the line; as he rises, he is caught "round the neck" as by a halter and, as "Turkish mutes bowstring their victim," is shot out of the boat and seemingly hanged and drowned by the line woven by the White Whale. Melville effectively brings his variation of the thread that binds back to its classical origins, suggesting once again that fate is character and that the hero himself participates fully in his fate. This time, however, he is not only, as Henn suggests, the fish/hero swimming into the trammel net, but also the joint weaver of that net of tragic bond/age. As he does in charting Moby Dick's circumnavigation upon his map, in forging the shank and plaiting the line connected to the harpoon, in welding all the varieties of crew members into oneness, and in casting his line at the White Whale, Ahab initiates the weaving of the net of his own tragic bond/age; Moby Dick completes it and finally wields it.

Moby Dick is the totemic, and thereby more uncanny, strange, and terrible sovereignty that finally manipulates and masters the threads of tragic bond/age. It is an androgynous primitive and savage divinity, the repository of the sacred force that can both benevolently provide man with the oil that warms, lights, and informs or justly weave the net that destroys man when he strives to overpower that natural majesty with the very resources provided him by nature. Moby Dick is also the totemic embodiment of nature or Being, from which man has [been] separated himself by virtue of the gifts of consciousness, by his own peculiar human-beingness. What torments Ahab is that the totem is a constant reminder of his chthonic origins in the earth and in human parents and of his separation from that inception. Moby Dick is also, therefore, in this world of abandoned orphans and foundlings, the mother and father from whom man has been separated, through whom he would be tethered and smothered, and by whom, in the eyes of the more paranoiac, he has been abandoned.

Ahab will make no compromise with that power, with that ambiguity of human bond/age. He is dissociated man—split into two irreconcilable halves by his "birthmark," that "whitish" scar "threading its way out from among his grey hairs, and continuing right down one side of his tawny scorched face and neck, till it disappeared in his clothing" (110), a mark which the old Manxman contends will be found splitting Ahab "from crown to sole." In this case the punishment precedes the crime, for that birthmark is but the mark of Cain, and Ahab is Cain insofar as he will slay all but one of his brothers. In bringing about the destruction of the brotherhood of the *Pequod*, one which he is primarily responsible for forging, Ahab, as in his final denial of the bonds offered by his wife, Pip, and Starbuck, destroys the primary family unit in *Moby Dick*. "Gifted with the [Apollonian] higher perception," and lacking "the [Dionysian] low, enjoying power," Ahab is also what Nietzsche calls the individuated, Socratic hero, who finally casts off vestiges of the collective Dionysian mask, isolates himself from the communal experience, and thereby transgresses the limits of the familiar. The irony and paradox of the tragic bond/age in *Moby Dick* are in many ways those of individuation. Ahab is a manifestation of Nietzsche's view of individuated man; Ishmael, of Jung's. In recognizing the sublimity of the other—of Queequeg, Moby Dick, and all those who squeeze hands and melt together in the sperm of the whale—Ishmael is the young voyager whose passage is a rite, by which he is drawn closer to "the wife, the heart, the bed" (323), to what in his world is female or feminine even in male strangers. Such a calling allows him to bond himself to others and thereby to develop a true identity and nurture a new kinship. In his expression of that newly-acquired selfhood and communion, Ishmael offers through his Jungian integrating individuation a contrast to Ahab's Nietzschean disintegrating individuation and demonstrates in his narrative one final variation of Melville's rich trope of weaving.

Early in the novel, Melville has Father Mapple refer to the story of Jonah and the whale as a book containing only four chapters, "four yarns . . . one of the smallest strands in the mighty cable of the Scriptures" (52). The metaphor establishes all long narratives as cables and thereby Ishmael/Melville's *Moby Dick* as one as well. It is a richly textured tapestry that enables both artist and narrator to confront and purge the shadowy parts of their and their society's psyches, and the result of that confrontation is a catharsis of tragic bond/age.

9
In *The Mayor of Casterbridge*

The relatively more realistic versions of tragic bond/age in the late nineteenth century lack the recurring net, chain, and rope images found in Greek, Shakespearean, Miltonic, and American gothic forms of the trope. What they lack in quantity, however, they compensate for in subtlety and multiplicity of meaning. The most significant variation of the image of tragic bond/age in Thomas Hardy's *The Mayor of Casterbridge* occurs in the vividly dramatic scene of the skimmity-ride, in which the citizens of Mixen Lane wreak their jealousy, resentment, and folk justice upon Lucetta and Farfrae by exposing what they consider to be her unfaithfulness to him. They make effigies of Lucetta and Henchard, the man with whom she reputedly has been unfaithful, and tie the two effigies together, elbow to elbow, back to back, with the Lucetta figure facing the head of a donkey and the Henchard one facing the tail. Thus, Hardy most effectively varies Shakespeare's image of the beast with two backs with his own with two fronts.

That the Lucetta likeness faces the masculine head with her back to the Henchard figure, who faces the feminine tail, suggests that their relationship has been sexually bestial with very little human face-to-face contact. It also suggests that, although both have tried to walk away from each other—Henchard when Susan appears and Lucetta when Farfrae does—they remain, as have Henchard and Susan, tied to each other by virtue of their past relationship. The ride has consequences beyond the crowd's expectations: Lucetta has an epileptic seizure and loses her child and then her life. It would appear to be a cruel hoax played on Lucetta, who in this instance seems more sinned against than sinning. If she has been unfaithful to anyone, Lucetta has been so to Henchard, to whom she has given her word in marriage, and not to Farfrae, since her relationship with Henchard came to one close even before she met Farfrae and ended once again immediately thereafter.

Despite what would seem to be the literal inappropriateness of the Mixen Lane ritual in decrying one sin of Lucetta and Henchard, the scene works symbolically to evoke another—the breaking of bonds and the resulting punishment of bondage. What is true of Lucetta's adulterous relationship with Henchard is described by Hardy in his summation of the presentness of Henchard's sale of wife and child: "But the act having lain as dead and buried ever since, the interspace of years was unperceived; and the black spot of his youth wore the aspect of a recent crime."[1] Lucetta's having kept her relationship with Henchard secret is tantamount to her having had that relationship recently. In that respect, Mixen Lane retribution is timely and appropriate.

Moreover, in a novel in which one of the most significant bonds is one's word, the failure to give that word is a sin of omission, if not commission. Lucetta's failure to confide in Farfrae is a failure to bond truly with him. Just as her letters have revealed what she would have kept secret, so the Skimmington reveals to all of Casterbridge what has become known to Mixen Lane. Since her error in judgment has been partly to withhold her word, her penalty is to have her secret revealed in public. Lucetta is being punished, as has Henchard and as will be Angel and Tess, for her attempt to run away from the past. That the Lucetta and Henchard effigies are facing away from, but still tied to, each other is an appropriate Dantean punishment for the sin of trying to deny the past.

Another reason why Mixen Lane is an agent of justice in its social condemnation of Lucetta is that she has broken her word to Henchard, whom she promised to wed. Moreover, she gave Henchard that word after she met and found herself attracted to Farfrae, and therefore the act of giving her word is ironically a betrayal of her feelings for Farfrae. The promise Lucetta makes to Henchard and the fact that Henchard was her first love take precedent in Hardy's world: "My God—what, married him whilst—bound to marry me?" (162), Henchard says to Lucetta. Lucetta counters, "I knew I should lose Donald if I did not secure him at once." Because Lucetta betrays her bond to Henchard and seeks to bind or "secure" Farfrae, the Skimmington authentically reveals and punishes betrayal and bondage. Even Elizabeth Jane, who comes as close as anyone to Hardy's authorial perspective, cautions Lucetta that it is her supposed father, Henchard, Lucetta should marry or no one.

The bond Lucetta has to Henchard, however, becomes bondage when she meets Farfrae; he is a man of the future, both literally and figuratively; Henchard is of the past, literally of her's and figuratively of Wessex's. In attempting to deny Henchard and embrace Farfrae, Lucetta is trying to sever the past from the present and the future, and thereby to deny the former. Lucetta Le Sueur, in her attempt to become Lucetta Templeman Farfrae, seeks to deny what she has been: "He's hot-tempered and stern, and it would be madness to bind myself to him knowing that. I won't be a slave to the past,—I'll love where I choose" (136). What Lucetta does not understand now, but will later as a result of the Skimmington, is that she is already bound to Henchard for, in Hardy's world, what one has been is integral to what one is. Consequently, the attempt to act independently of what one has been and what one has chosen is by necessity self-destructive and, as we see from the Skimmington, self-binding. What Mixen Lane does to its victims is but the social manifestation of what the victims have already done to themselves.

In that respect, as in so many, Lucetta's agon is a variation of Henchard's; furthermore, the Skimmington appropriately symbolizes Henchard's bondage to family and the past and his earlier crime against kinship in selling his wife and disinheriting his daughter. Feeling "the frustration of many a promising youth's high aims and hopes and the extinction of his energies by an early imprudent marriage," (7) intuiting that he has given hostages to fortune by marrying and begetting a child, and straining against the bondage of such domesticity, Henchard in a drunken stupor does what he (and perhaps many of Hardy's readers) heretofore only joked or dreamt of doing: he exchanges "stale familiarity" (4) for estranged liberation. Henchard sells his wife and daughter and seemingly frees himself from a past that would keep him from good fortune.

Fortune itself aids and abets in Henchard's liberation in the persons of the simple and ingenuous Newson, who buys Susan and, we might note, finances the Skimmington as well, and an even simpler Susan, who believes "that there was some sort of binding force in the transaction" (14). It is one of the most dramatic manifestations in all of Hardy's fiction of marriage as a form of bondage that the hero feels compelled to break; it is also a dramatic violation of a major taboo in Hardy's fiction: the sacredness of the first bond. Such sanctity is evident not only in Mixen Lane's social confirmation of Lucetta's first bond to Henchard, but also in the fact that, when she finds out that the transaction in the furmity tent lacked the authority she believed it had, Susan brings to an end her marriage to Newson and seeks to claim rightfully her kinship to Henchard. The result of Henchard's breaking that first bond is that the hero, instead of reversing the act of giving hostages to (potential) fortune, only gives to fortune (or necessity) more hostages.

As indicated earlier, one of the effects of Hardy's eliding the nineteen-year interim between Henchard's selling of his wife and daughter and their return to claim kinship is that the past is made to seem less distant—his past crime a recent one—a seeming that reinforces Hardy's idea that the past is always present in the web-like world of Wessex. Thus, when one of the citizens of Casterbridge questions Henchard about the bad wheat, "But what are you going to do to repay us for the past," (29), it is as though he were speaking as much for Susan and Elizabeth Jane as he is for the folk of Casterbridge. Also, by juxtaposing Henchard's disclaimer of the kinship of wife and child with his embrace of the youthful Farfrae to fill the emotional void in his life, Hardy suggests that Henchard's subsequent act is one of atonement: the adoption of a son to compensate for the disinheritance of a daughter.

For Henchard, it is always the vertical, intergenerational relationship, daughter or son, Elizabeth Jane or Farfrae, that takes precedence over the horizontal, generational relationship, Susan or Lucetta. Indeed, one could argue that the reason that Henchard anguishes over the Lucetta/Farfrae marriage is not so much that he has lost Lucetta, but rather that he has more completely lost Farfrae. Moreover, when Henchard seals this newfound relationship with Farfrae with the universal image of bonding, the shaking of hands, and with the claim that "my word is my bond," one cannot help but recall, because of the proximity of past with present, that Henchard's word and bond have been and no doubt will be easily broken.

Indeed, his contract with Jopp is broken in spirit, if not by letter, immediately after Farfrae and Jopp's arrivals, and, since his contract with Jopp precedes his commitment to Farfrae, Henchard once again breaks the first bond. Furthermore, he renounces his newfound relationship with Farfrae when the latter dares reverse Henchard's punishment of Whittle and upstage his employer by constructing a superior outdoor festival hall, where the populace throng to watch the Scotchman dance with admiring ladies. In this competition of festivities, Hardy reveals that the accomplished dancer and singer is the man of the future insofar as he is more the master of nature, the elements, and motion. Rather than continue to take advantage of his brief union and interdependence with the young man to control the elements and order his domestic life, Henchard repeats his crime, fires the young employee, and disinherits an adopted son. As in the first disclaimer of kinship, Henchard awakens the next day contrite but powerless to reverse the dismissal of Farfrae, who "was determined to take him at his word," determined to honor that which Henchard does not.

Being separated from Susan by death and from Farfrae by estrangement, Henchard seeks "the re-establishment of this tenderest human tie" (95) to the familiar through Elizabeth Jane. Desiring to make her his daughter in name and spirit as well as in blood, Henchard violates the word of the dead, takes advantage of the cracked seal on Susan's letter, and reads therein that Elizabeth Jane is not his natural daughter: "The mockery was, that he should have no sooner taught a girl to claim the shelter of his paternity than he discovered her to have no kinship with him" (97). Blind to the fact that she is at least his stepdaughter because of his remarriage to Susan and therefore has a claim in law to his kinship, Henchard rejects any paternity and once more tries to redeem his bond with fortune, this time not by selling away his inheritance, but rather by buying off her who would hold him hostage. He offers Elizabeth Jane an annuity when she decides to leave him and live with another; characteristically, he rues his action the very next day. Once again, Henchard violates the domestic bond of paternity and family by trying to calculate and negotiate its worth: he not only sells Susan and buys off his stepdaughter, but also, when anticipating a complete break with Lucetta upon his wife's return, contemplates similar compensation: "I must send a useful sum of money to her" (61).

Because of the greater economic worth of Lucetta and because, cut off from Farfrae, Elizabeth Jane, and Susan, he finds himself left with an "emotional void" (113), Henchard is motivated to woo Lucetta. With his diminishing fortune and her rising one, Henchard seeks to do the right thing and make Lucetta an honest woman and in so doing honor his word that, should he find himself free to marry her, he would. Before that act can be consummated, once again the upstart and seemingly ungrateful Farfrae comes between Henchard and his fortune. Farfrae rises as Henchard falls and inherits almost all of Henchard's property as well as his family—Lucetta and Elizabeth Jane. Humbled publicly once more, Henchard, with one of his hands tied behind him, fights Farfrae, overcomes him, but is unable to destroy him. He allows Farfrae to go free, confessing, "God is my witness that no man ever loved another as I did thee at one time" (210).

In Oedipal terms, Henchard is the failing mayor, king, father, whose place in the family and community is usurped by the growing son. His fall is complicated by the pact he has made with fortune: he swore an oath to have no drink of alcohol for twenty-one years. He keeps that word, and the reader infers that one of the reasons for his success has been the self-discipline resulting from honoring his oath. However, another result is that it is a manifestation of the man who knows no moderation; thus, when he goes off the wagon, he forces Farfrae to "snub" and thereby humble him before the folk of Casterbridge. In response, part of him wishes to revenge himself upon the usurper; another part of him loves the usurper despite his usurpation. In tragic terms, Henchard's agon is the conflict between resisting the necessity that requires all failing fathers to give over to all growing sons and accepting the interdependence that is required in human family and society. Because he resists interdependence, Henchard forces himself into either total independence or dependence and thereby manifests what Lucien Goldmann considers the essential trait of the tragic hero: "He makes this absolute and exclusive demand for impossible values . . . for 'all or nothing' . . . [he is] totally indifferent to degrees and approximations."[2]

In one of the most morally ambiguous acts of the novel, Henchard repeats the crime for which he is being punished. When Newson comes looking for his daughter, Henchard in a characteristic impulsive response tells him that Elizabeth Jane is dead. Once more Henchard is responsible for the "separation of father and child" (225). This time, however, his crime against kinship is more morally ambiguous for he is moved to act not so much because he wishes to keep Newson and Elizabeth Jane apart, but rather because he, like Lear, has finally accepted one form of paternity: he has grown to love and depend upon Elizabeth Jane and therefore wishes to keep her by his side. Again, Henchard fails to see that the truth, his admission to Newson that Elizabeth Jane is in the next room, could be the very word, the bond, that would not only reunite natural father and daughter, but perhaps keep stepfather and stepdaughter together. Once more Henchard reveals an almost perverted compulsion to repeat acts that are ultimately self-destructive. For Freud, such compulsiveness implies an attempt to control actively what one has been the victim of passively. Does Henchard's compulsion suggest any such trauma? As we shall see, the novel suggests so.

When the questions that he expects "to close in round him, and unmask his fabrication" to Newson fail to come forth, Henchard walks to the Ten Hatches in torment over his degenerative act. There, about to commit suicide, he encounters what he believes is an apparition of himself in the whirlpool; stunned, he aborts his suicide, leaves, and returns home, where he finds Elizabeth Jane waiting for him. She accompanies him back to the Hatches and discovers that the apparition is nothing more than the Skimmington effigy that has floated downstream from the town. What the figure in the pool suggests is that, separated from the Lucetta effigy, from what is both female and familiar, what is other, the Henchard effigy, like the ex-mayor himself, is a terribly isolated and alienated figure adrift in a strange land.

Henchard cannot, like Lucetta, die yet, for his suffering and thereby his atonement are not yet complete. In order for that to occur, the man who would be independent of the female must become once again, as in infancy, totally dependent upon her, and such is the case when Henchard takes refuge with Elizabeth Jane after having sent her father off believing she is dead: "he schooled himself to accept her will . . . as absolute and unquestionable . . . the dependence upon Elizabeth's regard into which he had declined (or, in another sense, to which he had advanced) denaturalized him" (232–33). The paradox is plain: Henchard, who is "uncultivated" (99) and has "no domestic finesse," (87), who, as John Holloway has noted,[3] is identified with animals throughout the novel, and who in his independence from all familiarity and domesticity has become somewhat "naturalized," is now "denaturalized" in his dependence upon his adopted daughter. It is both a decline insofar as it may be said to unman him and make him in his and the town's eyes less than the man he has striven to be and an advancement insofar as it tends to soften and feminize him and thereby lift him humanly above the chthonic. Such a change is also apparent in the denouement of his physical agon with Farfrae.

After Henchard finds himself incapable of killing Farfrae and subdued in a crouching attitude upon the sacks of corn, Hardy concludes, "Its womanliness sat tragically on the figure of so stern a piece of virility" (210). The lion has indeed been domesticated or "netted" by human bond/age; just as his disinheritance had been characterized by complete excessive independence, so his domestication is manifested in excessive dependence. What is lacking in this protagonist of heroic proportion is the moderation of compromise and interdependence, the integration of anima and animus.

The only two instances of "fresh familiarity" of Henchard's life occur during his brief adoption of both Farfrae and Elizabeth Jane. Indeed, one might argue that the strongest attraction Henchard feels for anyone is the one he feels for Farfrae because in him he finds a figure that reminds him not only of his brother, but also—because of what is soft and gentle in Farfrae—of the wife and daughter, from whom he has cut himself off, and perhaps the mother, from whom he has been separated by necessity. In turning himself away from all these persons, Henchard denies what is feminine and other, what Jung would call the *anima*, what is necessary not only for familiarity but also for individuation.[4]

Hardy draws his novel full circle by having his hero leave Casterbridge almost as he had entered a quarter of a century ago: "except, to be sure, that the serious addition to his years had considerably lessened the spring in his stride, that his state of hopelessness had weakened him, and imparted to his shoulders, as weighted by the basket, a perceptible bend" (239). Fearing the consequences of the return of Newson, whom he has sighted on the heath near Casterbridge, Henchard flees the town and Elizabeth Jane, lamenting the lost opportunity: "if I had only got her with me—if I only had. . . . Hard work would be nothing to me then! But that was not to be. I—Cain—go alone as I deserve—an outcast and a vagabond. But my punishment is not greater than I can bear!" (239)

When Henchard tries to leave Casterbridge for good, however, he discovers himself figuratively tethered to his adoptive home and daughter: instead of continuing away from Casterbridge, Henchard finds that the "centrifugal tendency imparted by the weariness of the world was counteracted by the centripetal influence of his love for his stepdaughter" and thus his wandering becomes "part of a circle of which Casterbridge [and Elizabeth] formed the centre" (244). Attempting in one final desperate act to renew his relationship with Elizabeth, Henchard comes to her wedding only to have her reject and disinherit him with the greeting, "Oh—it is—Mr. Henchard" (249). Henchard responds by asking Elizabeth "don't give all your thought to [Newson]! Do ye save a little room for me!" (249) But it is too late; Elizabeth cannot love a man who has "persuaded me that my father was not my father"; she cannot love a man who has disinherited her twice.

By developing the agon in the complex way he does, Hardy achieves several variations of tragic bond/age implicit in the Oedipal complex. Not only does Henchard emerge as a father who must suffer the loss of the intended wife, Lucetta, and the adopted daughter, Elizabeth Jane, to the upstart Farfrae, but, once he becomes so dependent upon Elizabeth Jane that he is connected almost umbilically to her, he must also suffer the trauma of the son who is supplanted by rival father figures, Newson and Farfrae. The rejections of Henchard by Lucetta and Elizabeth Jane are variations of the victimization Henchard has suffered at the hands of the female earlier in the novel: Susan by virtue of her letter from the grave avenges herself upon him and the furmity woman by virtue of her revelation of the past avenges society upon him. All of these configure in a pattern that suggests the goddesses who weave the threads that control man. When one considers the pain and suffering Henchard and women have caused each other, is it any wonder that he confides to Farfrae, "Being by nature something of a woman hater, I have found it no hardship to keep mostly at a distance from the sex" (60).

9 / In The Mayor of Casterbridge

The answer to the question posed earlier—what trauma is implied by Henchard's compulsion to repeat self-destructive acts in his relationship with the feminine?—is the original separation of the self from the female and the compensating splitting of the self into a male master who lords it over the female servant. According to Freud, such compulsion is motivated by a need to assume control over a situation in which one has been the passive victim and to satisfy the most primal of instincts, the desire to return to the inorganic state. By commencing the separation of himself from the female, Henchard precludes both the female's initiating a rejection of him and a repetition of the severance of the first bond to the mother when, according to Lacan, the infant ceases to be the object of desire of the mother in order to enter the linguistic realm of the no/name-of-the-father. By breaking with woman now, he thereby gains some psychological control over the original situation that lies latent in the unconscious. That power also manifests itself as an Hegelian master/servant relationship, in which, as Jessica Benjamin interpolates Hegel, the dialectical reciprocity of recognition between both is split and the male assumes the role of the master, who must be recognized, and the female, the servant who must recognize.[5]

That situation is reversed, however, as Farfrae grows stronger and more patriarchal rather than filial and as the women in Henchard's life become increasingly more independent. Susan becomes a little more so with the passing of time, and Lucetta and Elizabeth Jane are each increasingly more independent than the previous woman in Henchard's life. In time, the roles of master and servant are reversed, and Henchard becomes the Lear-like figure so desperately dependent upon the Cordelia-like Elizabeth, that he leaves her a bird in a cage, a wedding gift, whose acceptance would imply recognition by the new mistress of the ex-master and his new restricted situation. Henchard has become so dependent on the recognition by woman that he literally is no longer capable of keeping his "distance from the sex," and he circumscribes his life around Casterbridge in the hopes of a chance recognition by Elizabeth. When that is not forthcoming, the desire to be the object of desire, or at least of recognition, of the daughter/mother figure further retrogresses and manifests itself as the instinct to return to the inorganic, to die. Thus, Jeanette King concludes that within Henchard, "character and fate are woven into a net from which death is the only escape."[6]

Hardy's treatment of tragic bond/age in this novel is evocative not only of the earliest psychological instincts, but also of the crime against kinship and of the condition of the Hardy hero and heroine that often attends that crime: all the major figures of the novel—Henchard, Susan, Elizabeth,

Lucetta, Farfrae, Newson—are *déracines*; they have been uprooted and eventually come to Casterbridge to establish roots and family. They all share with Cain to one degree or another the punishment of deracination, and Henchard in particular shares the crime of disinheritance. Cain slays his brother; Henchard rejects his wife, daughter, stepdaughter, adopted son, and former mistress and in turn is rejected by Lucetta and Elizabeth. The reader discovers that, although much of what happens to him is not more than he can bear, the loss of Elizabeth Jane is. Because Henchard has willed much of what befalls him, the tragic net of bond/age in which he finds himself is the trammel. Such is not the case for Tess Durbeyfield, one more sinned against than sinning; the net that ensnares her is more of a seine.

10
In *Tess of the d'Urbervilles*

In one sense, the theme of *The Mayor of Casterbridge* is the "question of paternity" (240); Henchard rejects it when he sells his wife and thereby disinherits his daughter. He momentarily embraces it when he adopts Farfrae only to reject him as well when he discovers that paternity requires interdependence rather than independence. He suffers his most bitter agon in his relationship with Elizabeth Jane, vacillating between what he believes to be the bond of reunion and what he subsequently discovers is the separation of blood, until he finally acknowledges he loves her and is more dependent upon her than any other person in his life. For Henchard, the question of paternity is resolved in the realization that paternity and kinship are as much a matter of the heart as of the blood, of written law and society as much as of natural law and nature. Part of his tragedy is that at the very moment he experiences this new-found paternity, Elizabeth disinherits him because he has not been true to his word, which of course is his bond. Just as the question of paternity is one of the central themes of tragic bond/age in the *Mayor* so the question of patrimony and matrimony is at the core of tragic bond/age in *Tess of the d'Urbervilles*.

Literally, patrimony is the inheritance one receives from the father; by extension it is also the legacy or heritage one receives from the fatherland or the patriarchy. Matrimony in this context is the inheritance or legacy one receives from the mother and the residual legacy from the motherland or matriarchy that precedes patriarchal society. One of the central agons in *Tess* is the rival claims made upon a young milkmaid by the patriarchal and matriarchal forces in her life. Hardy asks on behalf of Tess Durbeyfield what is my kinship, what is my bond? In answering that question, he reappropriates ritual and mythology to demonstrate that the major claim made upon Tess by all her heritage is that she sacrifice herself in bondage in order to advance the well-being of those to whom she is bonded.

In "Phase the Fifth—The Woman Pays," Tess, after struggling at Flintcombe Ash for several months, decides to walk to the Emminster Vicarage and claim kinship and relief from the Clares. As she approaches the loamy Vale of Blackmoor in which Emminster lies, Hardy gives the reader this telling graphic variation of the net of tragic bond/age: "Instead of the great enclosures of hundred acres in which she was now accustomed to toil there were little fields below her of less than half-a-dozen acres, so numerous that they looked from this height like the meshes of a net. Here the landscape was whitey-brown; down there, as in Froom Valley, it was always green. Yet it was in that vale that her sorrow had taken shape, and she did not love it as formerly. Beauty to her, as to all who have felt, lay not in the thing, but in what the thing symbolized."[1]

What is symbolized in that meshed net of landscape is that for Tess the land and the families upon it are the bondage that ensnare the tragic heroine. Dorothy van Ghent is correct in her incisive conclusion that it is the landscape that is a primary antagonist to Tess;[2] moreover, it is the landscape as fatherland and motherland that is the antagonist in Tess's futile quest for kinship that enfolds rather than ensnares. Thus, her trek from Flintcombe Ash to Emminster and back results in fatigue that causes her to succumb to what seems a cold reception on the part of her brothers-in-law and Mercy Chant. Instead of finding relief in the charity of her father-in-law, she finds only condemnation in Mercy Chant's inference, on discovering Tess's abandoned boots, that they must be those of an "impostor who wished to come into the town barefoot, perhaps, and so excite our sympathies" (280).

Although Hardy does not spell out why Tess is wont to find in the circumstance a condemnation, it seems clear that the word "impostor" comes too close to home. Tess is a Clare in name only; her marriage has not been consummated; she has been abandoned by Angel, who feels she is no longer the woman he thought he married; and in both of their minds, as well as the mind of the narrator, she still remains joined to Alec by virtue of the first bond. Moreover, Mercy's comment must remind Tess that the very first time she set out to claim kinship at Trantridge she then too felt like an impostor, and she consequently suffered a fall. Furthermore, just as she once set out to claim kinship or connection with the family d'Urberville and wound up encountering a nouveau riche Alec Stoke d'Urberville, who was neither kin nor kind, so upon her retreat from Emminster she once again meets a new, reborn Alec and is made to repeat her fall.

Tess is sent on that initial quest to claim kinship by parents whose patrimony and matrimony are for the most part variations on original sin: she is made to pay for the transgressions of her immediate parents and subsequently for those of her d'Urberville ancestors. To begin, she compensates for Jack Durbeyfield's drinking: because Jack celebrates to drunkardness his new found heritage, Tess must drive Prince to market, and Prince is killed. The loss of the horse, upon which the Durbeyfields, of whom there are too many, have depended for their livelihood, leads her parents to send Tess off to claim kinship and relief from what they believe is another branch of the d'Urberville family. Tess acquiesces because she is overcome by her patrimony, a scrupulous sense of culpability that makes her feel fault for the death of Prince and the penury of her family, and by her matrimony, a tractability which she inherits from Joan, who has long ago learned that some things are just "meant to be."

Joan's fatalism and Tess's tractability reflect and foreshadow what Benjamin defines as the splitting of forces within the individual that leads to the imbalance of power between individuals: "Submission becomes the 'pure' form of recognition, even as violation becomes the 'pure' form of assertion. The assertion of one individual (the master) is transformed into domination; the other's (the slave's) recognition becomes submission. Thus the basic tension of forces within the individual becomes a dynamic between individuals."[3] Hardy dramatizes this tension in terms of class, social, and personal relationships.

Hardy also foreshadows the consequences of Tess's quest to claim kinship by having the Parson, a clerical patriarch, inform Jack Durbeyfield, in answer to his question as to where his d'Urberville family lives, "You don't live anywhere. You are extinct—as a county family" (7). The parson's comments will prove to be not only accurate in terms of any blood-begotten d'Urbervilles, but also prophetic in terms of the final outcome of Tess's journey. In addition, Jack himself, not realizing the possible consequences of having the past visited upon the present, boasts that "There's not a man in the county o' South-Wessex that's got grander and nobler skillentons in his family than I" (8). It is those very skeletons whose ghostly presence will preside over her fall in the Chase and whose stern portraits will haunt her at the Manor house when her revelation to Angel about her first encounter with a d'Urberville will cost Tess her marriage.

It is not only her patrimony that endangers Tess's innocence in the Chase, but also her matrimony, a voluptuousness she inherits from her mother—"a luxuriance of aspect, a fulness of growth, which made her appear more of a woman than she really was" (35). That sensuality impassions Alec to seduce Tess in the labyrinthine darkness of the oldest wood in England. It is her patrimony, however, that Hardy suggests might be the unseen cause behind the seeming happenstance of Tess's fall at the hands of the wrong man at the wrong time: "One may, indeed, admit the possibility of a retribution lurking in the present catastrophe. Doubtless some of Tess d'Durberville's mailed ancestors rollicking home from a fray had dealt the same measure even more ruthlessly towards peasant girls of their time" (63). Hardy qualifies what he has proposed by pointing out that "to visit the sins of the fathers upon the children may be a morality good enough for divinities, it is scorned by average human nature, and it therefore does not mend the matter."

It may not mend the matter; it may be scorned by human nature, and indeed Tess may not be suffering for the sins of her distant ancestors, but she is in fact suffering for the sins of her own parents. She would not have been in a position to be seduced by the wrong man had her father not gotten drunk in revelry over his newly discovered kinship; had his pride and his greed not gotten the better of him and impelled him to send his daughter off to sell her inheritance, their title, for twenty pounds; had he and Joan not seen the possibility of a way out of poverty by sending Tess off to claim kinship. Trying to benefit from the connection they believe they have with the d'Urbervilles at Trantridge and to use their daughter to establish a bond that will bring economic relief, they only send Tess into a form of bondage that can justifiably be called an act of prostitution. Thus, it is not so much Henry James, as Jeannette King suggests, but rather more so Thomas Hardy, who is the true literary successor of George Eliot for it is in the latter's work, and particularly in *Tess*, that "the 'bond of blood' everywhere exercises its stranglehold."[4]

When Tess discovers that she is pregnant and does not love Alec, she refuses both her matrimony—playing her trump card, which is the same as her mother's, "her face,"—and patrimony, forcing Alec to marry her because she is pregnant with his child and thereby becoming in name as well as in blood a d'Urberville instead of a Durbeyfield. When she returns home and confides to her mother her condition, Hardy delineates the nature of Tess's bond/age—a family bond transformed into family bondage—through Joan's response, "And yet th'st no got him to marry 'ee. . . . Any woman would have done it but you, after that!. . . . Why didn't ye think of doing some good for your family instead o' thinking only of yourself?" (69)

Hardy makes it clear that Tess is not any woman, that she is indeed herself as no other woman in South Wessex is, and that she is in such a way that makes her a "Durbeyfield," whose true heritage is other than that bequeathed by either Jack or Joan. On the hills of her native soil, Tess's "quiescent glide was of a piece with the element she moved in. Her flexuous and stealthy figure became an integral part of the scene" (72). He adds that in the field, where, "holding the corn in an embrace like that of a lover" bringing "the ends of the bond [of corn] together," Tess "is a portion of the field; she has somehow lost her own margin, imbibed the essence of her surrounding, and assimilated herself with it" (74–75). At the end of her first day's "pilgrimage" to Talbothay's dairy, entering a new part of Wessex, "she felt akin to the landscape" (86) and even en route to the bleaker landscape of Flintcombe Ash, Tess is "a figure which is part of the landscape" (234). The full significance of this association of Tess with the earth will be discussed in more detail later; suffice it to say now that in this identification of Tess with the landscape, Hardy suggests that Tess's true kinship is less with her immediate or distant families and more with a nature older than any patrimony or matrimony. That kinship is further reinforced in Hardy's depiction of Tess as an animal.

Even after her fall from grace, the "stir of germination" in spring moves Tess "as it moved the wild animals" (84). At Talbothays, conscious that Angel is regarding her for the first time, she begins "to trace imaginary patterns on the tablecloth with her forefinger with the constraint of a domestic animal that perceives itself to be watched" (102). When she says to Angel later, however, that he should have remained behind in Marlott at the Cerealia, it is with the torment of a "bird caught in a springe" (165). Thus, in his development of this identification of Tess with animals, Hardy moves from the stirring of a wild animal to a domestic animal who feels watched to one caught in a trap. Most of the images that follow emphasize the notion of Tess as an animal ensnared; when Angel suggests that maybe Tess does not really love him, she "wince[s] like a wounded animal" (184); at Flintcome Ash, standing before the master of the swede farm, she is described "like a bird caught in a clap-net" (242); and later at Flintcombe, Alec suggests to her that she looks as "weak as a bled calf" (278). Such patterns of imagery confirm that this novel is a fictive variation of Hardy's assertion that all "are caged birds; the only difference lies in the size of the cage."[5]

This evocation of Tess as a hunted animal is foreshadowed in a scene that takes place during a harvest just after Tess has returned to Marlott and given birth to Sorrow. There, the liquid fire arms of "the revolving Maltese cross of the reaping machine" cut a deep swath in the fields of corn as it moves up and down and back and forth in a shrinking square: "The narrow lane of stubble encompassing the field grew wider with each circuit, and the standing corn was reduced to smaller area as the morning wore on. Rabbits, hares, snakes, rats, mice, retreated inwards as into a fastness, unaware of the ephemeral nature of their refuge, and of the doom that awaited them later in the day when, their covert shrinking to a more and more horrible narrowness, they were huddled together, friends and foes, till the last few yards of upright wheat fell also under the teeth of the unerring reaper, and they were every one put to death by the sticks and stones of the harvesters" (74).

Tess is such an animal, and the scene is a symbolic recapitulation and foreshadowing of a patrimony—a phallo-techno-logocentric patriarchy that ravishes nature and women in its quest for mastery and one that victimizes Tess throughout the novel. It is evocative of a theology that is so scrupulous and exacting in its response to human weakness that it will not permit Tess to bury her son in holy ground nor allow her to forget her fall; of a technology that will waste Tess through the machinations of the tyrannical, despotic, and plutonic threshing machine and, in its encroachment upon Wessex, uproot Tess's family and thereby drive Tess once more into the arms of Alec; of a society so successful in its cultivation of the young that even Angel, who tries to reject his heritage, finds himself as much an instrument of its logocentrism as Alec is of its phallocentrism and thereby an instrument of torment for Tess.

Angel attempts to break the bondage of the conventions of his society. He refuses a university education that requires him to accept the teachings of Palestine instead of those of Greece. He tries to move away from a life centered on the mind to one close to the soil. In that effort, he is drawn both spiritually and sensually towards Tess, but he wavers in his denial of his patrimony even before Tess makes her confession as evidenced in the fact that, like Jack Durbeyfield, he wishes to claim kinship with the d'Urbervilles in order to placate his father. What he and Jack do not realize is that with the family name comes the family curse. Once Tess confides in him, Angel finds himself even more in the clutches of the very patrimony he has sought to break: "With all his attempted independence of judgement this advanced and well-meaning young man, a sample product of the last five-and-twenty years, was yet the slave to custom and conventionality when surprised back into his early teachings" (221). What surprises him is Tess's confession, and that revelation makes manifest the "hard logical deposit . . . that lay hidden . . . in the remote depths of his constitution" (202). Thus, Angel's affection is unlike the warm prismatic many-coloredness of Tess's; his "was less fire than radiance," and "when he ceased to believe he ceased to follow."

Angel suffers from a dissociation of sensibility that at this moment of crisis causes him to dwell upon the Tess that had been and might have been rather than the Tess that is. Angel, the lover whose music charms all of Talbothays, is an Orpheus-like figure, who has it in his power to lead Tess, a Eurydice-like one, out of the Hades into which her patriarchal masters have psychologically buried her. Like Orpheus, however, Angel too looks back and in reflection loses Tess. That is the significance of the sleepwalking scene during the aborted honeymoon: Angel, who instead of continuing to lead Tess out of her residence in the Hades of self-condemnation, instead carries her back into the grave, back into the darkness of the hell within, and Tess becomes a victim once more of her own scrupulous automachia and the malevolent Alec.

In describing the ill-timed meeting at Trantridge, Hardy reappropriates Plato's metaphor of the two halves of an original androgynous figure who seek to make themselves whole again through union with the other half and acknowledges that in the case of Tess and Alec "it was not the two halves of a perfect whole that confronted each other" (35). Contrastingly, when Angel and Tess drive the milk to the railroad depot, Hardy describes them as "forming one bundle inside the sail-cloth" (160). Angel and Tess are not only the two halves of the Platonic androgynous egg reunited, they are also the two halves of the androgynous Adam who cleave to one another after Eve's awakening. Thus, Hardy describes them at Talbothays, in the "spectral, half-compounded aqueous light which pervaded the open mead," as "Adam and Eve" (110). Later, Angel looks into the "deepness of the ever-varying pupils [of Tess] with their radiating fibrils of blue, and black, and gray, and violet, while she regarded him as Eve at her second waking might have regarded Adam" (143).

That is why, when Angel first meets and begins to court Tess, "he seemed to discern in her something that was familiar, something which carried him back into a joyous and unforeseeing past, before the necessity of taking thought had made the heavens gray" (102). Tess is the symbolic Eve of his youth, the sensuous part of his existence—the desire of the female—that has been sacrificed to the logical patrimony—the word of the father. That is also why Angel is attracted to what is "real vitality, real warmth, real incarnation" in Tess, to "that little upward lift in the middle of her red top lip [that] was distracting, infatuating, maddening . . . it was the touch of the imperfect upon the would-be perfect that gave the sweetness, because it was that which gave the humanity" (127). If it is Eve with whom Angel falls in love, it is Eve after the fall, after the seduction by the serpent Alec, after the "coarse pattern [has been] traced . . . upon the beautiful feminine tissue, sensitive as gossamer and practically blank as snow" (63). That is also why, when Angel calls her Artemis and Demeter, Tess responds, "Call me Tess" (111). Just as she does not want to be the sensual object of Alec's lust and domination, Tess does not want to be the object of Angel's idealism and adoration. What she wants is what Lacan suggests all human beings want: to be desired as a subject.

Hardy, however, in order to develop that self most completely, relies upon allusion to several mythological female archetypes. As Carl Wickens points out,[6] he clearly identifies Tess with the goddess figures in the myth of Demeter and Persephone. Like Kore, Tess is abducted in a chariot by Alec/Hades and eats of the forbidden fruit of the pomegranate/strawberry and is therefore confined to the underground world of both Trantridge and Flintcombe Ash as Persephone. Like Persephone, Tess enjoys a return to her mother Demeter, to the fields of Marlott and the dairies of Talbothays, only to fall once again into the darkness of Flintcombe Ash and Sandbourne. The major question posed by Hardy in this reappropriation of the myth is whether in her symbolic resurrections from Hades, Tess returns as the fallen Persephone or as the pure Kore: "Was once lost always lost really true of chastity? she would ask herself. She might prove it false if she could veil bygones. The recuperative power which pervaded organic nature was surely not denied to maidenhood alone" (84).

Persephone returns to Demeter as Kore, and thereby the myth symbolizes what Hardy says about the recuperative power that pervades organic nature. In the novel Hardy is more ambiguous. For Alec, who is a creature of the body, Tess remains "unsmirched in spite of all" (266). For Angel, Tess is what she is for Hardy, "pure woman," until he looks backward to the past and finds a Tess different from the one with whom he has fallen in love. For herself, Tess can never be the pure, untraced, unstained young woman who set out to Trantridge to claim kinship, for she cannot "veil bygones." Like Henchard and Lucetta, she cannot be separated from the past: the "almost physical sense of an implacable past which still engirdled her . . . intensified her consciousness of error to a practical despair; the break of continuity between her earlier and present existence, which she had hoped for, had not, after all taken place. Bygones would never be complete bygones till she was a bygone herself" (254).

The manner in which Tess becomes "a bygone herself" continues the identification of Tess with mythological female personae. Tess, who "never in her life . . . had ever intended to do wrong" (295), finally repudiates the tractability inherited from Joan and intentionally strikes back against the patriarchy that has demanded her earlier sacrifices. Her murder of Alec is a symbolic act, by which Tess repudiates her inheritance, acknowledges her true kinship, rejects male domination, and thereby defines herself. In killing Alec, she achieves the following: she annuls her common law bond/age and thus frees herself to consummate her marriage to a humanized Angel; she destroys the last of the d'Urbervilles, paradoxically and simultaneously repudiating her family patrimony while fulfilling the family curse; she disavows the scrupulous auto-machia of modern Protestant theology in favor of an older, simpler form of justice that requires blood for blood; she repudiates the splitting that effects male domination and female submission as a form of identity, and she willingly sacrifices her own life in order to free Angel and Liza-Lu from the patrimony that binds instead of bonds. She is then led to the altar at Stonehenge, upon which she is discovered at sunrise and consequently taken to Wintoncester to be hanged by the rope of tragic necessity. Thus, the tragic net that ensnares Tess ceases to be the seine and becomes the trammel.

What these reappropriations of mythology have in common is that through each Tess is identified with a mythological woman who is made to suffer at the hands of some patriarchal force. Like Eurydice, Eve, Kore, and even Antigone, with whom she shares the desire to bury her kin in accordance with a power that transcends the law of the fathers, Tess is identified with the fecund and luxurious garden in which a virgin woman is seduced by dark male forces; like Demeter and Kore, Tess is identified with the fields of grain that are ravished by a ruthless patriarchal technology. The concatenation between the mythological sacrifice of the woman and the modern technological ravishment of both field and female suggests that Tess is the virgin, the potential matriarch, who must be subjugated and sacrificed before an ascendant and overpowering patriarchy. Thus, upon approaching Stonehenge amid the plains of Salisbury, "a place older than the d'Urbervilles," Tess says, "One of my mother's people was a shepherd hereabouts, now I think of it. And you used to say at Talbothays that I was a heathen. So now I am at home" (326). Tess, the *déracine* who has been uprooted by family and patrimony, has indeed come home to the heath, where once more she must be sacrificed, this time upon a pagan altar of stone in worship of the phallogocentric sun.

The identification of Tess with the mythological female personae, the linking of Tess with the female landscape, the sacrifice of her own life in order to liberate Angel from the bondage of the past and Liza-Lu from that in the future, the bequeathing of Angel to Liza-Lu, of her husband to her sister, the fidelity of Tess and the three maidens at Talbothays, who despite all temptations to the contrary remain faithful to each other, all suggest that in the final analysis the answer to the question posed at the outset—what is Tess's kinship, her true bond—is sorority. She is sister not only to Liza-Lu, Marian, Izzy, Retty, Eurydice, Kore, Persephone, Demeter, Eve, Antigone and the women of the Cerealia, but also to the narcissistic, platonic, self-completing half of herself, Angel, who has discovered in Brazil that "we are all children of the soil" (305).

11
In *The Portrait of a Lady*

Separated by only a decade in their emergence in the world of English fiction (James's *Lady* was published in 1881 and Hardy's *Tess* in 1891), Tess Durbeyfield and Isabel Archer would seem to be diametrically opposite female protagonists. Tess is a pure woman of the field; Isabel Archer, a liberated lady of the drawing room. Tess is incapable of escaping the suppression of her family and distant relatives; her distant kin give Isabel a greater dimension of liberty that allows her to free herself more completely from her own family. Tess is overtaken by passion; Isabel manages to evade it. Tess is drawn as an "impressive" object moving throughout her environment; Isabel is evoked primarily through her impressions of her environment; indeed, bond/age in *Portrait* is manifested as what might be termed tragic "un/consciousness." Despite these obvious differences, Tess Durbeyfield and Isabel Archer have a great deal in common as tragic protagonists. Both are victims of the tendency of their relatives to claim kinship; both suffer the bondage of a patriarchal order; both need to redefine the bonds of their existence, and both choose sorority in so doing.

Isabel Archer is the personification of the American predilection towards freedom. She strikes almost everyone she meets in Europe as being an independent person; she herself declares to her newly discovered relatives at Gardencourt, "I'm very fond of my liberty."[1] She reinforces this commitment to personal freedom later in the narrative with her observation that "one should try to be one's own best friend and to give one's self, in this manner, distinguished company" (54), an observation which suggests that, although she may have been begotten by an Archer, she shares a New England kinship with the likes of Ralph Waldo Emerson and Emily Dickinson. Indeed, it is this very sentiment that will later attract her to Gilbert Osmond, who seems to live his life as though he has achieved what Isabel seeks.

It is her dedication to the free life that makes her resist the advantageous proposals of both Caspar Goodwood and Lord Warburton because "the idea of a diminished liberty was particularly disagreeable to her at present" (105). Having arrived at Gardencourt from Albany, having been liberated in body as well as in spirit, having sensed in the proposals of marriage from her two ardent suitors a confinement of both body and spirit, Isabel Archer has only one ambition, "to be free to follow out a good feeling" (293). James brings the development of Isabel's character as the exemplification of freedom to a climax when he confronts Isabel with Madame Merle's sense of individual identity.

Merle, speaking not only for herself, but also for European society, says to Isabel that "every human being has his shell and that you must take the shell into account. By the shell I mean the whole envelope of circumstances. There is no such thing as an isolated man or woman; we're each of us made up of some cluster of appurtenances" (175). Isabel's response once more reveals her connection to New England transcendentalism, and she answers as Thoreau might have: "I don't agree with you. I think just the other way. . . . Nothing that belongs to me is any measure of me; everything's on the contrary a limit, a barrier, and a perfectly arbitrary one" (175). Part of the "envelope of circumstances," of which Merle speaks and which Isabel regards as limitation, is family; thus, when the heiress Isabel says good-bye to her family in England, she experiences an abandonment that she has not known before: "She never had a keener sense of freedom, of the absolute boldness and wantonness of liberty, than when she turned away from the platform at the Euston Station . . . after the departure of poor Lily, her husband and her children to their ship at Liverpool" (272). Such passages confirm Ezra Pound's assertion that what Henry James, "the hater of tyranny," constantly "fights" in his fiction is "'influence,' the impinging of one personality on another."[2] Here it is the Archer family that would inhibit the freedom and therefore the identity of the heroine; later, it will be her husband and his mistress who would do so.

The discourse between Merle and Isabel on the matter of "appurtenances" and identity sets the parameters of the agon in *Portrait*: the American dedication to personal independence and liberty confronts the European sense of social network. Implicit in Madame Merle's position is the idea that bond/age is human relation: what connects us to others is both bond and bondage. Even Ralph Touchett agrees with Merle: "everything is relative; one ought to feel one's relation to things" (291). Moreover, the elder Henry James, who argued that human identity and individuality are a manifestation of one's relationship to others and that failure to relate to others negates human identity, would agree with Madame Merle.[3] Thus, James not only establishes the agon of the conflict between a particular American dedication to independence and European commitment to social network, but also implies the tragic outcome of that conflict.

James makes it clear that Isabel's freedom and independence are not without their dangers, one of which is to reverse the intention of free intellectual exploration so that it manifests itself as confinement within an intellectual labyrinth: "In matters of opinion she had had her own way, and it had led her into a thousand ridiculous zigzags"(53). Another peril is that her ambition to follow freely a good feeling can redound upon her strong desire for freedom when the feeling is a bad one: "She had resented so strongly, after discovering them, her mere errors of feeling (the discovery always made her tremble as if she had escaped from a trap which might have caught her and smothered her)" (54). Her intuitions about Warburton and Goodwood have been good ones insofar as they have kept her free; her impression of Osmond will be a bad one, insofar as it will deprive her of almost all liberty.

Isabel is not the only one to overestimate her imagination and her capacity for freely following the inclinations of that imagination. Ralph wishes to put a little wind into the sails of the imagining Isabel Archer, and he does so by convincing his father to leave her half the fortune intended for himself. He argues, "She wishes to be free, and your bequest will make her free . . . to meet the requirements of her imagination" (160). Ralph does so, however, assuming incorrectly that those requirements are incapable of realization in such a one as Gilbert Osmond. Isabel herself receives the money with more trepidation than Ralph gives it: "Yes, I'm afraid; I can't tell you. A large fortune means freedom, and I'm afraid of that" (193). And well she should; perhaps a fortune is one of those appurtenances of which Madame Merle speaks and which Isabel fears as limitation, or perhaps Isabel's reservation is merely the result of a fear of flying.

James metaphorically suggests that the Touchett legacy will not only put wind in Isabel's sails, but also enable her to soar above the chthonic, above earthly and natural limitation. Her aunt tells Isabel shortly after the latter receives her inheritance, "you're completely your own mistress and are as free as the bird on the bough," (190) and her cousin shortly thereafter admonishes her to "spread your wings; rise above the ground. It's never wrong to do that" (193). Later, when Ralph hears of his cousin's engagement to Osmond, he extends the simile with Isabel:

"You were the last person I expected to see caught."
"I don't know why you call it caught."
"Because you're going to be put into a cage." (285)

"You seemed to me to be soaring far up in the blue—to be, sailing in the bright light over the heads of men. Suddenly someone tosses up a faded rosebud—a missile that should never have reached you—and straight you drop to the ground. It hurts me," said Ralph audaciously, "hurts me as if I had fallen myself." (291)

"You talk about one's soaring and sailing, but if one marries at all one touches the earth." (293)

    It is apparent from the extension of his simile that James depicts Isabel's independence in Icarian terms. It seems that the notion is more her aunt and cousin's than hers; however, it is important to remember that Isabel's observation that marriage returns one to earth is one that comes only after her marriage to Osmond. Indeed, James indicates that Isabel's prospects in marrying Osmond were Icarian: "She had taken all the first steps in the purest confidence and then she suddenly found the infinite vista of a multiplied life [with Osmond] to be a dark, narrow alley with a dead wall at the end. Instead of leading to the high places of happiness, from which the world would seem to lie below one, so that one could look down with a sense of exaltation and advantage, and judge and choose and pity, it led rather downward and earthward, into realms of restriction and depression, where the sound of other lives, easier and freer, was heard as from above" (356).
    James demonstrates that the intention of Isabel has been reversed, and, instead of following freely a good feeling to a point above chthonic confinement, proudly and pityingly looking down upon the confined, Isabel finds herself looking upward, listening to those comparatively freer than herself. Once again Isabel's sensibility, her intelligence and imagination, has failed her. Like Oedipus, who could not read correctly the obvious signs of his own complicity in the death of Laius, or Macbeth, who could not interpret correctly the witches' prophecies about Birnam Wood and Macduff, Isabel fails in her understanding of Gilbert Osmond: "She had had a more wondrous vision of him, fed through charmed senses and oh such a stirred fancy!—she had not read him right" (357). Her failure to read Gilbert Osmond translates her dreams of Icarian transcendence into the nightmare of chthonic confinement, her dream of a special bond with her husband into the nightmare of common marital bondage.

11 / In The Portrait of a Lady

Just as her dreams of liberty and independence resonate with the teachings of Emerson and Thoreau, so her experience of marital bondage suggests the nightmares of Edgar Allen Poe. The house of Osmond is like the house of Usher: "It was the house of darkness, the house of dumbness, the house of suffocation. Osmond's beautiful mind gave it neither light nor air; Osmond's beautiful mind indeed seemed to peep down from a small high window and mock at her . . . his egotism lay hidden like a serpent in a bank of flowers . . . there was more in the bond than she had meant to put her name to" (360). The more that is in the bond is that she should become "an applied handled hung up tool, as senseless and convenient as mere shaped wood and iron" (459), an appurtenance of Gilbert Osmond. Thus, when Ralph tries to read the change in Isabel as a result of her marriage, he concludes that "she represented Gilbert Osmond" and laments, "Good heavens, what a function" (331).

It takes Isabel several years of marriage to discover what her cousin Ralph has always known about Osmond, that his entire life as an aloof gentleman of taste and refinement is nothing more than a pose to attract the attention and envy of society: "Osmond lived exclusively for the world" (331). For Isabel to become the reflection of the man who lives primarily for society is for Isabel to become, according to her cousin, "ground in the very mill of convention" (478) and because of that grounding, to become exactly what her aunt has said most American wives are—"the slaves of slaves" (89). Isabel's discovery of the bondage of her marriage after a few years of matrimony, however, is incomplete; it is not until the encounters with Osmond over visiting Ralph and with Merle over Warburton's aborted courtship of Pansy that Isabel becomes conscious of the true and somewhat malevolent dimensions of the envelope of circumstances surrounding her life.

When Isabel married Osmond, "she felt herself disjoined from every one she had ever known before"; she also felt that "to prefer Gilbert Osmond as she preferred him was perforce to break all other ties" (295). Having broken all relation to all others, Isabel's identity depends on her relationship to Osmond. When it becomes clear to her that it has assumed the aspect of marital war in which he seeks to make her entirely dependent on him—for her to become nothing more than the reflection or echo of his narcissistic and egocentric self—and that her resistance to such submission has effected his hatred of her, Isabel stands perilously close to losing what identity she still has. This recognition is initiated by the impression she receives when she witnesses Osmond and Madame Merle in a silent, intimate moment:

> Madame Merle was standing on the rug, a little way from the fire; Osmond was in a deep chair, leaning back and looking at her. Her head was erect, as usual, but her eyes were bent on his. What struck Isabel first was that he was sitting while Madame Merle stood; there was an anomaly in this that arrested her. Then she perceived that they had arrived at a desultory pause in their exchange of ideas and were musing, face to face, with the freedom of old friends who sometimes exchange ideas without uttering them. There was nothing to shock in this; they were old friends in fact. But the thing made an image, lasting only a moment, like a sudden flicker of light. Their relative positions, their absorbed mutual gaze, struck her as something detected. (342)

It is as though Isabel has a Lacanian "gaze" in which the subject (Isabel) sees in the mirror of the moment an alter ego (Madame Merle) displacing her as the subject of her husband's desire.[4] Isabel, like the Lacanian subject, is "arrested" by the gaze and has a flickering intimation of human bondage both to Madame Merle and Gilbert Osmond, one from which she will be able to liberate herself only after her midnight meditation, the Countess Gemini's revelation, her confrontation with Madame Merle, and the reintroduction into her life of those with whom she has severed ties—Lord Warburton, Henrietta Stackpole, Caspar Goodwood, and her cousin. It is in her relationship with them, but especially with Ralph, that Isabel begins to reassert her independence and reclaim her identity. Thus, after all have returned to England and she is informed of Ralph's impending death, Isabel confronts Osmond with her intention to go to her dying cousin.

The encounter on the surface is whether or not Isabel will honor her marriage vow to obey her husband or by defiance to dishonor him and his home by going to her cousin; on a deeper level it is also about whether or not Isabel will recover her identity by putting her relationship to others above her submissive and self-denying relationship to her husband. Osmond does not make it easy for her; he alludes to the bond of matrimony: "I assure you that we, we, Mrs. Osmond, is all I know. I take our marriage seriously; you appear to have found a way of not doing so. I'm not aware that we're divorced or separated; for me we're indissolubly united" (446). Osmond speaks not so much in the tones of a command but rather in those of an appeal, and he does so "in the name of something sacred and precious—the observation of a magnificent form." Isabel, who had resolved to defy her husband, suddenly recognizes that "the resolution with which she had entered the room found itself caught in a mesh of fine threads."

The mesh is that of the trammel, and to a great extent she, more than

Osmond, has woven it for it has been Osmond's observation of form that has attracted Isabel from the outset. James, however, as he is wont, gives the screw one more turn and has the Countess Gemini come to Isabel and, by revealing to her the role that Madame Merle has played in weaving the fine net in which Isabel finds herself caught, give her the means to sever it. Prior to this moment, Isabel had rejected the temptation to blame Madame Merle for her misfortune: "To associate Madame Merle with its disappointment would be a petty revenge—especially as the pleasure to be derived from that would be perfectly insincere. It might feed her sense of bitterness, but it would not loosen her bonds. It was impossible to pretend that she had not acted with her eyes open; if ever a girl was a free agent she had been.... There had been no plot, no snare; she had looked and considered and chosen" (340).

Isabel, when not blaming herself, is more inclined to attribute her confinement to some more powerful force than the other woman: "Madame Merle might have made Gilbert Osmond's marriage, but she certainly had not made Isabel Archer's. That was the work of—Isabel scarcely knew what: of nature, providence, fortune, of the eternal mystery of things" (339). When the two confront each other on the matter of Warburton's abandonment of Pansy, however, and Isabel asks, "Who are you—what are you? ... What have you to do with me?" and Madame Merle answers, "Everything!"; the reader is tempted to conclude with Isabel not only that Madame Merle has married Isabel to Osmond, but also that she is "a powerful agent in her destiny" (428). The concatenation between Isabel's identification of the force that made her marriage to Osmond with "fortune" and her discovery that it was indeed Madame Merle invites the reader to infer that, in this realistic novel of manners, Madame Merle is James's version of the divine mistress who weaves and holds the fine threads of cosmic bondage. That reappropriation of the goddess of terrible bondage is reinforced by James's suggestion that Isabel's aunt is another agent: "It suddenly struck her that if her Aunt Lydia had not come that day in just that way and found her alone, everything might have been different... her remarkable kinswoman resembled more a queen regent or the matron of a gaol" (472).

It is such a context that gives more meaning to the Countess's observation about Isabel as she sits caught in the fine mesh or envelope of circumstances: "You seem to have so many scruples, so many reasons, so many ties" (449). As has been the case so often for Isabel, those ties or that net is woven not only by the machinations of people like Merle, but also by Isabel's limited consciousness. The Countess frees Isabel from that limitation with the knowledge of Merle and Osmond's adultery and the true lineage of Pansy. In so doing, the Countess acts not only as a sister-in-law, but also as a sister-in-bondage in the "steel trap" of marriage. She also demonstrates for Isabel the bond that will release her from, or compensate her for the repressions of, marital bondage: sorority.

That sorority is the key to Isabel's relationship with others and thereby to her recovery of self is evident in the fact that Isabel will initially confide the true conditions of her marriage only to Henrietta Stackpole, because she was not Ralph or Warburton or Caspar, but "a woman, she was a sister" (407). The specialty of sorority or sisterhood is developed even more significantly when Ralph comes to Rome, and Isabel turns to him for comfort. Ralph's presence enlarges the orbit in which Isabel has felt increasingly entrapped: "There was something in Ralph's talk, in his smile, in the mere fact of his being in Rome, that made the blasted circle round which she walked more spacious" (364). Moreover her visits to her dying cousin shed light upon the Osmond house of darkness, take her out of her self-conscious narcissism, and recover for Isabel the relationship necessary to life: "Ralph's little visit was a lamp in the darkness; for the hour that she sat with him her ache for herself became somehow her ache for him. She felt today as if he had been her brother. She had never had a brother, but if she had and she were in trouble and he were dying, he would be dear to her as Ralph was" (363).

When Isabel finally defies Osmond and returns to Gardencourt to be with Ralph, she discovers the bond that had been heretofore reserved for Osmond and Merle, one that she had had an intimation of when she discovered both in silent and familiar communication. Like them, she and Ralph find communion "looking at the truth together" (478). In that moment, Isabel reveals what Ralph has already discerned, that she is not only an object of property to her husband, but also one of loathing. In their final moment together, however, Ralph reminds her, "But remember this, that if you've been hated you've also been loved. Ah but, Isabel—adored!" Isabel's response is not only the most compassionate that she utters in the novel, but also the most passionate, "Oh my brother!" (479). Derrida's gloss on Hegel's reading of *Antigone* is applicable to the experience of such sorority in the novel: "The infinite superiority of the bond between brother and sister [is a result of the fact that] brother and sister do not desire one another.... They are ... two single consciousnesses that, in the Hegelian universe, relate to each other without entering into war."[5] Another sense of sorority is evident in Isabel's separation from Pansy.

When, just before her departure for England, Isabel visits Pansy in the dark "dungeon" of the nunnery into which Osmond has punished his daughter for her love of Ned Rosier, she is confronted with a stepdaughter, who fears her father, dislikes her mother, and desperately reaches out for deliverance:

"Ah, Mrs. Osmond, you won't leave me!"
"I won't desert you."
"You'll come back?"
"Yes, I'll come back."
Then they held each other a moment in a silent embrace, like two sisters. (463)

Isabel gives her word not so much to a stepdaughter as to a stepsister, one who reflects the same man that she does, one who dwells in the same house of darkness and decay, and one who is as much in need of deliverance. Before Isabel can act on her words, however, before she can demonstrate that her word to Pansy is also her bond in sorority, she must act on her compulsion to repeat her rejections of any deliverance from her destiny with Osmond; she must once again reject the sanctuary proffered by Warburton and Goodwood. She defers Warburton's advances twice, once in Rome when she indirectly sends her former suitor back to England and away from Pansy and more importantly herself, and then again in England when she refuses once more his invitation to visit Lockleigh. Again, she rejects Caspar Goodwood, whose influence upon her had always "seemed to deprive her of the sense of freedom" (104). In the second rejection James renders that influence more corporeal in one of the most erotic passages in the James's canon: "He glared at her a moment through the dusk and the next instant she felt his arms about her and his lips on her own lips. His kiss was like white lightning, a flash that spread, and spread again, and stayed; and it was extraordinarily as if, while she took it, she felt each thing in his hard manhood that had least pleased her, each aggressive fact of his face, his figure, his presence, justified of its intense identity and made one with this act of possession. So had she heard of those wrecked and under water following a train of images before they sink. But when darkness returned she was free" (489).

There is a tendency to read Isabel's departure from England and Goodwood and her return to Rome and Osmond as renunciation. It is true only to the degree that life with Goodwood would spare her life with Osmond; however, it is not true insofar as life with Goodwood would only trade one kind of bondage, as reflective appurtenance of Gilbert Osmond, for another kind, as the smothered and possessed love slave of Caspar Goodwood. Thus, it is interesting to note that, when James earlier describes Isabel's bondage within the house of Osmond, he does so using the same image of darkness and the same idea of possession: "Her notion of the aristocratic life was simply the union of great knowledge with great liberty. ... When she saw this rigid system close about her, draped though it was in pictured tapestries, that sense of darkness and suffocation of which I have spoken took possession of her; she seemed shut up with an odour of mould and decay" (361).

James's trope at the end of the novel ironically reverses what he has suggested earlier in the depiction of the house of Osmond, that darkness is equated with bondage. When she recovers from the illuminating as well as searing embrace of Goodwood, darkness is equated with freedom; therefore, Isabel's decision to return to the dark house of Osmond implies not so much her renunciation of sanctuary with Goodwood, but rather her relative freedom with Osmond, relative in that her psychological bondage to Osmond is in its descendancy while her present condition makes her physical bondage to Caspar potentially in its ascendancy.

What will make her more free is that she will now enter the house of Osmond with her eyes open and with her mind less on her own condition and more on Pansy's; as she found more space in thinking of Ralph's ache more than her own, so will she now in thinking of Pansy's. As demonstrated also in her repeated rejections of Warburton and Goodwood, she will return to Osmond with a recovered independence that will probably make the house of Osmond as dark for its owner as it has been for its other residents. She will also return with a more realistic understanding of her own appurtenances, of her own social identity—her money—and the power that envelope of circumstances represents in freeing Pansy and staying Osmond. She will once more be free to live out her destiny: "When a woman had made such a mistake, there was only one way to repair it—just immensely (oh, with the highest grandeur!) to accept it" (340). Although she chooses to return to, and become a part of, the "magnificent form" before which her husband kneels, she does so more able to read that form and less likely, therefore, to subject herself completely to it.

In *The Portrait of a Lady* bond/age is a matter of "un/consciousness." To be unaware is to be in bondage; as Osmond says to Isabel during their courtship, "we're not under bonds to any kind of ignorance" (297). Ironically, however, the shock that comes with recognition contributes to one's subjugation insofar as the knowledge that one has been more confined than one has been aware of is initially an intensification of that bondage. Isabel's discovery that she is a mere reflection of Osmond and that it is Madame Merle who has woven the net that has caught her and brought her down to earth is the greatest blow to her sense of freedom, even her freedom to make the wrong choice. Subsequently and paradoxically, however, that same knowledge delivers Isabel from bondage: sharing the truth with a brother and confinement with a sister is the most self-identifying bond/age Isabel experiences.

12
In *Heart of Darkness*

The title of one of Conrad's most compelling novellas, *Heart of Darkness*, can be read in at least two literal ways. The heart of darkness is primarily the centrality or core of an awful or malevolent darkness that is the interior of Africa along one of the continent's most remote, snakelike rivers; thus, as Marlow pilots his ship along the Congo, he penetrates "deeper and deeper into the heart of darkness."[1] It is also a heart whose nature is predominantly dark, and it belongs to Kurtz; thus, towards the end of the novella, Marlow confronts the voice of Kurtz and suggests that it "survived to hide in the magnificent folds of eloquence the barren darkness of his heart" (84). Marlow's journey, traditional interpretation holds, is not only the literal one along the snake-like river to the Inner Station, but also the symbolic one to the center of the earth or to the center of his own soul. Because his knowledge of self is predicated on his knowledge of Kurtz, Marlow's journey is also one to the core of Kurtz. In order to comprehend the implications of tragic bond/age in those journeys, it is necessary to comprehend Marlow's voyage to and through Kurtz, and, in order to do that, it is necessary to understand Kurtz.

Whatever else he may be, Kurtz is, according to those who know and speak of him, the paragon of nineteenth-century man: an uncommon man, a very remarkable person, the emissary of pity and science, the prodigy of progress, a special being, a universal genius, a gifted one, an initiated wraith from nowhere, a first-class agent, the chief of the Inner Station. He is a first-rate journalist who paints or a first-rate painter who writes; he also could have been a musician of the first order and, because he was an extremist, the political standard-bearer of any party. He is the quintessential embodiment of what Nietzsche believes is humanity's "need to conquer, its lust or power, whether by means of arms or by trade, commerce or colonization."[2] He is the designated agent of the Society for the Suppression of Savage Customs, the explorer who charts new waters throughout the dark continent, one of many charged with the quest of bringing light to the savage. Not only is he cast in the mold of Prometheus, he is described as Prometheus unbound, and it is in his great freedom that Kurtz is rendered strange beyond the bonds of the familiar.

Marlow raises the specter of Kurtz's unboundedness when he poses this question about the hero: "He had taken a high seat amongst the devils of the land—I mean literally. You can't understand. How could you?—with solid pavement under your feet, surrounded by kind neighbours ready to cheer you or to fall on you, stepping delicately between the butcher and policeman, in the holy terror of scandal and gallows and lunatic asylums—how can you imagine what particular region of the first ages a man's untrammelled feet may take him into by the way of solitude—utter solitude without a policeman—by the way of silence—utter silence, where no warning voice of a kind neighbour can be heard whispering of public opinion?" (64).

The implication of Marlow's query is that his listeners—the director, lawyer, accountant, and narrator—are men connected to each other not only by the bond of the sea, but also by the human net of language and prohibition that not only warns and connects but also inhibits. Because one has butchers to procure one's meat and policemen to inhibit one's aggressiveness and the gallows and asylum to order the moral parameters of one's existence, one is arbitrarily restrained. When one puts off such chains, either through geographical distancing from the butcher and the policeman or through the absence of language in the terrible silence of the heart of darkness, then one is free to make one's own word the law. When that happens, a man's "untrammelled" feet can free him of the chthonic; thus, Marlow observes of Kurtz: "He had kicked himself loose of the earth. Confound the man! he had kicked the very earth to pieces. He was alone, and I before him did not know whether I stood on the ground or floated in the air" (82).

Free of the bond/age of European society, Kurtz apparently had succumbed to the "heavy, mute spell of the wilderness—that seemed to draw him to its pitiless breast by the awakening of forgotten and brutal instincts, by the memory of gratified and monstrous passions. This alone," Marlow tells his listeners "had driven him out to the edge of the forest, to the bush," away from the verbal warnings of neighbors, away from the words, "thou shalt not," away from social necessity "towards the gleam of fires, the throb of drums, the drone of weird incantations; this alone had beguiled his unlawful soul [like Milton's Lucifer] beyond the bounds of permitted aspirations" (82). Untrammeled, Kurtz is seduced by a female, fecund wilderness "that had taken him, loved him, embraced him, got into his veins, consumed his flesh and sealed his soul to its own by the inconceivable ceremonies of some devilish initiation" (64). By virtue of this new sealing or bonding, one evoked in the image of a savage union culminating in ritualistic cannibalism, of which his own flesh is figuratively the communal meal, Kurtz is estranged from civilized society.

Initially, Kurtz's journey is not unlike the journey of most of the pilgrims whom Marlow ferries down the river: it is a quest for the totemic ivory in the name of Christian conversion, an attempt to justify society's rapaciousness by spreading the light of civilization throughout the darkness of Africa, thereby eliminating savage customs. What it becomes, however, is a quest to deny mankind's past, its autochthonous origins in the earth, by casting into bondage the primitive, who is looked upon by the pilgrims as something not only to use in its rapaciousness, but also to exterminate when used up. Marlow, in seeking respite from the heat in the shade of some trees, discovers in that "gloomy circle of some inferno" the discarded laborer no more worthy of his labor in the eyes of the company and thereby "nothing but black shadows of disease and starvation" (31).

As Heidegger suggests, modern man in calculating everything in his sight, including here the black man, uses up whatever he calculates.[3] Civilization, in reducing the primitive to an object of production, denies its bond to primitive man by casting him into bondage; this subjugation is evident when Marlow observes six black men climbing up a path: "I could see every rib, the joints of their limbs were like knots in a rope; each had an iron collar on his neck, and all were connected together with a chain whose bights swung between them, rhythmically clinking" (30) The enchainment of the black man contrasts strikingly with the untrammeled feet of Kurtz and demonstrates once again that tragic bond/age is operative in man's self-estranging need to overpower his fellow man. Kurtz's strangeness is compounded as his denial of both his civilized and chthonic nature grows more absolute.

As the opening paragraphs of his monograph indicate, one of the first things Kurtz realizes in his confrontation with primitive man is the savage's propensity to regard the civilized man as a god: we "must necessarily appear to them in the nature of supernatural beings—we approach them with the might as of a deity. . . . By the simple exercise of our will we can exert a power for good practically unbounded" (65). Kurtz's submission to the temptation to be a god causes him to "preside at certain midnight dances ending with unspeakable rites, which . . . were offered up to him . . . to Kurtz himself" (65). This regression to overseeing human sacrifice and cannibalism as propitiations to himself takes Kurtz not only beyond the familiarity of the civilized human condition, but also beyond that of the primitive because in his regression Kurtz does not leave behind all that is civilized. Even in his transcendence he continues to accumulate all the ivory he can and thereby uses apotheosis not to do good but to do well. As Marlow tells him when Kurtz tries one last time to return to the wilderness, "You will be lost . . . utterly lost" (81)—to the society from which he has broken and to the tribal community for whom he has become a god.

It is too late; Kurtz was lost when he reversed his course three hundred miles en route to the outer station and returned to the savage woman for self-apotheosis and more ivory. The noble native woman, who worships him as god, literally becomes more seductive than the Intended in the whited sepulchre, who worships him only symbolically. That apotheosis becomes, however, nature's revenge: "But the wilderness had found him out early, and had taken on him a terrible vengeance for the fantastic invasion . . . it had whispered to him things about himself which he did not know, things of which he had no conception till he took counsel with this great solitude—and the whisper [resounding in the immense silence] had proved irresistibly fascinating. It echoed loudly within him because he was hollow at the core" (73), because he lacked restraint. It might be more precise to suggest that such vengeance is not just what the wilderness takes against the invading Kurtz, but also what Being itself takes upon an evolved human being when it wanders with its untrammeled feet beyond the boundaries of the familiar and the autochthonous.

Consequently, when Marlow says of penetrating deeper and deeper into the heart of darkness, "we could have fancied ourselves the first of men taking possession of an accursed inheritance," (50) one may appropriately understand such inheritance to be the primordial savage one that is always latently manifested in the mind of man, because, as both Marlow and Jung observe, "the mind of man is capable of anything—because everything is in it, all the past as well as all the future" (51). What brings what is latent to manifestation is modern man's confrontation with the heart of darkness. Kurtz's experience suggests, however, that the accursed inheritance is also the price that human beingness pays for its separation from Being, one manifested not only in its enslavement of primitive man, its regression to savage practices, but mostly in its acceptance of its own apotheosis.

The redeeming quality of the horror of Kurtz's separation is that it precludes Marlow's, and it does so because knowledge of what Kurtz has done and of Kurtz's realization of that horror is what saves Marlow from similar separation. That recognition comes after a voyage, which Lillian Feder and Robert Evans have likened to the long descent of Aeneas into Hades and of Dante into the Inferno.[4] Insofar as Marlow's journey is comparable to these symbolic descents, it is also a passage along the *via negativa*.

For Marlow, going up the river is a "weary pilgrimage" that "was like travelling back to the earliest beginnings of the world, when vegetation rioted on the earth and the big trees were king" (48). Like Lear, Marlow comes to realize that reality is ultimately "truth stripped of the cloak of time" (51), of "acquisitions, clothes, pretty rags," which "fly off at the first good shake." That first good shake for Marlow is the encounter with the heart of darkness which is both Africa and Kurtz. Moreoever, Marlow's voyage is one in which the ordinary light blinds and the darkness illumines: Conrad writes of Marlow's confrontations with a "blinding light" (29) and a white fog "more blinding that the night" (54), both of which tend to throw a veil over truth and reality. What rends that veil is a trip up the *via negativa*, an encounter with the heart of darkness that paradoxically "seemed to throw a kind of light on everything" (21) about Marlow. Like most men, he cannot bear too much reality, and consequently he turns away from reality to the surface matters of the art of riverboat maintenance.

He cannot, however, avoid the tragic recognition that occurs upon his meeting with Kurtz. He has been led to expect great things of the Inner Station Chief, not so much from what others have told him, but more so from the nature of the men he has heard speaking of Kurtz. It is Marlow's unconscious wish that Kurtz turn out better than the other pilgrims: to the degree that he has responded sympathetically to the heart of darkness, to what is dark, unconscious, and Dionysian in a way that the other patriarchal, Apollonian, capitalistic, phallogocentric pilgrims cannot, Kurtz meets Marlow's expectations. Moreover, although he is shocked to discover that in so many ways Kurtz is much worse, Marlow is also confirmed in his belief that Kurtz is much better because he came at last to know himself: "The most you can hope from [life] is some knowledge of yourself—that comes too late—a crop of inextinguishable regrets" (86). Marlow believes that Kurtz's final stare and utterance—"The horror! The horror!" (85)—is "an affirmation, a moral victory paid for by innumerable defeats, by abominable terrors, by abominable satisfactions. But it was a victory!" (87). It may be argued whether or not his final cry was indeed a victory for Kurtz, but it is indisputably one for Marlow because, in his encounter with the heart of darkness, Marlow discovers the true nature of tragic bond/age.

Marlow begins that discovery when he is moved by the thought of the humanity of the primitives, who are not the "shackled form of [the] conquered monster" that is modern man, but the savage "thing monstrous and free." Marlow is impressed that, despite their primordial freedom, they were not inhuman: "what thrilled you was just the thought of their humanity—like yours—the thought of your remote kinship with this wild and passionate uproar" (51). This relationship becomes even more intimate when Marlow finds himself responding to the death of his steersman in a manner that confirms the otherness of that otherwise "grain of sand in a black Sahara"—the savage: "Well, don't you see, he had done something, he had steered; for months I had him at my back—a help—an instrument. It was a kind of partnership. He steered for me—I had to look after him, I worried about his deficiencies, and thus a subtle bond had been created, of which I only became aware when it was suddenly broken. And the intimate profundity of that look he gave me when he received his hurt remains to this day in my memory—like a claim of distant kinship affirmed in a supreme moment" (66).

Marlow will respond once more to a similar look, the one that Kurtz gives him while he awaits death and just prior to his recognition of the horror. As he approaches the house of the Intended, Marlow recalls Kurtz: "I had a vision of him on the stretcher, opening his mouth voraciously, as if to devour all the earth with all its mankind. He lived then before me; he lived as much as he had ever lived—a shadow insatiable of splendid appearances, of frightful realities; a shadow darker than the shadow of the night, and draped nobly in the folds of his grand eloquence" (89). In the imagery, Conrad reveals that Marlow has developed between himself and Kurtz a kinship as well, a secret sharing of that which exists latent, on the edge of manifestation, within all men because the mind of man contains all things. Appropriately, Conrad describes that kinship in terms of shadow and thereby suggests that Kurtz is what Jung calls the psychic antetype of what the modern personal and social ego unconsciously desires and values.[5]

Marlow begins the telling of his tale with the observation that his commission to sail up the Congo not only enabled him to fulfill a dream of his childhood, one which becomes a nightmare, but also a "chance to find yourself" (22). What Marlow finds is that he is not only kin to the monstrously free savage, but also to the similarly free Kurtz, who uses his freedom to kick himself loose of the earth and to succumb to the temptations to deny his humanity, his autochthonous roots, and thereby become a self-appointed god. Marlow also discovers that such apotheosis is doomed because just as Kurtz is the beneficiary of the woman priestess who ordains his apotheosis, so is he the victim of another priestess who presides at the beginning of his ordination.

After Marlow discovers that Kurtz has jumped ship and is attempting to return to his people and decides to bring him back, he comes upon his trail and exclaims "He can't walk—he is crawling on all-fours—I've got him." Suddenly, there intrudes upon the memory of Marlow, "the knitting old woman with the cat . . . as a most improper person to be sitting at the other end of such an affair" (80). Like Oedipus and Macbeth before him, Kurtz suffers a return to the chthonic from the heights of self-apotheosis, and what better figure to preside over that return than the woman who must have presided over the initiation of Kurtz's journey as she did over the beginning of Marlow's. The tableau of Kurtz, the shadow of Marlow's psyche, reduced to crawling on all fours beneath the ominous presence of the "uncanny and fateful" knitting old woman also serves to remind the reader that in tragic bond/age all of man's grand attempts to transcend his chthonic roots through the crossing of forbidden boundaries are doomed to failure by the goddesses who control the threads that bind and by some innate flaw in man's character—his lack of restraint.

This is the lesson that Marlow learns from his encounter with the hearts of darkness that are Africa and Kurtz. By virtue of his recognition and acceptance of his kinship with that darkness and by the application of an inner restraint that serves him well, Marlow is able to benefit from the light that an encompassing darkness paradoxically throws on everything about him, "as a glow brings out a haze, in the likeness of one of these misty halos that sometimes are made visible by the spectral illuminations of moonshine" (20–21). Just as such lights illuminate the kernel within the narrator's tale, so does the revelation in the heart of darkness illuminate what is within Kurtz and Marlow. That knowledge allows Marlow, who has restraint and the distractions of riverboat maintenance, to discover the shadow side of his psyche without submitting, like Kurtz, totally to it. It also allows him to speak in the service of not only *veritas*, but also *caritas* when he confronts Kurtz's Intended during another, but this time ironic, encounter with the heart of darkness.

When Marlow approaches the home of the Intended, a house of death with its "high and ponderous door, between the tall houses of a street as still and decorous as a well-kept alley in a cemetery," he is haunted by the shadow of Kurtz, one "darker than the shadow of the night, and draped nobly in the folds of a gorgeous eloquence." The vision accompanies Marlow inside the house like "the heart of a conquering darkness." Once he meets the beautiful woman, who is dressed all in black and upon whose brow "all the sad light of the cloudy evening had taken refuge," the room seems to grow darker. As she speaks of her undying love for and faith in Kurtz and continues to celebrate her beloved's greatness, "the darkness deepens" and Marlow winces with the discrepancy between the man she loves and the one he has known. He also becomes increasingly aware that hers is a "great and saving illusion that shone with an unearthly glow in the darkness, in the triumphant darkness from which I could not have defended her—from which I could not even defend myself" (90–93).

Defend her, however, is exactly what Marlow does when confronted with her request to know Kurtz's last words. Rather than disillusion the Intended with the truth of Kurtz's final cry, a revelation that would have been "too dark altogether," Marlow charitably says to her that Kurtz's last words were "your name." Thus, Marlow in another quest becomes the knight who delivers the maiden from the dragon of the darkness of truth and leaves her with her illusion, her supreme fiction, her "inextinguishable light of belief and love" (91) in Kurtz. The identification here of the Intended as the bearer of an inextinguishable light that blinds her to what the light reveals about the surrounding darkness clearly identifies her with the figure in Kurtz's painting of the draped and blindfolded woman who bears the flaming torch through a similar darkness.

But in Marlow's mind, the Intended, when she puts out her arm towards the receding spirit of Kurtz, is identified with still another woman: "I shall see this eloquent phantom as long as I live, and I shall see her too, a tragic and familiar Shade, resembling in this gesture another one, tragic also, and bedecked with powerless charms, stretching bare brown arms over the glitter of the infernal stream, the stream of darkness" (93). Although one may question Marlow's estimate of the powerless charms—they were powerful enough to lure Kurtz back three hundred miles—one should note, nevertheless, that just as the savage woman is the image of one heart of darkness in the African jungle, so is the civilized woman the personification of the other heart of darkness that is the death house of the whited sepulchral city of Europe, the house that ironically contains the repository of the totemic ivory in the eloquent "grand piano [that] stood massively in a corner; with dark gleams on the flat surfaces like a sombre and polished sarcophagus" (90).

The Intended, who believed in Kurtz more than he believed in himself and who was the inspiration behind his rapaciousness in the heart of darkness, joins the savage woman, the priestess who attends Kurtz's apotheosis, and the fateful and knitting office woman, who presides at his fall back to earth on all fours, in a cluster of female presences that symbolically manipulate the threads that cast Kurtz into human bond/age. Marlow too is caught in that bond/age for he not only permits his aunt to grease the bow of his journey into the heart of darkness, but also allows the Intended to force him to commit the one deed he abhors and hates, to lie. That deed, however, is mitigated by the fact that, although it is concern for the Intended that moves Marlow to lie, it is his "choice of nightmares," a choice of *caritas* over *veritas*. What is more, that choice is not confined to the Intended. Clearly, the listeners and the reader do not lose sight of the symmetry and irony of Marlow's answer to the Intended: she and all that her home as whited sepulchre symbolize are part of the horror that is Kurtz's revelation. Just as clearly, however, the *caritas* that both the Intended and Marlow express are part of the warmth, if not light, of the torch that will comfort man in the heart of darkness.

13

In *Absalom, Absalom!*

Henry James Sr. maintains that one of the paradoxes of the American experience is that the American, who cherishes his individuality and often seeks it through separation from others, denies himself what he seeks for such identity can exist only through relationship with the other.[1] James's conclusion reaffirms Hegel's belief that the solitary self cut off from the universal plurality of individuals is "a powerless and unreal self."[2] Comparably, Ralph Ellison suggests that the most common theme of American fiction is the search for identity and adds that this is the case because the mobile American, who seems forever on the road, in losing his sense of where he is also loses a sense of who he is.[3] In *Absalom, Absalom!,* William Faulkner combines these elements of the American experience in a narrative that varies the ancient trope of tragic bond/age in the person of the hero who, in seeking to establish a dynastic posterity, ironically disclaims all kinship and thereby dooms the realization of that goal.

When young Thomas Sutpen comes down from the western Virginia mountains, he loses a sense of where and who he is: "he knew neither where he had come from nor where he was nor why."[4] When he is turned away from the front door of a plantation, his loss of identity is confirmed, and he withdraws into the woods to brood and to determine how to recover his identity. What he comes up with is his grand design, a Southern version of the American Dream. Like Jay Gatsby before him and Willy Loman after, Sutpen decides that the self he seeks is the kind that American society pays homage to: a successful one. For Sutpen, this means he must acquire the nearest thing to a fine rifle that he can; he must become a rich plantation owner. When he has neared success with the acquisition of plantation, power, and family, and the whole edifice suddenly seems to be coming down around him with tragedy's characteristic intrusion of the past upon the present in the guise of Charles Bon, he wonders aloud to Colonel Compson what mistake in his design this imminent fall of the house of Sutpen implies. Although Faulkner does not allow his protagonist to discern the error, the whole pattern of the novel suggests that the flaw is that, in attempting to realize his dream, he has allowed the end to justify the means, one of which is to use others to express the self. For Sutpen there is no other, and, since there is none with whom he can relate, his plan to recreate himself is destined to fail. It is Quentin Compson's fate to recognize this truth about the soul of Sutpen and the South.

What ought to be the other and a source of bonding for Thomas Sutpen—the family—becomes only the means by which he seeks to realize his dream. Sutpen initiates his design by withdrawing forever from his own Virginia family, an act of disinheritance that will be repeated throughout the novel. Sutpen then marries his first wife only because his plan requires that he have a son and "incidentally" a wife. When he discovers that she has Negro blood, he rejects her and disinherits the offspring of that marriage, Charles Bon. Between his first and second marriages he sires Clytie with one of his twenty black slaves, and the only advantage her blood connection to her father lends her is that she becomes a house, rather than a field, slave. He marries his second wife primarily because she and her family's reputation for Protestant uprightness will provide him with the means to legitimate his design: "he did want, not the anonymous wife and the anonymous children, but the two names, the stainless wife and the unimpeachable father-in-law, on the license, the patent" (39), the bond.

They have two children, and it is through Henry, who is more his mother's child and not Judith, who is more truly her father's child, that Sutpen develops the semblance of a conscious relationship because he hopes to establish through him his posterity and thereby the completion of his design. However, because his wife Ellen and his children are but elements of that ambition and because the Southerner, Faulkner tells us, has a habit of reducing his women to "ladies," who are then reduced by the war to "ghosts," there is no viable relationship—one predicated on interdependence. None of the Sutpens exists except as subordinate elements in Sutpen's design, and their primary inheritance from their father is his tendency to use other human beings as objects.

This curse upon the house of Sutpen is most fully realized in each Sutpen's response to Charles Bon. Thomas Sutpen denies him thrice. The first instance occurs in his putting aside his mulatto wife and their offspring when he finds out she has Negro blood and thereby cannot be a part of his goal to establish himself as part of Southern aristocracy. The second takes place when Charles Bon comes to the Sutpen household at Christmas, "thinking maybe now he would walk into the house and see the man who made him and then he would know; there would be that flash, that instant of indisputable recognition between them and he would know for sure and forever" (255). There is no acknowledgment, and thereby Faulkner works out a most effective ironic inversion of the tragic recognition scene. Sutpen recognizes Bon and sees that his house is about to fall, but does not indicate such recognition—Sutpen does not personally or publicly acknowledge Bon as his son—and Bon sees that the man who made him will not now or ever admit their kinship. The third denial comes about at the brothers' campsite when their father arrives to inform Henry that Bon has Negro blood, and Bon puts himself in his father's way so that he has to see him, but Sutpen seems to gaze through Bon as though he were what Ralph Ellison will later call an "invisible man." Bon consequently sees in Henry's face "my father's, out of the shadow of whose absence my spirit's posthumeity has never escaped" (254). One might add that Bon himself is Sutpen's own shadow, out of whose presence Sutpen's desired posterity never escapes and through which Sutpen's dreaded posthumeity, in the person of Jim Bond, survives.

Although her relationship to Bon is not as complicated as her husband's, Ellen responds in similar fashion. She sees in Bon an "inanimate object for which she and her family would find three concordant uses": a garment for Judith to wear, a piece of furniture to complete the furnishing of her home, and a mentor to correct Henry's provincial manners (59). Bon becomes much more than mentor and garment to Henry and Judith, but in order to understand their use of him in Faulkner's gothic ménage à trois, one has to consider first the relationship of brother and sister. Jason Compson, reflecting on the courtship of Judith by Bon, speculates that it must have been Henry, who, on behalf of Charles, seduced Judith from that distance between Oxford and Sutpen's Hundred and did so using a rapport not so much like that of twins, but "such as might exist between two people, who, regardless of sex or age or heritage of race or tongue, had been marooned at birth on a desert island: the island here Sutpen's Hundred; the solitude, the shadow of [their] father" (79).

Sutpen has enisled himself and family on his one hundred acres. He has thereby isolated his children from others and forced them to turn to each other. They are separated from their heritage by Sutpen's rejection of his own family and by their limit of one visit a year to their mother's family. This isolation has been furthered by a mother, who as lady and ghost has left the rearing of the children to others, and by a father, whose design and shadowy existence keep him more absent than present, prevent him from seeing or "recognizing" others, including his own wife and children. In the absence of mother and father, Henry and Judith turn to one another as the substitute for that which is missing: mother or father as other. Thus, the desired incestuous relationship between Henry and Judith implies the incestuous relationship between child and parent as well as the one between brother and sister. Also, through the comparison of both to twins who disregard metaphorically the boundaries of their society, they also manifest that violation of difference, which Girard says undermines the unity of society.

Henry and Judith are "a single personality with two bodies" (73). Social taboo prohibits the coupling of those two bodies, but not the use of another as an object to unite them. Both need to act through an alter ego; Charles Bon is that androgynous object: "perhaps this is the pure and perfect incest: the brother realizing that the sister's virginity must be destroyed in order to have existed at all, taking that virginity in the person of the brother-in-law . . . by whom he would be despoiled, choose for despoiler, if he could become, metamorphose into the sister, the mistress, the bride" (77). Faulkner's complex trope suggests that not only would the brother vicariously commit incest with the sister through the prospective brother-in-law, but also he would experience a Platonic, homosexual union with the brother-in-law through the sister. Thus, Henry uses not only Bon, but also Judith; and Bon uses Henry to seduce Judith, Judith to seduce Henry, and both to force Sutpen to recognize him as son. Faulkner also suggests that in their use of Judith, Charles and Henry also strive to perpetuate their ironic master/bondsman relationship.

Judith is the "blank shape" that embodies the illusion of what each brother conceives the other believes him to be. For Henry, Judith is the seducer Charles, by whom the younger brother is conquered; for Charles, she is the seduced Henry, whose very weakness vanquishes the elder brother. In this way, Judith is, much more than Aunt Rosa, "Polymath love's androgynous advocate" (117), and it is the condition of Judith and Rosa, as well as of Ellen Coldfield and Clytie, that dramatizes the contention of Jessica Benjamin that "the three pillars of oedipal theory—the primacy of the wish for oneness, the mother's embodiment of this regressive force, and the necessity of paternal intervention—all combine to create the paradox that the only liberation is paternal domination. Oedipal theory thus denies the necessity of mutual recognition between man and woman."[5]

Implicit in this use of human beings, and of women in particular, as objects in order to extend and complete oneself is a particular variation of tragic bond/age, one manifested in another myth that Faulkner reappropriates in *Absalom, Absalom!*—that of Narcissus. Sutpen overcompensates for having lost a sense of self by projecting that sense upon everything and everybody out there. By that, he has deprived his children of others and in so doing has turned them inward towards each other—towards the mirrored image of the self. Their narcissistic need is so great that Sutpen's sons would violate the universal taboo against incest; indeed, incest would accomplish not only the completion of self but also the perpetuity of self. Shreve/Quentin reasons that in the act of incest between brother and sister, where "there were sin too, maybe you would not be permitted to escape, uncouple, return" (259). The violation of taboo then would make possible eternal bond/age.

Because all taboo is an institutionalization of order, the desire to violate it is also a wish to undo an order that, in the case of the ante-bellum South, renders the self incomplete. The intention to commit incest is not only a symbol of narcissistic desire but also a protest against a Southern mythos that nurtures an incompleteness based on the rejection of the other. The ménage à trois that would violate the incest taboo in order to perpetuate the narcissistic self is doomed by another taboo of the Southern mythos, which posits that, although in this instance the brother may be different, he is not other because he is not white. That part of the mythos holds Henry within its grip, and against that prohibition he is helpless. The irony is that it may very well have been Bon's blackness that constituted his otherness; could the younger Sutpens have related to Bon rather than use him, they might have repudiated the Sutpen or Southern heritage, discovered their identities, and thereby more truly completed themselves. But the mythos gets in the way; Bon is different, less than human, and Judith's union with that "it," that not-human, would undo all that Henry wished to accomplish by it.

What Judith wishes to accomplish may very well be love, but it would have to be a love predicated on the idea, as much as the person, of Bon. One is led to conclude that what Judith hopes to accomplish by marriage to Bon is to have escaped from the bondage that she confesses to Mrs. Compson she feels constrained by. Judith hands over to her, in hopes that it might be handed down to other Compsons (perhaps she, like Cassandra, has already envisioned the end of the house of Sutpen and therefore can rely upon no Sutpen for the handing down of tradition), the letter sent to her by Bon. She hopes that, by bestowing the letter, she may leave behind the one "scratch" or "mark" that would say at least that she and the Sutpens had been, and that would enable the Sutpen men to endure: "Read it if you like or dont read it if you like. Because you make so little impression, you see . . . you are born at the same time with a lot of other people, all mixed up with them, like trying to, having to, move your arms and legs with strings only the same strings are hitched to all the other arms and legs and the others all trying and they dont know why either except that the strings are all in one another's way like five or six people all trying to make a rug on the same loom only each one wants to weave his own pattern into the rug" (100–101).

In Faulkner's variation of the archetypal symbol of the threads that bind, women as well as men (and especially the Afro-American) are the ones held in bondage, and what manipulates those binding threads are everyone else's movements. Moreover, the interconnecting strings form a variation of the trammel net; as one moves and tries to weave one's own independent pattern, one is only made more intensely aware of one's interdependence with everyone else and, consequently, of one's bond/age. Through this metaphor of Judith's, Faulkner details what he orchestrates throughout his five-told tale: that identity and individuality are interdependent with the other and each person is bound to those born not only at the same time, in the same place, and of the same blood, but also at other times and other places and of other bloods. The lives of the generations of the Sutpens and of the South are interconnected with those of other generations and of the North, and thus do Henry and Judith work out their inheritance in conjunction with Charles, and Quentin Compson, his in conjunction with Judith, Henry, Charles, and Shreve. In his orchestration, Faulkner repeats, varies, and develops the leitmotif of the cord that binds in his descriptions of the rippling effect of time, of the New Orleans ritual of the duel, and of Rosa's encounter with Clytie on the night Henry kills Charles.

On the day that he receives a letter from his father telling him of Rosa Coldfield's death and he and Shreve try to fill in the gaps of the Sutpen legend, Quentin questions whether anything ever happens just once. He imagines that the past is a ripple made by a pebble thrown into a pool, which is "attached by a narrow umbilical water-cord to the next pool" and that the past event moves as a ripple from one pool in time and space into another, moving across the surface of the new pool "at the original ripple-space, to the old ineradicable rhythm" (210). The metaphor suggests not only the repetition of event in the history of the Stupens and the South, but also the rhythm of recitation in the retelling of the event: all the narrators—

Jason Compson, Quentin Compson, Rosa Coldfield, Shreve McCannon, and the omniscient third person narrator—fall into the same rhythm of storytelling that seems to repeat and vary the narration. More of that later; for now the image of the ripple that umbilically feeds and connects pool to pool offers a variation on the bond/age trope that emphasizes the compulsion of the Sutpens and of necessity to repeat the past. The original pebble may be understood as either young Thomas Sutpen's being turned away from the front door of the Tidewater plantation, a rejection that denies his individuality, or his initial response to that rejection, which is to disinherit his own family in seeking to recreate himself and thereby initiate his plan.

We have already detailed how Sutpen repeats the crime done to him by refusing to recognize the individuality of the other and by disinheriting his own family. Another repetition is that each male Sutpen who weds—Thomas Sutpen, Charles Bon, and Charles Etienne Bon—marries a woman with Negro blood; the variation is the increasingly greater degree of black blood, until the whiteness of the Stupen line and, therefore, the design of its patriarch are almost darkened out of existence in the nonperson of Jim Bond. Not only is each Sutpen progenitor decreasingly white, but each is increasingly rootless and, by the standard of Henry James and Ralph Ellison, selfless. Thomas Sutpen enters Jefferson seemingly out of nowhere; Charles Bon leaves no more trace in Rosa's house than he has in Ellen's, where he has been but "a shape, a shadow" (120); Charles Etienne, in jail in Jefferson, is questioned, "What are you? Who and where did you come from?" (165), and Jim Bond is the vague heir apparent, who disappears into the same nowhere from which his great grandfather had emerged over one hundred years (of solitude) ago.

The leitmotif of the figure from nowhere is repeated once more in the person of Wash Jones, and with him, the event that triggered Sutpen's design: "Clytie would not let him come into the kitchen with the basket even, saying, 'Stop right there, white man. Stop right where you is. You aint never crossed this door while Colonel was here and you aint going to cross it now'" (226). Although Jones accepts this rejection more so than Sutpen does his, Faulkner furthers the rippling repetition by having Sutpen repeat not only what was done to him upon that earlier threshhold, the negation of his otherness or individuality, but also what he has been doing ever since, ignoring the otherness of the not-me. After Sutpen denies the humanity of the fifteen-year-old Jones's granddaughter and implicitly the grandfather himself, Wash Jones, as grim reaper and father time, picks up the scythe and balances the moral ledger of the "ubiquitous Creditor."

It is as though Thomas Sutpen's father, who may have been about Jones's age when he, along with the rest of the family, was repudiated by Sutpen, or even the ghost of the young Thomas Sutpen, who might have become were it not for the rejection and the dream, rise up through another ripple in time in the person of Wash Jones-from-nowhere to exact justice for the wrongs done them and all the other Sutpens whom the patriarch has failed to recognize or relate to in the execution of his design. None has been wronged more and suffered more than his own children through their connection to the dynast, a fate that is evoked in the second variation of the bond/age trope.

In that one, Charles describes for Henry the manner of dueling in New Orleans, in which each of the duelists grasps the cloak of the other, proceeds to walk away from his opponent, and, when he feels the cloak tauten, turns and fires (90). Faulkner's description is a most effective foreshadowing of the doomed bond/age that will cause Henry to shoot his brother Charles while defending his sister Judith's honor. Like the threads of the loom of time, which bond and bind each weaver to every other, the brothers are bound to shoot and be shot by their recognition of the code of the fathers and by their need for recognition by the father. The other variation occurs when Rosa, having been summoned by Wash Jones, rushes into the Sutpen mansion to attend Judith.

When she momentarily halts Rosa's movement up the stairway, Clytie, by addressing Rosa by her first name, ironically does her "More grace and respect than anyone else" (111) Rosa knows, for she responds to Rosa as an adult and not as the child everyone else acknowledges. Later, when Clytie arrests her movement with the touch of her black hand, flesh on flesh, Rosa realizes "the fall of all the eggshell shibboleth of caste and color" and "the bitted bridle-curb to check and guide the furious and unbending will" (112). When she responds by crying out—"Take your hand off me, nigger!"—Rosa expects no answer because she realizes that both she and Clytie understand that it was not Clytie to whom she spoke nor only Clytie who rendered her motionless: "the two of us [were] joined by that hand and arm which held us, like a fierce rigid umbilical cord, twin sistered to the fell darkness which had produced her" (112).

What engenders Clytie are, among other things, Sutpen's use of one of his black female slaves for the purpose of satisfying his own lust and economic need, a Southern mythos that makes Sutpen feel his right to so breed, and a Southern catastrophe that leaves Rosa as orphaned as Clytie. That Rosa is held twin-sistered by that umbilical cord clearly indicates that she is as much bound by the same darkness as is Clytie and that so are her niece and nephew to their half-caste brother, and all whites to all blacks. As she remains at the house during and after the war, Rosa, together with Clytie and Judith, become as "one being, interchangeable and indiscriminate, which kept the garden growing, spun thread and wove the cloth" (125).

More than Rosa and Clytie, Judith and Clytie are twin-sistered by the darkness out of which Thomas Sutpen emerges and which he personifies. Both distinguish themselves from all the other children of Thomas Sutpen insofar as they are the ones who use and objectify others the least. What they mostly do is serve, and by that they become, as Hegel suggests, the truly individuated because they recognize the other through service.[6] As much as Faulkner obviously draws parallels between the other personae of the novel and mythological archetypes and as sparse as his treatment of Judith and Clytie are, their relationship is not so much to their namesakes but rather to Antigone. Judith buries her outcast brother/fiance; she raises and recognizes her blood-tainted nephew and her more-than-half-black-blooded grandnephew; and more than anyone else, she tries to perpetuate through memorial and memory the Sutpen posterity. Clytie is the only one who dares, with an individual will that she has developed ironically in service, defy the shibboleth of caste and color. She not only recognizes her cousin Rosa as adult individual and helps bury her brother, but also ignites the fire that simultaneously protects her brother from capture and confinement and expiates the "mark" or defilement that is the house of Sutpen.

In so doing, Judith and Clytie dramatize what Derrida in his gloss on Hegel suggests is the distinctive bond/age of woman: "In embalming [the male corpse], in shrouding it, in enclosing it in bands of material, of language, and of writing, in putting up the stele, this operation raises the corpse to the universality of spirit" while she "remains glued, limed in the natural, in sensibility."[7] Through this relationship of the three principal female characters of the novel and through the service that Clytie and Judith (and to a lesser extent Rosa) render the other Sutpens, Faulkner demonstrates that in *Absalom, Absalom!*, as in *Antigone*, *Tess of the d'Urbervilles*, and *The Portrait of a Lady*, the most enduring familial relationship in a degenerate patriarchy is sorority.

Not only do the three principal female figures of the novel blend into one identity, but so do the four young male protagonists. When Henry repudiates his paternal heritage, just as Sutpen had a score ago, and Henry and Charles leave the Sutpen household that Christmas, it is not just the two brothers riding off, but four young men: Charles-Shreve and Quentin-Henry" (267). In the figure of Faulkner's narrative carpet, the lives of the characters are the interconnection of people's wills upon the loom of time, and so there are also "four of them there, in that room in New Orleans in 1860, just as in a sense there were four of them there in [the] tomblike room in Massachusetts in 1910" (268). This fusion of character in composite personae not only recapitulates Faulkner's theme of the strung, rippled interconnectiveness of humanity, it also manifests another characteristic of tragedy as defined by Nietzsche and reappropriated by Faulkner. All these characters are but different manifestations of the same suffering tragic hero: "interchangeable not only from scene to scene but from actor to actor and behind which the events and occasions took place without chronology or sequence" (49).

Indeed, Faulkner's fictive mode of multiple narratives through and beyond which the reader must discern the truth serves to effect a choral rendering of the novel and thereby to recover the early tragic mode in which the chorus has more lines than the individual personae; Ilse Dusoir Lind suggests such a choral presence.[8] One of the most startling aspects of Faulkner's novel is the relative absence of dialogue and, with the exception of the imagined brief encounters between Sutpen and Henry, Henry and Charles, Henry and Judith and the colloquy of Shreve and Quentin at the end of the novel, very little that amounts to stichomythia. In *Absalom, Absalom!*, something approximating tragic form reinforces something approaching tragic theme, and, in a novel in which the primary action is a futile attempt to establish individuality through separation, there is very little personal or individual testimony and dialogue. When it does come, however, stichomythia appears with great dramatic power because it brings to a climax what heretofore Faulkner's orchestrated narratives of events have only established through leitmotif and variation and delayed through indirection. Such orchestration not only serves to fuse the many personae into a suffering Dionysian hero, it also forces the reader, in inferring the single meaning or "might-have-been conclusion" of the five narratives, to undergo the very essential phenomena of the tragic experience: recognition (of what has happened) and cartharsis (of having had the experience and inferred its meaning).

Faulkner introduces the concept of the paradoxical verity of the conditional in the following passage: "there is a might-have-been which is more true than truth" (115). Five pages later, he has the same narrator, Rosa Coldfield, vary the theme with this statement: "there is that might-have-been which is the single rock we cling to above the maelstrom of unbearable reality" (120). In the latter passage, the context suggests that the might-have-been is an escape from an unbearable reality; in the former, it emphasizes that which is only implied in the word "rock" in the latter: that the might-have-been is paradoxically or illogically truer than truth. The reader might be tempted to attribute all of this to the gothically-felt ruminations of an American grotesque in the person of Rosa Coldfield were it not for the fact that much of the narration, spoken or inferred, is by way of what might have been.

Much of the narration in *Absalom, Absalom!* takes the form of the narrator's filling in gaps in the story with what is construed to be what might have been. The might-have-been is, however, not so much what could have happened, but also what did not; it is that essential feature of Shakespearean tragedy, the waste of human potential. The might-have-been may also be what we do not know for certain happened, but, given all that we do know, may very well have happened. Such seems to be the case in the inferred encounters among the Sutpens—Thomas, Henry, and Charles—in the culminating days of the Civil War. Of course, it is also possible, that Quentin, who is no disinterested and therefore objective narrator and who participates not altogether vicariously in these events, may be contributing much more to the might-have-been than might have been. Here, T. S. Eliot is illuminating:

> Time past and time future
> What might have been and what has been
> Point to one end. which is always present.[9]

Whatever occurred in the past that is known, whatever might have occurred that is not known, and whatever might have occurred that did not but is attributed by Quentin to having occurred, all point to the one end that is the narrative-history-myth of Sutpen and the South. Within the context of *Absalom, Absalom!* it is the primary heritage Quentin receives from his father, Miss Rosa, and the South, and it is one that informs his contribution to the might-have-been of the Sutpen myth. Moreover, within the greater context of *The Sound and the Fury* and the theme of incest as a might-have-been that is truer than truth, that contribution is even more understandable. In a novel that reappropriates the ancient motif of original sin as the primary mode of tragic bond/age, is it any wonder that Quentin Compson—a young man traumatized by the gothic and tragic narratives of Thomas Sutpen told to him respectively by Rosa and his father—should seek simultaneously both to evade and elevate the truth of history with the might-have-been of myth.

The trauma derives from the fact that the gothic and statuesque Thomas Sutpen of Rosa's narrative is an image from Lacan's mirror stage of the ego. In that state, the world is "strangely petrified and static, a sort of immense museum peopled with immobile 'statues,' 'images' of stone, and heiratic 'forms.'" It is the most *"unheimlich"* and "shadowy" of worlds, in which "every image of the ego is already an uncanny harbinger of its death."[10] Before that mirror of uncanny images, Quentin's soul quakes at what it beholds—the reflection of his own Southern self. It responds similarly to the mask personified in his father's tragic version of the Sutpen legend because, as Vernant suggests, the mythological hero (the figure of the nineteenth-century Sutpen mask) in tragedy becomes the contemporary protagonist (the twentieth-century exiled Southerner): "Even as the setting and the mask confer upon the tragic protagonist the magnified dimensions of one of the exceptional beings that are the object of a cult in the city, the language used brings him closer to the ordinary man, and even as he lives his legendary adventure his closeness makes him, as it were, the contemporary of the public, so that the tension . . . between past and present, beween the world of myth and that of the city, is to be found again with each protagonist."[11]

When Quentin seems to protest too much that he does not hate the South, one cannot help but wonder if the protest issues from all the Sutpen offspring. One cannot help but also consider if, in that protest and in the idea that the only Sutpen left is a Jim Bond—the idiot whose only possible narrative of the past can be filled with sound and fury—there is a hopelessness that precludes the possibility of cathartic restoration and therefore the possibility that the novel is tragic. The suggestion here, however, is that, although there is nothing in *Absalom, Absalom!* equivalent to the restoration of religious integrity in Greek tragedy or social order in Shakespearean tragedy, Faulkner does indicate that some force is at work that will punish the crimes of Sutpen and the South and that this force is tragic necessity. For example, Faulkner suggests that the individual's attempt to weave independently a design upon the loom of time is contrary to the idea that individuation of the self necessarily requires an other. Those who oppose the integrity of the weave are certain to have their intentions reversed, to be punished by an instrument of justice that "presides over human events which, incept in the individual, runs smooth, less claw than velvet; but which, by man or woman flouted, drives on like fiery steel and overrides both weakly just and unjust strong" (107). Not unlike the circular wheel (of fortune), the circular ripple (of time) also overrides both the weakly just and the unjust strong, and does so as well through the umbilical connection of the pool of the past with that of the present.

In a novel so richly orchestrated as *Absalom, Absalom!*, one is not surprised to find meaning that is dialectic or tropes that are oxymoronic. Indeed, the novel could be interpreted as a dialectic on the mutually exclusive nature of justice and love. What Sutpen seeks in his design is justice, a wrong righted. What he loses in that quest is love, a recognition of the other. What Henry seeks in his quest is love; what he loses is justice, a recognition of the rights of the other. What Quentin comes to recognize and elevate in his retelling of the curse on the house of Sutpen is the love, justice, and posterity that Sutpen, Henry, and the South have wasted in their valiant, but misguided and futile, expressions of self. What the reader intuits, despite the crimes of slavery, disinheritance, fratricide, and denial of the other, is that life does matter "because you keep on trying," because man and woman do endure, if not prevail, and because out of the bondage of slavery, patriarchy, and posterity, ironically flower the bonds of a fraternity and sorority beyond time.

14
The Tragedy of Bond/age

Thus far the purpose of this study has been to read texts of tragic drama, poetry, and fiction within the context of the trope of tragic bond/age developed in the first chapter. Henceforth, it will be to review that trope within the context of those manifestations and to examine what those readings reveal about the tragedy of bond/age and perhaps about tragedy itself. Tragic bond/age is evident in the works of the three Greek playwrights through the metaphor of the harness. Man's evolving dominion over nature is evoked by the image of the reins that curb, check, and master nature as personified by the horse. When man, in seeking to control nature by virtue of bridle, yoke, language, numbers, and other husbandry, goes too far in his evolution from Being, from an existence free of a conscious and self-conscious human-beingness, Being avenges itself upon humanity for the violation by turning the reins on the hero and thereby curbing his aspirations and punishing him. The symbol of the harness is but one of several variations of the threads that bind the tragic hero and permeate Greek tragedy; others are the chain, the net, and the burning fabric.

All are used against man when he violates not only the just precincts of Being, but also the delicate cadences of kinship. The tragic hero often finds himself being pulled in opposite directions among conflicting threads of kinship. Prometheus and Oedipus must choose between god and man; Oedipus, between being a son and being himself; Agamemnon and Creon, between nuclear and tribal families; Antigone and Creon, between brother and brotherhood; Hippolytus, between the Apollonian and Dionysian goddesses; Medea, between husband and sons. The protagonist must choose between equally demanding claims, and his choice by necessity must violate at least one bond.

In developing the trope of tragic bond/age, the Greek dramatist uses the following variations: in its primitive manifestation, human bond/age is both rootedness and deracination; it is often recognized through traces of the chthonic in the human; the primacy of the crime against kinship is evoked through the symbol of defilement or stain; the necessity of tragic bond/age is dramatized through variations of the compulsion to repeat an original sin; and the discontent is a character, and discontentment a characteristic, inevitably resulting from civilization, the wresting of human and social beingness from Being. The latter leitmotif is apparent in the tragic heroes of Shakespeare; the effect of such discontentment, however, is somewhat different.

Hamlet, Lear, and Macbeth share an extraordinary trait: all three protagonists manage to effect the end not only of their own lives, but also of their families. In Shakespeare's world the denouement that concludes the fall and initiates the restoration requires the sacrifice of the hero and all immediate kin. It may very well be that the repetition of this leitmotif of the end of the royal line in Shakespeare reflects Elizabethan concern over royal succession resulting from the imminent end of the reign of the progeny-less Elizabeth; it also, however, adds a measure of the apocalyptic to the domestic dimension of the agon, underscores the integrity of the greater familial bond and the totality of its disintegration, and intensifies the terrible nature of the justice that punishes such crimes against kinship.

In *Hamlet*, kinship is revealed as a complicated network of counter claims that leaves the hero helpless and drives him to the brink of madness. The plight of the hero is repeated and varied, and therefore made more richly textured, through the agons of the other young heroes, who must also choose between rival claims for their fidelity. The primary result of that intricate network of relationship is that Hamlet is "benetted round with villainies" without and imprisoned by "bad dreams" within. Hamlet is the modern tragic hero burdened by the consequences of a scrupulous soul; because he sees and senses so much more than all the other characters, he suffers more difficult and painful decisions. As Hegel has demonstrated, it is the rich transformation of the tragic agon to the arena of the psyche that is the significant variation of tragedy (and of the trope of tragic bond/age) in Shakespearean tragedy.[1]

In *King Lear*, kinship is further confused by the outrageous demands made by Lear upon his daughters, a complication repeated in, and reinforced by, Lear's decision to divide and thereby multiply kingdom in England. When complexity itself becomes unbearable for the aged and self-deposed monarch, he seeks relief along the *via negativa*, a course that requires he withdraw from all things, including kinship. In that withdrawal, Shakespeare suggests that deliverance from the curse of human beingness may reside in the encounter with a nothingness that is a recognition of Being. Although the outcome of his journey down the *via negativa* in terms of his experiencing Being or God may be in doubt, it is clear that the journey enables Lear, through reunion with Cordelia, to recover, if only temporarily, the "sacred knot" of kinship "too intrinsic to be loos'd."

Macbeth enjoys no such momentary clarity for his crime against kinship is much greater than either Lear or Hamlet's. His situation is neither complicated by rival claims nor mitigated by a need to be loved; instead, he is motivated only by hubris, a desire to be more powerful than any other and a need to express himself beyond limitation. In order to achieve that power and expression, he cuts all family cords, including those with Lady Macbeth, and chooses deracination from all past tradition and disinheritance from all future generation. Moreover, in denying himself participation in the benevolent and sacred banquet with the brotherly band of noblemen and unholy communion with the coven of witches, in refusing to acknowledge the presence and otherness of those who serve his masterful self, and in fleeing or seeking to destroy those mirror images of self—Duncan, Banquo, and Macduff—Macbeth destroys himself long before the scourge of fate, Macduff, does.

In its manifestation of the trope of tragic bond/age, *Paradise Lost* is more like *Macbeth* and less like *Hamlet* and *King Lear* insofar as the claims of kinship are less ambiguous and ironic in the former than they are in the latter. The God of Milton's poem establishes clear boundaries in the hierarchy, and all three tragic heroes—Satan, Eve, and Adam—transgress them because each lacks self-restraint. Moreover, in his dramatization of the motivation of the rebellious band of angels in Hell and of the sibling couple in Eden, Milton offers a corrective to the heresy suggested in *Hamlet*: that a viable fraternity is restorative for an absent or defiled paternity and maternity. Milton also effectively imbues his version of tragic bond/age with a rich reappropriation of the dialectic between the chthonic and the transcendent evident in *Oedipus Rex* and with meaningful variations of the handclasp, a symbol of humanity's early experience of bond/age in its situation in the world. Nathaniel Hawthorne and Herman Melville in turn use dynamic variations of the symbols of the handclasp and the net in their tragic fiction.

In classical manifestations of tragic bond/age in Greek and seventeenth-century dramatic literature, the net is already there, woven and restraining the hero at the outset, prepared to fall upon him after the crisis in retribution for his crimes. In the romantic versions of the trope in American gothic fiction, a more organic and dynamic weaving of the net by the hero, a weaving with which he wishes to bind others and by which he himself is ironically bound, augments the more static classical net. The same change is effected in the romantic depiction of the handclasp; both Dimmesdale and Ishmael experience in their clasps of the hand of the other an energy that rejuvenates, one missing in the more serene and static unions of Adam and Eve before and after the fall. The two gothic novels also offer variations on classical themes of tragic bond/age evident in *Paradise Lost*: they dramatize what Ricoeur sees as the psychological transference of bondage from within, seduction of the self by the self, to bondage from without, seduction of the self by the other. Dimmesdale and Ahab are guilty of such transference. Both also suffer from a compulsion to repeat, one intended to give them more control over their fates. Dimmesdale would do so through the agonizing self-scrutiny of soul, thereby precluding the stare of the public, and Ahab through the equally agonizing mapping of the white whale's circumnavigation of the globe, thereby reversing what he believes is the whale's scrutiny of himself.

As Sophocles does with Antigone and Creon, and Euripides with Hippolytus and Phaedre, both novelists split the tragic figure: Hawthorne, into Hester and Dimmesdale, and Melville, into Ahab and Ishmael. Like the classical protagonist, the American tragic heroes also are required to choose among conflicting claims of kinship; their choice, however, often redefines kinship. The nuclear family is already dissolved; most characters are already deracinated, disinherited, or disinheriting; and the restoration of order and the self is found in the transformation of a congregation of exiles into a community of saints. In his nineteenth-century fiction, Thomas Hardy also reappropriates two ancient themes to develop further the dramatization of disinheritance growing out of tragic bond/age.

Near the end of a Greek tragedy, hero, chorus, and audience all stand in terror at the prospect that "here come the Gods"; in the more secular fiction of Hardy, one is awed more by the intimation that "here comes the past." Indeed, this pattern of the intrusion of the past upon the present, combined with two others—the sacrality of the first bond and the compulsion to repeat self-destructive acts—distinguishes Hardy's interpolation of the trope of tragic bond/age. That Hardy was obsessed with these subjects throughout his career is evident even in his final novel, *Jude the Obscure*, in which he repeats all three. Jude and Sue are never completely divorced from

Arabella and Phillotson; just after Jude seems to establish some semblance of familial life with Sue, Father Time—that grotesque embodiment of Jude's past life with Arabella—intrudes upon that short-lived domestic bliss. Moreover, Jude throughout the novel repeats unions with the opposite sex that forestall any hope of his achieving a university education and/or a ministry in the world of the father.

In *The Mayor of Casterbridge* and *Tess of the d'Urbervilles*, these leitmotifs are interrelated in the evocation of tragic bond/age. The hero repeats the self-destructive act because he is bound to a primogenitive force, from whose grip he can or will not free himself. Torn as he is between the present and the past, the hero is also divided between counter claims of kinship and finds himself ambiguously the perpetrator and victim of crimes against family. What Freud and his disciples outline in the psychological narrative, Hardy intuits in the fictive one: the more civilized man becomes the more discontent he is because he remains bound to his origins at the breast, in the womb, and in the inorganic. That connection is tensive: part of him wishes to transcend those chthonic connections in order to establish an independent self, but another part, in the trying conditions of reality, needs to return to them. Thus, in Hardy's fiction, all first bonds of sex, marriage, or troth in the world of the father are paradoxically variations of the original connection to the mother, and the intrusions of the past and the compulsions to repeat traumatic acts tighten that original connection until the hero's noble suffering ends.

Henry James adapts several of the characteristics of tragic bond/age surveyed above: like Tess, Isabel suffers the claims of a restrictive kinship; like Eve and others, the recurrence of the chthonic; like Hamlet and Macbeth, the failure of hermeneutics in reading prophecy and people, and, like Antigone and Tess, the redefinition of family through the commitment to sorority. What James adds to his adaptations is something relatively new: the American myth of total freedom. Until James, none of the tragedians studied here suggests the possibility of such liberation. James, schooled in the dreams of mid-nineteenth-century New England transcendentalism, bases his novel on several of his characters' premise that financial independence can purchase the freedom to follow one's feelings or impressions. The irony is that, in affording her that luxury, the Touchetts only give Isabel enough financial rope with which to ensnare herself in the complex trammel net of Euro-American social convention.

James's fiction is also distinguished from that which precedes and succeeds it by an extraordinary generic achievement. Nineteenth and twentieth-century fiction, by its very nature, is relatively more realistic than Greek, Shakespearean, or Miltonic tragic poetry; it concentrates on the development of the particular and the individual in evoking both social and human beingness. The challenge then is, according to Jeannette King, "to find ways of isolating and universalising the individual experience, to make [the protagonist] at once exceptional and representative without destroying this sense that each element in society is inseparable from the whole."[2] Hawthorne and Melville achieve this primarily through the blending of realism with the sur-realism of American gothic, a distortion that magnifies the social measure of bond/age through the evocation of the psychological and demonic dimension. Hardy, Marlowe, and Faulkner achieve similar resonance through the use of what might be called "ur-realism," the reappropriation of myth that situates the local agon in a primordial landscape—the ring of Casterbridge, the sacrificial altar of Stonehenge, the heart of dark Africa, Sutpen's one hundred acres in ante-bellum South—and thereby evokes what is both immediate and universal about human bond/age.

In *The Portrait of a Lady,* James, adhering to a realism that uses neither sur-realism nor ur-realism, also manages to transcend historical limitation. He does so primarily through the nuance of style. For example, most of the allusions to flight and fear of flying are confined to the dialogue of Ralph Touchett and Isabel Archer, rendering its manifestation more realistic as the allusive conversation of the learned and imaginative, while still evoking the archetypal desire to transcend chthonic limitation. James's fictive world is an uncommonly intricate network of familial and social boundaries, of "appurtenances," requiring a more subtle sensitivity and more incisive hermeneutics from protagonist and reader alike. The failure therefore to read any one person rightly is a failure to read the whole world so; more significantly, the recognitions, when they rarely and finally come, do so with a force equal to any in tragic drama. In so doing, both the error and accomplishment of consciousness resonate with Greek *metis*, the failure of which binds the hero and the power of which effects transcendence.

In the twentieth-century novels, *Heart of Darkness* and *Absalom, Absalom!,* the historical fact of the enslavement of the primitive black man by the civilized white man lends significant impact to the trope of tragic bond/age. The heroes of both novels seek to calculate the worth of human flesh and blood in monetary terms and in so doing destroy what they calculate. In *Heart of Darkness,* Conrad renders the deeds of Kurtz as a crime against Being, against the unconscious *participation mystique* of the black man with the dark continent. His fall from apotheosis to chthonic crawling and his recognition of the horror of both his mission and his existence is Being's vengeance for Kurtz's intrusion into the heart of darkness. In Conrad, the net that ensnares the fallen protagonist is woven by goddess-like women who preside not only over Kurtz's fall, but also over Marlow's journey. This variation of the trope is enhanced and intensified by Conrad's situating his narrative in Africa, where primitive and cultured conspire in the unspeakable rite of the surrogate sacrifice.

Faulkner's variation is also enriched by a unique situating of the agon that dialectically juxtaposes an ur-realism—Jason Compson's Greek tragic version of the myth of Thomas Sutpen and his dark one hundred acres—and a sur-realism—Rosa Caufield's gothic interpolation of the demonic Sutpen and his plantation mansion of terror. Here, the absence of the patriarchal father breeds both incest and fratricide in his progeny; the breaking of those taboos are the sins for which succeeding generations do penance. In Faulkner's tragedy, both protagonist and antagonists weave the tragic tapestry, the figure of which is made more complex by the synchronicity of past, present, and future and whose meaning must be inferred from the interpenetrating yarns of five story-tellers.

This reflective examination on the manifestation of tragic bond/age in selected works of drama, epic, and fiction sheds light not only on the complexity and richness of the trope, but also on the essence of the genre. It reveals that the world of the tragedy of bond/age is one of integrity, implicitly so in the realm of the universally cosmic and explicitly so in the domains of the historically social and psychologically individual. In both his general philosophy and his particular observations about tragedy, Hegel posits that the absolute spirit/mind (*geist*) is a network of universal connections, an "absolute pure notion itself, viewed as being, relation bare and simple, but imperturbable, irresistible, and immovable." He adds that "in the world of existence [it] scatters itself into many manifestations."[3] One such manifestation is the evolution of a conscious and subsequently self-conscious humanity, which is a rift in what Foucault calls the unthought Order of things. Schopenhauer suggests that "the true sense of tragedy is the deeper insight, that it is not his own individual sins that the hero atones for, but original sin, i.e. the crime of existence itself," the rift in the fabric of existence that is a violation of pure Being by an emerging human beingness.[4]

Schopenhauer contends, however, that for such crimes there is no redemption; other commentators on the genre as well as the pattern of tragic bond/age unraveled in this study contradict such a conclusion. For example,

Richard Sewall reiterates and extends Schopenhauer's insight: "What does it mean to be? It recalls the original terror, harking back to a world that antedates the conceptions of philosophy, the consolations of the later religions, and whatever constructions the human mind has devised to persuade itself that its universe is secure. It recalls the original un-reason, the terror of the irrational. It sees man as questioner, naked, unaccommodated, alone, facing mysterious demonic forces in his own nature and outside, and the irreducible facts of suffering and death." Sewall, however, indicates that tragedy also points towards ultimate redemption: it "affirms a cosmos of which man is a meaningful part. . . . it speaks, however vaguely or variously, of an order that transcends time, space and matter."[5]

Like others, Sewall adds that prior to any final reintegration with Being, man-in-society re-orders existence. Thus, in Renaissance tragedy "there was order in the universe which should find its counterpart (and did, when society was in a healthy state) in the ordered life of man on earth."[6] Raymond Williams points out a similar version of social integrity in Greek drama, which "was rooted in history, and not a human history alone. Its thrust came, not from the personality of an individual but from a man's inheritance and relationships, within a world that ultimately transcended him."[7] Both Sewall and Williams reappropriate a major idea of Hegel about the essence of tragedy: what reconnects man with the absolute is its "highest spiritual form" in life, "the spirit of the community."[8]

In tragedy, social integrity is the weave by which the hero is knit or linked to nature, gods, family, woman, society, even the dead. In the Greek world, that chain implicitly possesses vertical degree, proportion, and plenitude; in the world of Shakespeare it more explicitly and complicatedly does so, and in that of Milton, most absolutely so. Even in the more democratic nineteenth and twentieth-century fictional tragic worlds, where boundary becomes more horizontal than vertical, more a matter of interrelationship among equals, verticality of boundary is still manifested in the filial relationship of parents and progeny. In tragedy, humanity repeats the original crime of existence—violating the boundaries of Being—by seeking to break the boundaries of social integrity. Thus, Steiner notes that Sophoclean tragedies "are penetrated throughout by a sense of the fragility of human institutions. . . . Man's animality, the creative-destructive atavisms of the organic and animal kingdom inside his own evolved person, threaten to restore to archaic solitudes and exposures the fabric of human existence."[9]

Implicit in this oscillating movement from cosmic integrity to existential disintegration to social reintegration and subsequent fragmentation of the community is an essential component of tragedy, an ironic and sometimes paradoxical dialectic. Max Scheler observes that the most tragic action occurs when "the same power which has brought either itself or another object to a very high positive value becomes its destroyer—especially if this takes place in the very act of its achievement.... The use of the phrase 'the tragic knot,' is a pertinent metaphor. It illustrates the inner entanglement between the creation of a value and the destruction of a value as they take place in the unity of the tragic action and the tragic event."[10] In the tragedy of bond/age, the figure who effects his own rise and fall through the paradoxically liberating and destructive power of transcending boundaries is the extraordinary hero.

According to Northrup Frye, what elevates the hero is his connection with something beyond the reach or vision of ordinary man: the hero "is typically on top of the wheel of fortune. halfway between human society on the ground and the something greater in the sky ... between a world of paradisal freedom and a world of bondage ... wrapped in the mystery of their communion with that something beyond which we can see only through them, and which is the source of their strength and their fate alike."[11] David Lenson reiterates two qualities of the tragic hero, that delegate of the absolute: he "lives by the upright flame while the remainder of mankind live by the floor, the ceiling and the walls" and in his defeat he "beats on the boundaries of existence and makes them less limiting."[12] Hegel sees such heroes not only as "immaculate celestial types or presences," but also as ones "who preserve within their differences and divisions of self the never-deconsecrated innocence and integrity of their being."[13] Hegel, however, as we shall see, also notes that in many tragic heroes such integrity is doomed.

What brings the tragic hero to a very high position is his power to penetrate the borders of Being, that boundary between mere organic existence and human beingness. Such power derives in large measure from what Detienne and Vernant call *metis*, the cunning intelligence manifested as fire, circle, and bond; it is also the source of the protagonist's undoing. Harold Watts concurs: the tragic hero is driven out of the paradise of Being and community "not by any flaming sword but by his own nature whose destiny it is to exercise choice and thus deny or qualify all cyclically-based perceptions."[14] Freer than most men, the hero wants even more freedom from the restraint imposed by Being and society. What in the world of mythology or even epic would be a paradigm of the heroic becomes in the world of tragedy one of the problematic. Thus, Vernant concludes, in "the new framework of tragic interplay, then, the hero has ceased to be a model.

He has become, both for himself and for others, a problem . . . [tragedy] confronts heroic values and ancient religious representations with the new modes of thought that characterize the advent of law within the city-state."[15] Also, as Frye points out, tragic choice is "a use of freedom to lose freedom"[16] because, as Vernant notes, "for there to be tragedy it must be possible for the text simultaneously to imply two things: It is his character, in man, that one calls *daimon* and, conversely, what one calls character, in man, is in reality a *daimon*; . . . Religious powers . . . intervene at the heart of [the hero's] decision, subjecting him to constraint even in what were claimed to be his 'choices.'"[17]

This irony is evident in the tragic world of interrelationship or integrity where the favored hero masters the natural and social environment and freely prospers within it, but such power, prosperity, and freedom end abruptly. That end is often brought about by a desire to master and prosper more and more freely, and the hero feels a greater need to express himself in an environment that for him is becoming increasingly repressive. The inevitable consequence of this growing conflict between the paradoxical powers of the world to connect and to constrain is that the hero, stirred by hubris, strives too much against and too far beyond the boundaries of the social and cosmic order. A. C. Bradley, in summarizing the essence of Hegelian theory on tragedy, concludes: "The family and the state, the bond of father and son, the bond of mother and son, the bond of citizenship, these are each and all, one as much as another, powers rightfully claiming human allegiance. It is tragic that observance of one should involve the violation of another."[18]

As we have seen, from Hegel's perspective, such violation operates when the hero has to choose between the family, the *philoi*, and the state, the *nomoi*, and consequently that choice results in what Lenson calls "the major paradox of tragedy: the individual in conflict with his community."[19] There are, however, as Bradley suggests, other meaningful choices for the hero, which reside within the narrower boundaries of the *philoi* or family. The tragic hero's struggle manifests itself as a crime against kinship, very often as disinheritance, and can therefore be said to result in tragedy that is essentially domestic. "Domestic" literally means of the house; by extension it means of the same family, tribe, or nation. "Family" itself derives from *famulus* or servant and thereby relates back to another meaning of domestic, which is servant. Taking these words together, one may conclude that the domestic tragedy of bond/age concerns itself with the internal conflicts among those who serve under the extended house whose lineage is blood, land, law, and obedience. The nature of kinship is connection, and the essence of crimes against kinship is that they disconnect, impede, or sever by disobedience and uprooting. Such crimes, however, extend beyond the nuclear to the tribal or racial family of men and women.

One such severance is disinheritance—to cut off, or to be cut off from—one's birthright. Both dictionary and usage suggest that disinheritance is a loss peculiar to heirs, to children. Heritage, however, is not only that which children expect from their progenitors by right of birth, but also that which parents may expect from their children by the same right. Thus, inheritance or heritage is that which is handed down or offered up; it is tradition, tribute, and tributary. Disinheritance is the cutting off, or away from, that which should connect and bond. Although much of the enormity of the hero's act derives a great deal from the repercussive nature of his crime as it reverberates throughout the world's web or chain, the major part of the magnitude of his crime derives from the fact that his is a crime against what is ontogenetically and phylogenetically primary, primordial, primo-genitive, and therefore sacred. This is the condition behind Oscar Wilde's assertion that heredity is "nemesis without her mask. It is the last of the fates and the most terrible."[20]

Because the focus here has been on tragedies composed in the Hellenic and post-Hellenic western world, the crimes against kinship take place in the world of the father. Either the father disinherits his son or daughter, or they rebel against him or his authority and law. In some cases, the conflict comes about because of the dominating presence of the father; in others, his absence creates a gap in the webbed world, one by which the hero seems to be unbound. He thereby reaches beyond the limits that are, despite the father's absence, still operative. In a few works, the tragic conflict eventuates paradoxically as a result of both the presence and absence of the father: although he is physically there, his failure to recognize his progeny invalidates the very law of which he is the originator and personification, or, although the father is physically absent, his presence, as spirit or memory, continues to bind the hero.

In this tragic world of the father, woman often serves as antagonist, either as a member of the nuclear family whose presence is a restraint, from which the hero futilely strives to liberate himself, or as an agent of the mistresses that bind the hero in retribution for his crime against the *philoi*. In some tragedies, bond/age is not vertical, between parent and child, but rather horizontal, between man and woman, husband and wife, one manifested in the image of the clasped hand, the knit or knot of marriage, and one therefore violated by the unclasping of hands or the rending of such knits. In those tragedies in which woman is the protagonist, the conflict with phallogocentric authority leads the heroine to question paternity and redefine kinship; sometimes she reaffirms an older, matriarchal force; other times she places her faith and fidelity in sorority. In those tragedies where the conflict along the vertical plane becomes patriarchically inter-generational, the young hero chooses a viable fraternity over an inhibiting paternity. In still others, the bond is extended from family to tribe, to a community of companions, of those who break bread together in the holy banquet that connects; in such cases the crime is against kind, and the unholy banquet or rite defiles and ruptures.

The decision of the hero to move beyond the nuances of relationship transforms the web into—or makes manifest what the web potentially always was—the net or spring or trap, the release of which has repercussions throughout the webbed world and beyond and in direct opposition to the intentions of the hero. Extending what has been a virtue—the expression of a proud self—to the point of diminishing return so that it becomes the flaw of an excessive defiance and a renunciation of the other, one resulting from excessive pride (hubris), error in judgment (hamartia), and obsession with but one strand in the world's complex web, the hero triggers his own nemesis. Aspiring to rise above his human state, he falls to a less-than-human chthonic condition; striving to gain Apollonian dominion, he loses Dionysian communion; wanting to free himself from a bondage, he deprives himself of a nurturing and self-identifying bond and, as Hegel acknowledges, violates his own integrity: "For individuality, which involves peril to the whole in the maintenance of its own self-existence (*Fursichseyn*), has thrust its own self out of the community, and is disintegrated in its own nature. . . . He who came to affront the highest spiritual form of conscious life, the spirit of the community, must be stripped of the honour of his entire and complete nature."[21] In defining the protagonist of Greek tragedy, Vernant confirms Hegel's conclusion: "Cut off from his familial, civic, and religious roots the individual was nothing; he did not find himself alone, he ceased to exist."[22]

The effect of the retribution of nemesis is not confined to the hero. Partly because of the integral nature of life, disturbance in one link effects disturbance throughout the weave; and partly because the justice of Being is often indifferent to moral or legal distinction, the consequence of the hero's wrong choice retraces itself throughout the world. Clifford Leech makes this clear in his examination of tragedy: "the divine justice mirrored in [tragedy] is an indifferent justice, a justice which cares no whit for the individual and is not concerned with a nice balance of deserts and rewards. . . . [It] operates like an avalanche or an echo in an enclosed space."[23]

In the Greek world the gods punish the crimes of kinship with a plague or net upon the familial house and tribal polis. In Shakespeare's world, disinheritance leads to seizures within or bindings of the bodies personal, politic, and Ptolemaic. In the modern world, deracination transforms the inner as well as the outer landscape into a labyrinth with seemingly no exit, in which one's movements are metaphorically tied to the motions of others. The justice released by the hero's action is so terrible that both guilty and innocent are caught in the exacting net: his children are punished with Jason; Ophelia, with Hamlet; Pearl, with Hester.

Despite the enormity of his act and of the reverberation it triggers throughout the domain of the tragedy, the spectator (including chorus, audience, and reader) is reluctant to judge the hero or at least mitigates the judgment rendered. Several reasons exist for this response. The acts of the hero and the reaction of justice are in their degree so terrible that they seem beyond the pale of social prohibition and punishment. As indicated earlier, it is as though the hero were in touch with a force beyond, one which chorus and audience can infer only by having witnessed the hero's act and the force's reaction. Thus, no one on the mere human plain can judge the degree or extent of guilt. Another reason is that the crime against kinship is related to and shares in the culpability of the crime against Being, a crime evoked symbolically in Milton's version of the Fall of Man. When Adam eats of the tree of the knowledge of good and evil, the rupture of the boundary between him and God reverberates with similar ruptures throughout the Garden as beast turns on beast. Adam's crime is not so much that he wants to be as God, but that he wants to be (more) human—more above the other beasts in the garden. That is why he eats of the apple, why he chooses Eve before God, and why his act symbolizes, among other things, the rupture made in Being by human beingness.

Can we blame primal man for willing his rise above his chthonic roots, for developing his own nature as human, for seeking not only to rise above the chthonic, but also to master it: to mine what is mineral, harness what is animal, and plot what is vegetable? Can we blame him for wanting deliverance from darkness and silence and thereby for organizing letters and sound to create language and controlling fire to create light? Is it not a matter of necessity that human nature evolve, that the rest of nature feel the rupture of that evolution and react, and that man's jurisdiction over nature violate the just precincts of Being? Does not such necessity mitigate whatever excessiveness may exist in the human being's evolution from, and attempt to exercise authority over, nature?

It is one of the major ironies of tragic bond/age that the hero's attempt to harness and plot is his participation in the weaving of the net of nemesis by which he will be punished for his violation of Being. Such is the moral ambiguity of human bond/age in phylogenetic man's attempt to transcend his chthonic roots; that same ambiguity characterizes man's crimes against community and kinship. Thus, Hegel concludes that "the original essence of tragedy consists then in the fact that within such a conflict each of the opposed sides [*philoi* or *nomoi*], if taken by itself, has justification; while each can establish the true and positive content of its own aim and character only by denying and infringing the equally justified power of the other. The consequence is that in its moral life, and because of it, each is nevertheless involved in guilt."[24]

The tribal and familial bonds protect; they also restrain. Restraint may be good, particularly if what is limited is that which threatens both the individual and his society. Restraint may be excessive, if what is confined is human potentiality. Noble rebellion against such restraint is also morally ambiguous, condemnable primarily because it goes too far. That the hero strives initially to realize his human potential more fully in the expression of his self compensates somewhat for his over-reaching in that expression—for example, in his having broken his word, his bond. Crimes against kinship are also morally ambiguous because the hero, seeking to free himself of bondage, necessarily dissolves a bond. Vernant sees such agons in terms of conflicting *dikes*: "What tragedy depicts is one *dike* in conflict with another, a law that is not fixed, shifting and changing into its opposite. . . . It takes as its subject the man actually living out this debate, forced to make a decisive choice, to orient his activity in a universe of ambiguous values where nothing is ever stable or unequivocal."[25] The audience, because it has been engaged in the same drama of human bond/age both phylogenetically and ontogenetically, feels complicity in the hero's act and thereby empathy for the hero. That is why in tragedy guilt is felt to be communal.

Another reason for the mitigation of judgment against the hero is that no punishment could be as severe as that meted out by himself: "It is the heroic spirits who say Yes to themselves in tragic cruelty; they are hard enough to experience suffering as a pleasure."[26] The hero's crime is his punishment; to react against bond/age leads to isolation, alienation, deracination, and disinheritance. Moreover, the hero often recognizes (*anagnorisis*) that he has transgressed, asks what have I done and to whom have I done it, and discovers that he has severed himself from the other or has committed crimes against an other who is both kin and kind. Additionally, what he often learns is that he has failed to recognize or understand, to read nature or others or the situation correctly. He has been found wanting in hermeneutics, in the very art that identifies him as human being and separates him from Being.

More severe than the audience, who has participated only by indirection, the hero, who has acted directly and blindly against kinship, curses and punishes himself and by more excess tempts fate to punish him further. Because his crime is one against the human bonds of the word and the light, his punishment is silence and darkness. Because he also has transgressed against Being, he and the world he embodies or represents must suffer death or apocalypse. What A. P. Rossiter observes about Shakespearean tragedy is applicable to the whole genre: "Suffering beyond solace, beyond any moral palliation, and suffering because of a human greatness which is great because great in passion: that, above everything else, is central to Shakespeare's tragic conception."[27] For all these reasons, judgment of the hero is reluctant and mitigated; thus, Scheler concludes: "In general, then, the quality of the tragic is lacking when the question 'Who is guilty?,' has a clear and definite answer. . . . 'Tragic guilt' is a kind for which no one can be blamed and for which no conceivable 'judge' can be found."[28]

The moral ambiguity of the act, the audience's complicity in the deed, and the degree of suffering explain not only the mitigation of judgment against the hero but also the arousal and purgation of pity and terror in the audience. The hero has suffered well, nobly, and courageously; like Shakespeare's thane of Cawdor, nothing in the life of the tragic hero "doth become him like the leaving of it." What becomes him is not only that he suffers, but that his suffering often leads to a recognition of the necessity of bond/age, of that person or power or society, of that Dionysian communion, of that Being, from which or beyond which he has sought separation and transcendence and to which he is ironically compelled to return. Vernant extends such *anagnorisis* to self-recognition: "In his purely human dimensions the agent is not the sufficient cause and reason for his actions: On the contrary, it is his action, recoiling upon him as the gods have, in their sovereignty, ordered, that reveals him to himself, showing him the true nature of what he is and what he does."[29] Sewall relates that knowledge of self to knowledge of existence: "But all who are involved [in tragedy] have been witness to new revelations about human existence, the evil of evil and goodness of good. They are more 'ready.' The same old paradoxes and ambiguities remain, but for the moment they are transcended in the higher vision."[30]

In the terrible reaction of an indifferent justice and necessity, there is a compensating reaffirmation of order and design; moveover, through the sacrificial death of the hero, the survivors—chorus, audience, and readers—have been brought into greater communion. The action has led up to what Frye calls "an epiphany of law, of that which is and must be"[31] and what Hegel suggests is the essence of catharsis: "The Greek who has within him the feeling of the necessity calms his soul with that. It is so: there is nothing to be done against it; with this I must content myself; just in this feeling that I must be content with it, that this even pleases me, we have the freedom which is implied in the fact that it is mine."[32] Moreover, in the case of those who have taken the *via negativa*, the trauma of recognition has been assuaged: "The darkness of terror is pierced by the radiance of blessedness and grace."[33]

Those scholars who examine the possible occurrence of the tragic in modern literature conclude that, lacking essential components of the traditional genre summarized above, tragedy is essentially altered or non-existent in the twentieth century. Murray Kreiger, whose *The Tragic Vision* differs significantly from Richard Sewall's *The Vision of Tragedy* not only in the syntax of title, but also in the substance of content, argues that "the unrelieved tragic vision. . . . [in] its denial of any totality . . . is an heretical vision; and in its defiance of all rational moral order it is a demoniac vision . . . a distillate of the rebellion, the godlessness which, once induced by crisis, purifies itself by rejecting all palliatives."[34] In *Modern Tragedy*, Raymond Williams reinforces Krieger's analysis by adding that modern tragedy in evoking "the loss of human connection at anything more than a private level . . . expresses sympathy and pity between private persons, but tacitly excludes any positive conception of society, and thence any clear view of order or justice."[35]

What causes Krieger and Williams to distinguish modern from traditional tragedy—the heretical concentration on the individual at the expense of totality and the absence of any transcendent order or justice in society or the cosmos—leads George Steiner to conclude that tragedy no longer exists in the modern world. For Steiner, the death of tragedy has been brought about by the loss of a "controlling mythology" that is the outcome of crystallized "sediments [of a mythos] accumulated over long stretches of time" and not the product of individual genius, by the decline of an "organic world view" with its attendant content of symbolic and ritualistic reference, and by the withdrawal of God's shadow, which no longer falls upon the modern hero as it once did upon Agamemnon and Macbeth.[36] Although Krieger and Williams see fit to conclude that such voids alter the form and Steiner that they destroy it, all three share one observation: it is the absence of integrity in the world that precludes the presence of traditional tragedy. It is such absence that partially explains why some manifestations of bond/age in modern dramatic literature are not tragic. Tennessee Williams's *The Glass Menagerie*, Arthur Miller's *Death of a Salesman*, and Eugene O'Neill's *Long Day's Journey Into Night* are three modern American examples of such drama.

In its own way, each of these plays dramatizes a variation of the symbol of the loom in Faulkner's *Absalom, Absalom!*, the one in which each member of the Sutpen family, connected to every other member, cannot help but feel the constriction of family ties as each moves to enact a design upon the fabric of existence. In all three plays, the audience is presented with a quartet of family members—Amanda, Tom, Laura, and absent father Wingfield (or the figure of Jim O'Connor who stands in for the father); Willy, Linda, Biff, and Hap Loman; and James, Mary, James Jr., and Edmund Tyrone—who in their attempt to love or communicate that love only repel or bind the other. The bond/age, the back and forth movement of personal and psychological connection and constraint, can be imagined metaphorically as a pavan, a stately dance, in which each performer is tied to the other three by a gossamer chiffon, which connects or restricts, but also gives form to, their movement.

The problem with the plays themselves is that, unlike every other work discussed in this study, there are only limited manifestations of images of bond/age and consequently no indication that what bonds and binds the agonists has any effect beyond the situation of the family. Laura Wingfield wears a brace and thereby is reminded of her chthonic condition; Tom's retreat to the fire "escape" reiterates what a confinement his home is; Willy Loman's dreams and nightmares demonstrate that he is caught up in the past; and the dense fog that rolls in from the Atlantic submerges the Tyrone family in blindness and guilt. More than any of the images in the other plays, this fog is so all-pervasive that it comes closest to evoking the nemesis of traditional tragedy, but in the end it is rendered more naturalistic than tragic. What little imagery of connection and constraint exists in the plays does not suffice to extend bond/age beyond the personal or domestic.

All three plays lack other essential components of the tragedy of bond/age: character is not in touch with that something beyond the ordinary (indeed in Williams and O'Neill, it is difficult to discern who the hero is); the crime and punishment of the hero do not reverberate throughout society and the cosmos; unlike that in James's fiction, the realism here does not reach beyond the real of the letter to the more real of the spirit and thereby confirms Lukac's conviction that "realism is bound to destroy all the form-creating and life-maintaining value of tragic drama."[37] Finally, because there is no significant orchestration of imagery of bond/age and its parallel evocation of a world of integrity, the conflict remains primarily domestic and does not reflect the original trauma of existence, the violation of Being by human beingness.

* * *

In the final pages of *The Death of Tragedy*, Steiner cites three incidents as signs of the potential recovery of tragedy in the modern world. One is a recollection of Helene Weigel's portrayal of Mother Courage, in which the actress reacts to the sight of her dead child: "As the body was carried off, Weigel looked the other way and tore her mouth wide open. The shape of the gesture was that of the screaming horse in Picasso's *Guernica*. The sound that came out was raw and terrible beyond any description I could give of it. But, in fact, there was no sound. Nothing. The sound was total silence. It was silence which screamed and screamed through the whole theater so that the audience lowered its head as before a gust of wind . . . it was the same wild cry with which the tragic imagination first marked our sense of life."[38]

Steiner's association of silence with tragedy is consistent with Walter Benjamin's observation that "the inarticulacy of the tragic hero . . . is one of the foundation stones of the theory of tragedy." Benjamin supports his assertion by quoting Franz Rosenwieg: "In his silence, the [tragic] hero burns the bridges connecting him to God and the world, elevates himself above the realm of personality, which in speech, defines itself against others and individualizes itself, and so enters the icy loneliness of the self. . . . How else can it activate this loneliness, this rigid and defiant self-sufficiency, except in silence."[39]

Although Steiner's anecdote is a moving illustration of Benjamin and Rosenwieg's point about the silence of the hero as the essence of tragedy, one cannot help but observe a seeming contradiction: how can one reconcile such theory with the facts that in Greek drama it is the separation of the hero's dialogue from that of the chorus that initiates the form, that in

Shakespearean and Miltonic tragedy the hero voices the richest of blank verse, and that even in Melville the prose narration serves as a frame for the declamations of the demonic hero. The resolution is perhaps implied in the last lines of one of tragedy's most vocal heroes: "The rest is silence." It is often towards the end of the hero's agon and of the drama that silence realizes itself as an important part of the essence of tragedy. This qualification is further illustrated by Lenson, who equates the absence of sound with catharsis: "the moment of silence that follows the conclusion of a tragic drama, . . . is, among other things, the moment of greatest unity among the author, players, and audience, for the author's form is complete. . . . The wordlessness between the last sentence and the applause is a special precinct, intrinsic to theatre and no other genre. . . . Whatever Aristotle meant by catharsis it is hard to think of it as anything other than an attempt to describe this moment. It is drama's most sacred point, the closing of the circle."[40]

Throughout this study, we have used the term "orchestration" figuratively to describe the complex and richly textured statement, repetition, and variation of leitmotifs of bonds and binding in the trope of tragic bond/age. We now extend the metaphor to suggest that such point/counterpoint is an essential part of the music that both Aristotle and Nietzsche felt intrinsic to tragedy. Within such a context the essential silence of tragedy is not unlike that which follows the climactic note of any musical composition and is best evoked perhaps by T. S. Eliot, who writes,

> Words, after speech, reach
> Into the silence. Only by the form, the pattern,
> Can words or music reach
> The stillness.[41]

Such stillness follows the last repetition of the orchestration of tragic bond/age variously and uniquely scored in each work studied herein; it informs pity and terror and makes possible catharsis and transcendence, without which, Jasper says, "there is not tragedy."[42] In the silence that ends such orchestration also resonates the reintegration of human beingness with Being and resides the resolution of tragic bond/age.

Notes

CHAPTER 1: THE NATURE OF TRAGIC BOND/AGE

1. Aristotle, *Poetics,* quoted in *Criticism: The Major Texts,* ed. Walter Jackson Bate (New York: Harcourt, Brace and Company, 1952), 30–31.
2. T. R. Henn, *Harvest of Tragedy* (New York: Barnes & Noble Inc., 1969), 36–37.
3. Mircea Eliade, *Images and Symbols: Studies in Religious Symbolism,* trans. Philip Mairet (New York: Sheed & Ward and London: Harvill Press, 1961; New York: Sheed & Ward Search Book, 1969), 114.
4. Eliade, *Images,* 95–96.
5. Marcel Detienne and Jean-Pierre Vernant, *Cunning Intelligence in Greek Culture and Society,* trans. Janet Lloyd (Sussex, England: The Harvester Press and New Jersey: Humanities Press, 1978), 284, 294–95.
6. Detienne and Vernant, *Cunning,* 286, 291, 105.
7. Eliade, *Images,* 124, 116–17.
8. Jacques Lacan, *Les complexes familiaux dans la formation de l'individu* (Paris: Navarin Editeur, 1984) quoted in Mikkel Borch-Jacobsen, *Lacan: The Absolute Master,* trans. Douglas Brick (Stanford: Stanford University Press, 1991), 49.
9. Mikkel Borch-Jacobsen, *Lacan, The Absolute Master,* trans. Douglas Brick (Stanford: Stanford University Press), 60.
10. Jessica Benjamin, *The Bonds of Love: Psychoanalysis, Feminism, and the Problem of Domination* (New York: Pantheon Books, 1988), 149.
11. John Muller, "Psychosis and Mourning in Lacan's *Hamlet*," *New Literary History* 12 (1980): 150.
12. Michel Foucault, *The Order of Things: An Archaeology of the Human Sciences* (New York: Pantheon Books, 1970), 21, 310, 239, 314, 63, xx.
13. Sigmund Freud, "The 'Uncanny,'" in vol. 4 of *Collected Papers,* ed. Ernest Jones and trans. Joan Riviere (London: Hogarth Press and The Institute of Psychoanalysis, 1924–50; reprint, New York: Basic Books, 1959), 140–50.
14. René Girard, *Violence and the Sacred* (Baltimore: John Hopkins University Press, 1977), 8, 18, 36, 65.
15. Claude Lévi-Strauss, "The Structural Study of Myth," in *Myth: A Symposium,* ed. Thomas A. Sebeok (Bloomington and London: Indiana University Press, 1972), 91.
16. G. W. F. Hegel, *The Phenomenology of Mind,* ed. and trans. J. B. Baillie (London: George Allen & Unwin, 1910), 232–34.
17. Benjamin, *Bonds,* 32, 73.
18. Martin Heidegger, quoted in George Steiner, *Antigones: How the Antigone Legend has Endured in Western Literature, Art, and Thought* (New York: Oxford University Press, 1984), 173.

19. George Steiner, *Antigones*, 129.
20. Sigmund Freud, *Totem and Taboo and Other Works*, vol. 13 of *The Standard Edition of the Complete Psychological Works of Sigmund Freud*, ed. James Strachey and trans. Joan Riviere (London: Hogarth Press, 1955), 368–407.
21. Sigmund Freud, *Beyond the Pleasure Principle*, in *The Freud Reader*, ed. Peter Gay (New York: W. W. Norton & Company, 1989), 612, 614, 613.
22. Friedrich Nietzsche, *The Will to Power*, ed. Walter Kaufmann and trans. Walter Kaufmann and R. J. Hollingdale (New York: Random House, 1967), 386.
23. Friedrich Nietzsche, *The Birth of Tragedy*, in *Basic Writings of Nietzsche*, ed. and trans. Walter Kaufmann (New York: The Modern Library, 1966), 75.
24. Sophocles, *Antigone*, in *Greek Tragedies*, ed. David Grene and Richmond Lattimore and trans. David Grene (Chicago and London: The University of Chicago Press), 194.
25. Nietzsche, quoted in Erich Heller, *The Artist's Journey into the Interior and Other Essays*, (New York: Random House, 1965), 218–19.
26. Maurice Merleau-Ponty, *The Visible and the Invisible*, quoted in M. C. Dillon, *Merleau-Ponty's Ontology* (Bloomington: Indiana University Press, 1988), 221; *The Primacy of Perception*, 7, quoted in Dillon, *Ontology*, 198.
27. M. C. Dillon, *Merleau-Ponty's Ontology* (Bloomington: Indiana University Press, 1988), 219, 214.
28. Mikhail Bakhtin, "From Discourse in the Novel," in *The Critical Tradition: Classical Texts and Contemporary Trends*, ed. David Richter (New York: St. Martin's Press, 1989), 75.
29. See T. S. Eliot, "Tradition and the Individual Talent," Virginia Woolf, "Shakespeare's Sister from *A Room of One's Own*," and Hélène Cixous, "The Laugh of the Medusa" in *The Critical Tradition*, ed. David Richter (New York: St. Martin's Press, 1989).
30. See Roland Barthes, "From Work to Text," in *The Critical Tradition*, ed. David Richter (New York, St. Martin's Press, 1989), 1008–9 and J. Hillis Miller, *Ariadne's Thread: Story Lines*, (New Haven and London: Yale University Press, 1992), 21–22.
31. Jacques Derrida, "Structure, Sign, and Play in the Discourse of the Human Sciences," in *Critical Tradition*, 963, 965.
32. See Derrida, "Structure, Sign" and Paul DeMan, "Semiology and Rhetoric," in *Critical Tradition*, 959–70, 1011–20.
33. Dylan Thomas, "Fern Hill," in *The Collected Poems of Dylan Thomas* (New York: New Directions, 1957), 180.

Chapter 2: In Greek Tragedy

1. Aeschylus, *Prometheus Bound*, in *Greek Tragedies*, vol. 1, trans. David Grene and ed. David Grene and Richmond Lattimore (Chicago and London: The University of Chicago Press, 1991), 65. Hereafter all references to *Prometheus Bound* will be to this edition and will be documented by page number in the text.
2. Anaximander, *Die Fragmente der Vorsokratiker*, trans. Rollo May, in Rollo May, *Love and Will* (New York: W. W. Norton & Co., 1969), 134.
3. T. S. Eliot, *Notes Toward a Definition of Culture*. (New York: Harcourt, Brace & Co., 1949), 16.
4. Aeschylus, *Agamemnon*, in *Greek Tragedies*, vol. 1, 44. Hereafter all references to *Agamemnon* will be to this edition and will be documented by page number in the text.
5. Jean-Pierre Vernant and Pierre Vidal-Naquet, *Myth and Tragedy in Ancient Greece* (New York: Zone Books, 1988), 263.

6. Vidal-Naquet, *Myth and Tragedy*, 740.
7. Vidal-Naquet, *Myth and Tragedy*, 116.
8. Paul Ricoeur, *Symbolism of Evil*, trans. Emerson Buchanan (New York: Harper & Row, 1967; reprint, Boston: Beacon Press, 1969), 27.
9. Sophocles, *Oedipus Rex*, in *Greek Tragedies*, vol. 1, 115. Hereafter all references to *Oedipus Rex* will be to this edition and will be documented by page number in the text.
10. Erich Neumann, *The Origins and History of Consciousness*, trans. R. F. C. Hull (Princeton: Princeton University Press, 1954) 307–12; Lévi-Strauss, "Structural Study," 91.
11. Ricoeur, *Symbolism*, 43, 44, 30.
12. Steiner, *Antigones*, 231.
13. Jean-Pierre Vernant, *Myth and Tragedy*, 41.
14. G. W. F. Hegel, *Aesthetics: Lectures on Fine Arts,* ed. and trans. T. M. Knox (Oxford: Clarendon Press, 1975), 1213.
15. Sophocles, *Antigone*, in *Greek Tragedies,* vol. 1, 198. Hereafter all references to *Antigone* will be to this edition and will be documented by page number in the text.
16. Jacques Derrida, *Glas,* trans. John P. Leavey, Jr. and Richard Rand (Lincoln and London: University of Nebraska Press), 143.
17. Girard, *Violence*, 57.
18. G. W. F. Hegel, *The Philosophy of Fine Art,* trans. F. P. B. Osmaston, in *Hegel on Tragedy,* ed. Anne and Henry Paolucci (Garden City, New York: Doubleday and Company, Inc., 1962), 73.
19. Steiner, *Symbolism,* 129.
20. George Meredith, "Modern Love," XLIII, in *Victorian Poetry and Poetics*, 2nd edition, ed. Walter E. Houghton and G. Robert Stange (New York: Houghton Mifflin Company, 1968), 645.
21. Euripides, *Hippolytus*, in *Greek Tragedies,* I:239. Hereafter all references to *Hippolytus* will be to this edition and will be documented by page number in the text.
22. Ralph Waldo Emerson, "Society and Solitude," in *The Complete Works of Ralph Waldo Emerson,* ed. Edward Waldo Emerson, 12 vols (Boston: Houghton Mifflin & Co., 1903–4), 7:15.
3. Hegel, *Philosophy*, 489.
24. Euripides, *Medea,* vol. 1, trans. Philip Vellacott, in *Literature of the Western World,* ed. Brian Wilkie and James Hurt (New York: Macmillan Publishing Company, 1992), 296. Hereafter all references to *Medea* will be to this edition and will be documented by page number in the text.

Chapter 3: In *Hamlet*

1. Hegel, *Philosophy*, 84, 86–87.
2. Hegel, *Philosophy,* 89, 25; *Aesthetics*, 583–84.
3. William Shakespeare, *Shakespeare: The Complete Works,* ed. G. B. Harrison (New York: Harcourt, Brace & World, 1952), 1.1.69. Hereafter all references to Shakespeare will be to this edition and will be documented by act, scene, and line numbers in the text.
4. Jacques Lacan, "Desire and the Interpretation of Desire in *Hamlet*," *Yale French Studies*, ed. Jacques-Alain Millter and trans. James Hulbert, 55–56 (1977), 31.
5. Ricoeur, *Symbolism,* 137–39.
6. Dylan Thomas, "A Refusal to Mourn the Death, by Fire, of a Child in London," *The Collected Poems of Dylan Thomas,* (New York: New Directions, 1957), 127.
7. See Janet Adelman's "'Man and wife is one flesh'; *Hamlet* and the Confrontation with the Maternal Body" in *Hamlet,* ed. Susanne T. Wofford (New York: Bedford Books,

1994), 256–82, for a similar examination of the effect of Gertrude's sexuality on Hamlet.
   8.   Anika LeClaire, *Jacques Lacan*, trans. D. Macey (London, 1977), in Muller, "Psychosis and Mourning," 155–56.
   9.   Muller, "Psychosis and Mourning," 150–51.

Chapter 4: In *King Lear*

   1.   *The Cloud of Unknowing*, ed. Clifton Wolters (Baltimore: Penquin Books, 1961), 61.
   2.   Pseudo-Dionysius Areopagite, *The Divine Names and Mystical Theology*, ed. and trans. John D. Jones (Milwaukee: Marquette University Press, 1980), 211.
   3.   John Caputo, *The Mystical Element in Heidegger's Thought*, (N. P., 1978), 14.
   4.   Juliana of Norwich, *Revelations of Divine Love Shewed to Mother Juliana of Norwich 1373* (London: Kegan Paul, Trench, Trubner & Co., 1902), 51, 195, 195.
   5.   Martin Heidegger, "What is Metaphysics?" in *Martin Heidegger: Existence and Being*, ed. Werner Brock and trans. R. F. C. Hull and Alan Crick (Chicago: Gateway Editions, 1967), 357, 335–36.
   6.   Heidegger, "Metaphysics," 336–39.
   7.   Jacob Johann Bachofen, *Myth, Religion and Mother Right*, trans. Ralph Manheim (Princeton: Princeton University Press, 1967), 143.

Chapter 5: In *Macbeth*

   1.   Steiner, *Antigones*, 26–27.
   2.   Douglas J. Canfield, *Word as Bond in English Literature from the Middle Ages to the Restoration* (Philadelphia: University of Pennsylvania Press, 1989), 191, 193.
   3.   Emile Durkheim, *The Elementary Forms of the Religious Life*, trans. Joseph Ward Swain (New York: The Free Press, 1965), 61.
   4.   Hegel, *Philosophy*, 504.

Chapter 6: In *Paradise Lost*

   1.   C. S. Lewis, *A Preface to Paradise Lost*, (New York: Oxford University Press Galaxy Book, 1961), 73–74.
   2.   John Milton, *Paradise Lost*, ed. Roy Flannagan (New York: Macmillan Publishing Company 1993), 2:891–96. Hereafter all references to *Paradise Lost* will be to this edition and will be documented by book and line number in the text.
   3.   Ricoeur, *Symbolism*, 156.
   4.   Norman O. Brown, *Love's Body*, (New York: Random House, 1966; New York: Vintage Books, 1966), 161.

Chapter 7: In *The Scarlet Letter*

   1.   Nathaniel Hawthorne, *The Scarlet Letter: An Authoritative Text, Essays in Criticism and Scholarship*, ed. Seymour Gross, et. al. (New York: W. W. Norton & Company, 1988), 54. Hereafter all references to *The Scarlet Letter* will be to this edition and will be

documented by page number in the text.
2. Ricoeur, *Symbolism*, 52.
3. Ibid., 146.
4. Sacvan Bercovitch, *The Puritan Origins of the American Self* (New Haven and London: Yale University Press, 1975), 15.
5. Ricoeur, *Symbolism*, 146.
6. Ibid., 151–57.
7. Benjamin, *Bonds*, 63–65.
8. Muller, "Psychosis and Mourning, " 151.
9. Benjamin, *Bonds*, 110.

Chapter 8: In *Moby Dick*

1. Herman Melville, *Moby Dick or The Whale* (Boston: Houghton Mifflin Company, 1956), 374. Hereafter all references to *Moby Dick* will be to this edition and will be documented by page number in the text.
2. Leslie Fiedler, *Love and Death in the American Novel* (New York: Criterion Books, 1960; reprint, Cleveland: World Publishing Co. Meridian Books, 1962), 329–70.
3. Foucault, *Order*, xvii.

Chapter 9: In *The Mayor of Casterbridge*

1. Thomas Hardy, *The Mayor of Casterbridge: An Authoritative Text, Backgrounds, Criticism*, ed. James K. Robinson (New York: W. W. Norton Company, Inc., 1977), 167. Hereafter all references to *The Mayor of Casterbridge* will be to this edition and will be documented by page number in the text.
2. Lucien Goldmann, *The Hidden God*, trans. Philip Thody (London: Routledge and Kegan Paul, 1976), quoted in *Tragedy*, John Drakakis and Naomi Conn Liebler, ed. (London and New York: Longman, 1998), 68.
3. John Holloway, "Hardy's Major Fiction," in Hardy, *The Mayor of Casterbridge*, 346.
4. Benjamin, *Bonds*, 62–63, 81.

Chapter 10: In *Tess of the d'Urbervilles*

1. Thomas Hardy, *Tess of the d'Urbervilles: An Authoritative Text, Hardy, and the Novel Criticism*, ed. Scott Elledge (New York: W. W. Norton & Company, 1979), 247. Hereafter all references to *Tess of the d'Urbervilles* will be to this edition and will be documented by page number in the text.
2. Dorothy Van Ghent, *The English Novel: Form and Function* (New York: Holt, Rinehart and Winston, 1953), 202.
3. Benjamin, *Bonds*, 62.
4. Jeannette King, *Tragedy in the Victorian Novel*, (Cambridge: Cambridge University Press, 1978), 19.
5. Florence Hardy, *The Early Life of Thomas Hardy*, (London: Studio Editions Ltd, 1994), 224.
6. Glen C. Wickens, "Hardy and the Aesthetic Mythographers: The Myth of Demeter

and Persephone in *Tess*," *University of Toronto Quarterly* 53:1 (Fall 1983), 105.

CHAPTER 11: IN *THE PORTRAIT OF A LADY*

1. Henry James, *The Portrait of a Lady: An Authoritative Text, Henry James, and the Novel Criticism*, ed. Robert D. Bamberg (New York: W. W. Norton & Company, Inc., 1975), 30. Hereafter all references to *The Portrait of a Lady* will be to this edition and will be documented by page number in the text.
2. Ezra Pound, "Brief Note," *Little Review* 5 (1918), 7 quoted in King, *Victorian Novel*, 67.
3. Henry James, Sr., *Society, The Redeemed Form of Man and The Earnest of God's Omnipotence in Human Nature, Affirmed in Letters to a Friend* (Boston: Houghton, Osgood & Co., 1879), 485, 430.
4. Jacques Lacan, *Ecrits: A Selection*, trans. Alan Sheridan (New York: W. W. Norton & Company, 1977), 1–7; "The Split Between the Eye and the Gaze," *The Four Fundamental Concepts of Psycho-Analysis*, ed. Jacques-Alain Miller and trans. Alan Sheridan (New York: W. W. Norton Company, 1978), 67–78.
5. Derrida, *Glas*, 148.

CHAPTER 12: IN *HEART OF DARKNESS*

1. Joseph Conrad, *Heart of Darkness: A Case Study in Contemporary Criticism*, ed. Ross C. Murfin (New York: St. Martin's Press, 1989) 50. Hereafter all references to *Heart of Darkness* will be to this edition and will be documented by page number in the text.
2. Nietzsche, *The Will to Power*, 386.
3. Heidegger, "What is Metaphysics," 357.
4. Lillian Feder, "Marlow's Descent into Hell," *Nineteenth-Century Fiction* 9 (March, 1955), 280–92, in Conrad, *Heart of Darkness,* 186–89; Robert O. Evans, "Conrad's Underworld," *Modern Fiction Studies* 2 (May, 1956), 56–62 in Conrad, *Heart of Darkness,* 191–93.
5. Carl. G. Jung, *Psyche and Symbol: A Selection of the Writings of C. G. Jung,* ed. Violet S. deLaszlo and trans. R. F. C. Hull and Cary Baynes (Garden City: New York: Doubleday Anchor Books, 1958), 1–60.

CHAPTER 13: IN *ABSALOM, ABSALOM!*

1. Henry James Sr., *Society*, 382, 430.
2. Hegel, *Philosophy,* 504.
3. Ralph Ellison, *Shadow and Act* (New York: Random House, 1964), 300; *Invisible Man* (New York: Random House, 1952), 436.
4. William Faulkner, *Absalom, Absalom!* (New York: Random House Vintage Books: 1990), 184. Hereafter all references to *Absalom, Absalom!* will be to this edition and will be documented by page number in the text.
5. Benjamin, *Bonds*, 81.
6. Hegel, *Phenomenology,* 238.
7. Derrida, *Glas,* 144, 164.
8. Ilse Dusoir Lind, quoted in David Lenson, *Achilles' Choice: Examples of Modern*

Tragedies (Princeton: Princeton University Press, 1975), 110.
   9.   T. S. Eliot, *The Complete Poems and Plays: 1909-1950* (New York: Harcourt, Brace & World, Inc., 1952), 118.
   10. Borch-Jacobsen, *Lacan*, 59.
   11. Vernant, *Myth and Tragedy*, 34.

CHAPTER 14: THE TRAGEDY OF BOND/AGE

   1.   Hegel, *Hegel on Tragedy*, 88-89.
   2.   King, *Victorian Novel*, 20.
   3.   Hegel, *Philosophy*, 387, 494.
   4.   Arthur Schopenhauer, quoted in Raymond Williams, *Modern Tragedy* (Stanford: Stanford University Press, 1966), 37.
   5.   Richard Sewall, *The Vision of Tragedy* (New York: Paragon House, 1990), 4-5; "The Tragic Form," in *Tragedy: Modern Essays in Criticism*, ed. Laurence Michel and Richard B. Sewall (Englewood Cliffs, N.J.: Prentice-Hall, 1963), 121.
   6.   Sewall, *Vision*, 69.
   7.   Raymond Williams, *Modern Tragedy*, (Stanford: Stanford University Press, 1966), 88.
   8.   Hegel, *Philosophy*, 494.
   9.   Steiner, *Antigones*, 261.
   10. Max Scheler, "On the Tragic," in *Tragedy: Modern Essays* , 34.
   11. Northrop Frye, *Anatomy of Criticism: Four Essays* (New York: Atheneum, 1968), 208.
   12. David Lenson, *Achilles' Choice: Examples of Modern Tragedies* (Princeton: Princeton University Press, 1975), 54, 160.
   13. Hegel, quoted in Steiner, *Antigones*, 30.
   14. Harold H. Watts, "Myth and Drama," in *Modern Essays*, 34.
   15. Vernant, *Myth and Tragedy*, 25.
   16. Frye, *Anatomy*, 71.
   17. Vernant, *Myth and Tragedy*, 37, 52.
   18. A. C. Bradley, "Hegel's Theory of Tragedy," *Oxford Lectures in Poetry* (London, 1950), 69-95 in Hegel, *Hegel on Tragedy*, 372.
   19. Lenson, *Achilles' Choice*, 161.
   20. Oscar Wilde, "The Critic as Artist," *The Artist as Critic: Critical Writings of Oscar Wilde,* ed. Richard Ellmann (1970), 383; in King, *Victorian Novel*, 60.
   21. Hegel, *Philosophy*, 494.
   22. Vernant, *Myth and Tragedy*, 82.
   23. Clifford Leech, "The Implications of Tragedy," in *Modern Essays*, 169.
   24. Hegel, *Aesthetics*, 1196.
   25. Vernant, *Myth and Tragedy*, 26.
   26. Nietzsche, *Will*, 450.
   27. Arthur Percival Rossiter, *Angel with Horns,* ed. Graham Storey (New York: Theatre Arts Books, 1961), 190.
   28. Scheler, "On the Tragic," 38-39.
   29. Vernant, *Myth and Tragedy*, 80.
   30. Sewall, "Form," 129.
   31. Frye, *Anatomy*, 212.
   32. Hegel, *Hegel on Tragedy*, 309.
   33. Karl Jaspers, *Tragedy is not Enough*, trans. Harold A. T. Reiche, Harry T. Moore,

and Karl W. Deutsch (N. P.: Archon Books, 1969), 13.

34. Murray Krieger, *The Tragic Vision: Variations on a Theme in Literary Interpretation* (Chicago and London: The University of Chicago Press, 1960), 145.

35. Williams, *Modern Tragedy*, 92.

36. Jaspers, *Tragedy,* 15.

37. George Steiner, *The Death of Tragedy* (New York: Alfred A. Knopf, 1961), 292, 298, 353.

38. Steiner, *Tragedy,* 292; Georg Lukacs, "The Metaphysics of Tragedy," *Soul and Form*, trans. Anna Bostock (London 1974) quoted in *Tragedy*, ed. John Drakakis and Naomi Conn Liebler (London: Longman, 1998), 11.

39. Steiner, *Tragedy*, 354.

40. Walter Benjamin, *The Origins of German Tragic Drama*, trans. John Osborne (London: NLB, 1977), 107–8.

41. Lenson, *Achilles'*, 167.

42. T. S. Eliot, "Burnt Norton," *Four Quartets* in *T. S. Eliot: The Complete Poems and Plays* (London: Faber and Faber, 1969), 175.

43. Jaspers, *Tragedy*, 15.

Bibliography

Adelman, Janet. "'Man and wife is one flesh': *Hamlet* and the Confrontation with the Maternal Body." In *Hamlet*, edited by Susanne T. Wofford. New York: Bedford Books, 1984.

Aeschylus. *Agamemnon*. In *Greek Tragedies*, vol. 1, edited by David Grene and Richmond Lattimore and translated by Richmond Lattimore, 1–60. Chicago and London: The University of Chicago Press, 1991.

———. *Prometheus Bound*. In *Greek Tragedies,* vol. 1, edited by David Grene and Richmond Lattimore and translated by Richmond Lattimore, 61–108. Chicago and London: The University of Chicago Press, 1991.

Anaximander. *Die Fragmente der Vorsokratiker*. In *Love and Will* by Rollo May. New York: W. W. Norton & Co., 1969.

Aristotle. *Poetics*. In *Criticism: The Major Texts,* edited by Walter Jackson Bate, 19–38. New York: Harcourt, Brace and Company, 1952.

Bakhtin, Mikhail. "From Discourse in the Novel." In *The Critical Tradition: Classical Texts and Contemporary Trends,* edited by David Richter, 781–90. New York: St. Martin's Press, 1989.

Barthes, Roland. "From Work to Text." In *The Critical Tradition: Classic Texts and Contemporary Trends,* edited by David H. Richter, 1006–9. New York: St. Martin's Press, 1989.

Bachofen, Johann Jacob. *Myth, Religion and Mother Right*. Translated by Ralph Manheim. Princeton: Princeton University Press, 1967.

Benjamin, Jessica. *The Bonds of Love: Psychoanalysis, Feminism, and the Problem of Domination.* New York: Pantheon Books, 1988.

Benjamin, Walter. *The Origin of German Tragic Drama*. Translated by John Osborne. London: NLB, 1977.

Bercovitch, Sacvan. *The Puritan Origins of the American Self.* New Haven and London: Yale University Press, 1975.

Borch-Jacobsen, Mikkel. *Lacan: The Absolute Master.* Translated by Douglas Brick. Stanford, Calif.: Stanford University Press, 1991.

Bradley, A. C. "Hegel's Theory of Tragedy." In *Hegel on Tragedy, Oxford Lectures in Poetry,* edited by Anne and Henry Paolucci. Garden City, N.Y.: Doubleday and Company, Inc., 1962.

Brooks, Peter. "Freud's Masterplot." In *The Critical Tradition: Classical Texts and Contemporary Trends,* edited by David H. Richter, 710–20. New York: St. Martin's Press, 1989.

Brown, Norman O. *Love's Body.* New York: Random House. Reprinted, New York: Vintage Books, 1966.

Canfield, J. Douglas. *Word as Bond in English Literature from the Middle Ages to the Restoration.* Philadelphia: University of Pennsylvania Press, 1989.

Caputo, John. *The Mystical Element in Heidegger's Thought.* N. P., 1978.

Cixous, Hélène. "The Laugh of the Medusa." In *The Critical Tradition: Classic Texts and Contemporary Trends,* edited by David H. Richter. New York: St. Martin's Press, 1989.

The Cloud of Unknowing. Edited by Clifton Wolters. Baltimore: Penquin Books, 1961.

Conrad, Joseph. *Heart of Darkness: A Case Study in Contemporary Criticism.* Edited by Ross C. Murfin. New York: St. Martin's Press, 1989.

Derrida, Jacques. *Glas.* Translated by John P. Leavey, Jr. and Richard Rand. Lincoln and London: University of Nebraska Press, 1986.

———. *Structure, Sign, and Play in the Discourse of the Human Sciences.* In *The Critical Tradition: Classic Texts and Contemporary Trends,* edited by David H. Richter, 959–70. New York: St. Martin's Press, 1989.

Detienne, Marcel and Jean-Pierre Vernant. *Cunning Intelligence in Greek Culture and Society.* Translated by Janet Lloyd. Sussex, England: The Harvester Press and New Jersey: Humanities Press, 1978.

Dillon, M. C. *Merleau-Ponty's Ontology.* Bloomington: Indiana University Press, 1988.

Durkheim, Emile. *The Elementary Forms of the Religious Life.* Translated by Joseph Ward Swain. New York: The Free Press, 1965.

Eliade, Mircea. *Images and Symbols: Studies in Religious Symbolism.* Translated by Philip Mairet. New York: Sheed & Ward and London Harvill Press, 1961. Reprinted, New York: Sheed & Ward Search Book, 1969.

Eliot, T. S. *T. S. Eliot: The Complete Poems and Plays.* London: Faber and Faber, 1969.

———. *The Complete Poems and Plays: 1909–1950.* New York: Harcourt, Brace & World, Inc., 1952.

———. *Notes Toward a Definition of Culture.* New York: Harcourt, Brace & Co., 1949.

———. "Tradition and the Individual Talent." In *The Critical Tradition: Classic Texts and Contemporary Trends,* edited by David Richter. New York: St. Martin's Press, 1989.

Ellison, Ralph. *Invisible Man.* New York: Random House, 1952.

———. *Shadow and Act.* New York: Random House, 1964.

Emerson, Ralph Waldo. "Society and Solitude." In *The Complete Works of Ralph Waldo Emerson,* vol. 7, edited by Edward Waldo Emerson, 12 vols. Boston: Houghton Mifflin & Co., 1903–4.

Euripides. *Hippolytus.* In *Greek Tragedies,* vol. 1, edited by David Grene and Richmond Lattimore and translated by David Grene, 233–95. Chicago and London: The University of Chicago Press, 1991.

———. *Medea.* In *Literature of the Western World,* vol. 1, edited by Brian Wilkie and James Hurt and translated by Philip Vellacott, 853–85. New York: Macmillan Publishing Company, 1992.

Evans, Robert O. "Conrad's Underworld." *Modern Fiction Studies* 2 (May, 1956): 56–62. Reprinted in *Heart of Darkness: An Authoritative Text, Backgrounds and Sources, Essays in Criticism,* edited by Robert Kimbrough, 189–94. New York: W. W. Norton & Company, Inc., 1963.

Faulkner, William. *Absalom, Absalom!* New York: Random House: Vintage Books, 1990.

Feder, Lillian. "Marlow's Descent into Hell." *Nineteenth-Century Fiction* 9 (March, 1955): 280–92. Reprinted in *Heart of Darkness: Authoritative Text, Backgrounds and Sources, Essays in Criticism,* edited by Robert Kimbrough, 186–89. New York: W. W. Norton & Company, Inc., 1963.

Fiedler, Leslie. *Love and Death in the American Novel.* New York: Criterion Books, 1960. Reprinted, Cleveland: World Publishing Co. Meridian Books, 1962.

Foucault, Michel. *The Order of Things: An Archaeology of the Human Sciences.* New York: Pantheon Books, 1970.

Freud, Sigmund. *Beyond the Pleasure Principle.* In *The Freud Reader,* edited by Peter Gay, 594–625. New York: W. W. Norton & Company, 1989.

———. *Totem and Taboo and Other Works.* In *The Standard Edition of the Complete Psychological Works of Sigmund Freud,* vol. 13, edited by James Strachey and translated by Joan Riviere. London: Hogarth Press, 1955.

———. "The 'Uncanny.'" In *Collected Papers,* vol. 4, edited by Ernest Jones and translated by Joan Riviere. London: Hogarth Press and The Institute of Psychoanalysis, 1924–50. Reprinted, New York: Basic Books, 1959.

Frye, Northrop. *Anatomy of Criticism: Four Essays.* New York: Atheneum, 1968.

Goldmann, Lucien. *The Hidden God.* Translated by Philip Thody. London: Routledge and Kegan Paul, 1976.

Hardy, Florence. *The Early Life of Thomas Hardy,* London: Studio Editions Ltd, 1994.

Hardy, Thomas. *The Mayor of Casterbridge: An Authoritative Text, Backgrounds, Criticism.* Edited by James K. Robinson. New York: W. W. Norton & Company, 1979.

———. *Tess of the d'Urbervilles: An Authoritative Text, Hardy, and the Novel Criticism.* Edited by Scott Elledge. New York: W. W. Norton & Company, 1979.

Hawthorne, Nathaniel. *The Scarlet Letter: An Authoritative Text, Essays in Criticism and Scholarship.* Edited by Seymour Gross, et.al. New York: W. W. Norton & Company, 1988.

Hegel, G. W. F. *Aesthetics: Lectures on Fine Art.* Edited and translated by T. M. Knox. Oxford: Clarendon Press, 1975.

———. *Hegel on Tragedy.* Edited by Anne and Henry Paolucci. Garden City, New York: Doubleday and Company, Inc., 1962.

———. *The Phenomenology of Mind.* Edited and translated by J. B. Baillie. London: George Allen & Unwin Ltd, 1910.

Heidegger, Martin. "What is Metaphysics?" In *Martin Heidegger: Existence and Being,* edited by Werner Brock and translated by R.F. C. Hull and Alan Crick. Chicago: Gateway Editions, 1967.

Heller, Erich. *The Artist's Journey into the Interior and Other Essays.* New York: Random House, 1965.

Henn, T. R. *Harvest of Tragedy.* New York: Barnes & Noble Inc., 1969.

Holloway, John. *The Chartered Mirror: Literary and Critical Essays.* London: Routledge and Kegan Paul Ltd., 1960. In *The Mayor of Casterbridge: An Authoritative Text Backgrounds Criticism,* edited by James K. Robinson, 342–45. New York: W. W. Norton Company, 1977.

James, Henry. *The Portrait of a Lady: An Authoritative Text, Henry James and the Novel*

Criticism. Edited by Robert D. Bamberg. New York: W. W. Norton & Company, Inc., 1975.

James, Henry, Sr. *Society: The Redeemed Form of Man, and The Earnest of God's Omnipotence in Human Nature: Affirmed in Letters to a Friend.* Boston: Houghton, Osgood & Com., 1879.

Jaspers, Karl. *Tragedy is Not Enough.* Translated by Harold A. T. Reiche, Harry T. Moore, and Karl W. Deutsch. N. P.: Archon Books, 1969.

Juliana of Norwich. *Revelations of Divine Love Shewed to Mother Juliana of Norwich 1373.* London: Kegan Paul, Trench, Trubner & Co., 1902.

Jung, Carl. G. *Psyche and Symbol: A Selection of the Writings of C. G. Jung.* Edited by Violet S. deLaszlo and translated by R. F. C. Hull and Cary Baynes. Garden City: New York: Doubleday Anchor Books, 1958.

King, Jeanette. *Tragedy and the Victorian Novel.* Cambridge: Cambridge University Press, 1978.

Krieger, Murray. *The Tragic Vision: Variations on a Theme in Literary Interpretation.* Chicago and London: The University of Chicago Press. 1960.

Lacan, Jacques. "Desire and the Interpretation of Desire in *Hamlet.*" In *Yale French Studies,* edited by Jacques-Alain Millter and translated by James Hulbert, vol. 55/56 (1977): 11–52.

———. *Ecrits: A Selection.* Translated by Alan Sheridan. New York: W. W. Norton & Company, 1977.

———. *Les complexes familiaux dans la formation de l'individu.* Paris: Navarin Editeur, 1984.

———. *The Four Fundamental Concepts of Psycho-Analysis.* Edited by Jacques-Alain Miller and translated by Alan Sheridan. New York: W. W. Norton & Company, 1978.

Leech, Clifford. "The Implications of Tragedy." In *Tragedy: Modern Essays in Criticism,* edited by Laurence Michel and Richard B. Sewall, 161–74. Englewood Cliffs, N.J.: Prentice Hall, Inc., 1963.

Lenson, David. *Achilles' Choice: Examples of Modern Tragedies.* Princeton: Princeton University Press, 1975.

Lévi-Strauss, Claude. "The Structural Study of Myth." In *Myth: A Symposium,* edited by Thomas A. Sebeok, 81–106. Bloomington and London: Indiana University Press, 1972.

Lewis, C. S. Preface to *Paradise Lost.* New York: Oxford University Press Galaxy Book, 1961.

Lukacs, Georg. "The Metaphysics of Tragedy." In *Soul and Form,* translated by Anna Bostock. London: 1974. Reprinted in *Tragedy,* edited by John Drakakis and Naomi Conn Liebler. London: Longman, 1998.

Melville, Herman. *Moby Dick or The Whale.* Boston: Houghton Mifflin Company, 1956.

Meredith, George. "Modern Love." In *Victorian Poetry and Poetics*, 2d ed., edited by Walter E. Houghton and G. Robert Stange, 936–45. New York: Houghton Mifflin Company, 1968.

Miller, J. Hillis. *Ariadne's Thread: Story Lines.* New Haven and London: Yale University Press, 1992.

Milton, John. *Paradise Lost.* Edited by Roy Flannagan. New York: Macmillan Publishing Company, 1993.

Muller, John P. "Psychosis and Mourning In Lacan's Ha*mlet*." *New Literary History* 12 (1980): 147–65.

Neumann, Erich. *The Origins and History of Consciousness*. Translated by R. F. C. Hull. Princeton: Princeton University Press, 1954.

Nietzsche. Friedrich. *The Birth of Tragedy*. In *Basic Writings of Nietzsche,* edited and translated by Walter Kaufmann, 4–146. New York: The Modern Library, 1966.

———. *The Will to Power.* Edited by Walter Kaufmann and translated by Walter Kaufmann and R. J. Hollingdale. New York: Random House, 1967.

Pound, Ezra. "Brief Note." *Little Review*, 5 (1918). Reprinted in *Tragedy and the Victorian Novel,* Jeanette King. Cambridge: Cambridge University Press, 1978.

Pseudo-Dionysius Areopagite. *The Divine Names and Mystical Theology*. Edited and translated by John D. Jones. Milwaukee, Wisc.: Marquette University Press, 1980.

Ricoeur, Paul. *Symbolism of Evil*. Translated by Emerson Buchanan. New York: Harper & Row, 1967. Reprinted, Boston: Beacon Press, 1969.

Rossiter, Arthur Percival. *Angel with Horns*. Edited by Graham Storey. New York: Theatre Arts Books, 1961.

Scheler. Max. "On the Tragic." In *Tragedy: Modern Essays in Criticism,* edited by Laurence Michel and Richard B. Sewall, 27–44. Englewood Cliffs, NJ: Prentice-Hall, Inc., 1963.

Sewall, Richard B. "The Tragic Form." In *Tragedy: Modern Essays in Criticism,* edited by Laurence Michel and Richard B. Sewall, 117–80. Englewood Cliffs, NJ: Prentice-Hall, 1963.

———. *The Vision of Tragedy*. New York: Paragon House, 1990.

Shakespeare, William. *Shakespeare: The Complete Works*. Edited by G. B. Harrison. New York: Harcourt, Brace & World, 1952.

Sophocles. *Antigone*. In *Greek Tragedie,* vol. 1, edited by David Grene and Richmond Lattimore and translated by David Grene, 177–232. Chicago and London: The University of Chicago Press, 1991.

———. *Oedipus Rex*. In *Greek Tragedies,* vol. 1, edited by David Grene and Richmond Lattimore and translated by David Grene, 107–76. Chicago and London: The University of Chicago Press, 1991.

Steiner, George. *Antigones: How the Antigone Legend has Endured in Western Literature, Art, and Thought*. New York: Oxford University Press, 1984.

———. *The Death of Tragedy*. New York: Alfred A. Knopf, 1961.

Thomas, Dylan. *The Collected Poems of Dylan Thomas*. New York: New Directions, 1957.

Tragedy. Edited by John Drakakis and Naomi Conn Liebler. London: Longman, 1998.

Van Ghent, Dorothy. *The English Novel: Form and Function*. New York: Holt, Rinehart and Winston, 1953.

Vernant, Jean-Pierre and Pierre Vidal-Naquet. *Myth and Tragedy In Ancient Greece*. New York: Zone Books, 1988.

Watts, Harold H. "Myth and Drama." In *Tragedy: Modern Essays in Criticism,* edited by Laurence Michel and Richard B. Sewall, 83–105. Englewood Cliffs, NJ: Prentice-Hall Inc., 1963.

Wickens, Glen C. "Hardy and the Aesthetic Mythographers: The Myth of Demeter and Persephone in *Tess.*" *University of Toronto Quarterly* (Fall 1983): 85–106.

Wilde, Oscar. "The Critic as Artist." In *The Artist as Critic: Critical Writings of Oscar Wilde,* edited by Richard Ellmann. Reprinted in *Tragedy in the Victorian Novel* by Jeanette King. Cambridge: Cambridge University Press, 1978.

Williams, Raymond. *Modern Tragedy.* Stanford, Calif.: Stanford University Press, 1966.

Woolf, Virginia. "Shakespeare's Sister From *A Room of One's Own.*" In *The Critical Tradition: Classic Texts and Contemporary Trends*, edited by David Richter. New York: St. Martin's Press, 1989.

Index

Adrasteia, 12
Aeschylus: *Oresteia*, 30; *Prometheus Bound*, 25–27, 154–55; and Shakespeare, 54, 56; and Sophocles, 21, 31; tragic bond/age in *Agamemnon*, 27–30, 41, 154–55
Allecto, 12
Anaximander: penance of separation, 25
Aphrodite, 13, 39; Hippolytus's neglect of, 39; Phaedre, as agent of, 39
Apollo, 13
Apollonian: bondage, 62; dominion, 165; goddesses, 154; individuation, 21, 32, 81; in *Macbeth*, 72; patriarchal, 136; perception, 99; spirit, 41
Ares, 13
Aristotle: on denouement, 11–12; on music in tragedy, 172
Artemis, 28–29; Hippolytus's devotion to, 39; in *Tess*, 118
Atropos, 12

Bachofen: *Myth, Religion and Mother Right*, 58
Bakhtin, Mikhail: on dialectical discourse, 22
Being, 62; borders of, 162; crime against, 159, 166; embodiment of, 99; evolution from, 154; hermeneutics as separation from, 168; house of, 36; and human beingness, 155, 161, 172; just precincts of, 167; justice of, 165; of Lacan, 15; paradise of, 162; purity of, 33; recognition of, 156, 169; restraint of, 162; rupture in, 166; separation from, 35, 135, 168; and speech, 22; static, 15; vengeance of, 135, 160; violation of, 160–61, 167–68, 171, 199, 204
Benjamin, Jessica: on absent father, 90; on domination of master, 19, 113, 144; on master/servant balance, 109; on narcississtic nostalgia, 15; on sado-masochism, 88
Benjamin, Walter: on silence and tragedy, 171–72
Bercovitch, Sacvan: on *auto-machia*, 87
binding: of body politic, 166; of Hamlet, 47; of hero, 32, 45; infantile, 14; leitmotif of, 36, 172; Ophelia as agent of, 45; paternity as, 53–54; power of, 13; of protagonist, 24; self-, 103
bond(s), 92; according to, 33; adjacencies and, 16; in Antigone, 31, 33, 36; beneficiary of, 24; of blood, 114; to blood brother, 33; and bondage, 12, 19, 24, 74, 102, 165; breaking of, 102; of brother and sister, 128; of child and father, 55; of childhood, 55; to chthonic, 21; circular, 13; of citizenship, 163; of corn, 115; cracked, 56; customary, 84; denial of, 20, 99; Dionysian, 21; dissolves a, 167; to earth, 19; of economic relief, 114; epitomy of, 13; of existence, 121; extension of, 165; familial, 12, 27, 30, 34, 105, 114, 133, 155, 167; fatalistic, 12; of father and son, 51, 163; first, 103–4, 112, 157–58; forsaking all, 82; with fortune, 105; of fraternity and sorority, 153; of God, 79; great, 66; in Greek culture, 13; of Hamlet and Ophelia, 48; of hand, 14; Hephaestus's, 13; Hester's, 84, 88; human, 56; of ignorance, 130; of indissoluble bronze, 25; Isabel's, 127–28; of king and subject, 48; of kinship, 33; legitimate, 142; leitmotifs of, 172; of life, 22; between lovers, 48; marriage, 12, 40;

187

matriarchal, 89; of matrimony, 126; of men and women, 12; as *metis*, 13, 162; more in, 125; of mother and son, 163; of nature, 79; Oedipus's, 32; Ophelia's, 46; parental, 55, 86; of paternity, 105; penal, 83; pious, 47; to primitive man, 134; in question, 63; real, 89; redefined, 121; redemption from, 56; of Renaissance order, 16; restoration of, 24; of reunion, 111; rooted, 36; of sea, 133; with self, 77; self-identifying, 165; -slave, 84; sleep as, 68; social, 12, 16–17, 58; of sorority, 47, 128–29; soul-saving, 94; special, 124; subtle, 137; in *Tess*, 111; of world and language, 22; unbreakable, 25; to unborn, 70; violation of, 35, 39, 81, 86, 154; word as, 102, 104, 106, 111, 167–68

bondage, 76, 146; in *Absalom*, 145; Apollonian, 14, 62; Babylonian, 87; of birth, 32; and bonds, 19, 24, 74; of business, 58; casting into, 134; of chthonic, 25, 80; and consciousness, 27, 76; cosmic, 12; of darkness, 27, 37, 130; Dimmesdale's, 86; of domesticity, 103; of eros, 37; eternal, 80, 146; to family, 103, 112, 114; of father, 17; fear of, 93; freedom from, 165, 167; goddess of terrible, 20, 127; and *Hamlet*, 45, 50; of handclasp, 14, 83; Henchard's, 102; hermeneutics and, 20, 131; of House of Atreus, 27; human, 79, 97, 126; idle, 55; image of, 56; of Incarnation, 80; individuated, 21; infernal, 81; infinite, 80; instrument of, 13; Isabel's, 129–30; of language, 21; of law of Zeus, 25; in *Macbeth*, 66; marriage as, 32, 103, 124–25; matriarchal, 16; in nature, 25; necessary, 27; of past, 139; patriarchal, 16, 121, 153; of patrimony, 56; penal, 84; phallogocentric, 24; physical, 130; in *Portrait*, 130; prostitution as, 114; psychological, 130; punishment of, 101; rejection of, 19; of self-consciousness, 26; sexual, 17; of single meaning, 23; sister-in-, 128; of slavery, 153; of social convention, 116; source of, 15, 21; strictest, 76; symbol of, 85; of terrible sovereignty, 14; Tess's sacrifice in, 111; threadlike, 13; threads of, 39; and tradition, 63; transference of, 157; victim of, 24, 75; and woman, 30, 39; world of, 162; woven, 96; of Zeus, 25

bond/age: common law, 118; cosmic, 12; and defilement, 33; definition of, 24; Dionysian, 62; domestic, 170–71, 196; doomed 148; eternal, 145; of European society, 133; of external world, 42; free of, 168; of Gertrude, 49–50, 53; heavenly, 81; human, 89, 99, 107, 122, 155, 167, 184; in internal world, 42; moral ambiguity of, 167; necessity of, 24, 168; net of, 110; netted by, 13, 110; orchestration of, 171; as pavane, 170; resisting, 78; self-, 75–76; self-identifying, 131; social measure of, 159; of terrible sovereignty, 14; Tess's, 114; tragedy of, 33, 154–72; of tragic necessity, 95; as un/consciousness, 130–31

Borch-Jacobsen, Mikkel: on Lacan's mirror state, 15

boundary(ies): of Being, 161; of existence, 162; of familiar, 135; forbidden, 138; of gender, 43–44; in *Hamlet*, 43, 45, 49; in *King Lear*, 56; in modern tragedy, 161; of nature, 44; in *Paradise Lost*, 73–82, 156; rupture of, 166; of social integrity 161; of social order, 163; of society, 43, 159

Bradley, A. C.: on Hegelian bonds, 163
Brown, Norman O.: on Dionysus in *Love's Body*, 81

Canfield, J. Douglas: on Freud and *Macbeth*, 71
Cassandra, 145
chain(s), 24, 84, 109, 133–34; adamantine, 76, 84; of being, 16, 56, 74, 161; that bind, 84, 154; breakable, 37; broken, 87; of communal sin, 89; connecting, 134; of darkness, 76; electric, 89; in Greek tragedy, 154; in *Moby Dick*, 103; in *Oedipus*, 32; Prometheus's, 37; Renaissance, 43; suspended in, 95; world's, 164

chthonic, 78, 165; beginning, 79; bound to, 21; confinement, 124–25, 170; connection, 158; crawling, 159; nature, 174; origins, 99, 134; return to, 60, 138;

roots, 14, 138, 166–67; separation from, 27; traces of, 155; transcendence of, 22, 25, 74, 89, 107, 122, 133, 156, 159

Cixous, Hélène: *The Laugh of the Medusa* and the canon, 23

Clotho, 12

compulsion to repeat, 59, 87, 88, 106, 109, 129, 147, 155, 157–58, 168

Conrad, Joseph: tragic bond/age in *Heart of Darkness*, 132–40, 159–60

cord(s): that bind, 146, 148; that connects and inhibits, 41; familial, 17, 20, 156; first, 14; holy, 20; linguistic, 22; natural, 12, 20; psychological, 22; umbilical, 14, 148; woven, 93

Darzales, 12

Demeter, 118, 120

deracination, 110, 119; in *Antigone*, 36; bond/age as, 156; in gothic fiction, 157; of Io, 26; of Jason and Medea, 41; labyrinth of, 166; in *Macbeth*, 64, 66, 72, 156; in *Mayor*, 110; from place, 20

Derrida, Jacques: on Lévi-Strauss, 23; on Hegel, 34, 128, 149

Detienne, Marcel: on *metis*, 13, 162

Dickinson, Emily: Isabel Archer and, 121

difference: deconstructive, 23; in Foucault, 16; in *King Lear*, 56–57; and social order, 17–18; violation of, 17, 144

Dike, 21

Dionysian: and Apollonian tension, 82; bondage, 62; communion, 21, 165–68; dark, 136; goddesses, 154; hero, 150; impulse, 81; integration, 81; mask, 99; oneness, 32; power, 99; spirit, 41; tension, 82

Dionysus, 81; and catharsis, 26; masks of, 21; and Nietzsche's theory, 21

disinheritance, 164, 168; in *Absalom*, 142; in *Antigone*, 36; and bond/age, 168; crime of, 163; of daughter, 104; in gothic fiction, 157; in *Macbeth*, 72, 156; in *Mayor*, 108, 110; in Shakespeare, 166

Durkheim, Emile: magic and *Macbeth*, 78

Eliade, Mircea: integrity of universe, 19; invisible web of world, 16; nets and knots, 13–14; religious symbol of knots, 12

Eliot, George, 114

Eliot, T. S.: on bond of family, 27; on bond to unborn, 70; on canon, 23; on dissociation of sensibility, 39, 117; on might-have-been, 151; on music and silence, 172; *Notes Towards a Defintion of Culture*, 27

Ellison, Ralph: invisible man in *Absalom, Absalom!*, 143; on search for identity, 141, 147

Emerson, Ralph Waldo: Isabel Archer and, 121, 125; on society and solitude, 38

Erinyes, 12–13

eros: in Antigone, 34; and Eumenides, 13, 87; Hamlet bound by, 52; net of, 34; and thanatos, 20, 38

Euripides: splitting of tragic hero, 157; tragic bond/age in *Hippolytus*, 34–37, 154–55; *Medea*, 37–40, 154–55

Eurydice, 117, 120

Evans, Robert: on Dante and *Heart of Darkness*, 136

fabric(ation): burning, 154; of existence, 17, 160–61, 170; of experience, 90; in *Hamlet*, 53; language as, 32; of signification, 16; social, 17

family, 163; acquisition of, 142–43; Archer, 122; bond of, 27, 105, 114, 142; and bondage, 103, 112, 114; commitment to, 91; cords, 156; crimes against, 158; curse, 119, 121; difference within, 17; disinherit, 147; and domestic tragedy, 163–64; flower, 66; freedom from, 121; in *Hamlet*, 50; in Lévi-Strauss, 18; as limitation, 141; name, 116; as network, 17; nuclear, 164; redefinition of, 158; rejection of, 143; and roots, 110; in Shakespeare, 155; situation of, 169; and state, 163; ties, 170; tree, 66; unit, 99; uprooted by, 120; violation of, 28

Faulkner, William: and modern American drama, 170; *The Sound and the Fury*, 170; tragic bond/age in *Absalom, Absalom!*, 141–53, 159–60

Feder, Lillian: on Aeneas and *Heart of Darkness*, 136

INDEX

Fiedler, Leslie: on *heirogamous* relationship, 92
Foucault, Michel: on integrity 19; *The Order of Things*, 16; and rift in order, 160; table of, 95–96
fraternity: bonds of, 153; in *Hamlet*, 49, 53–54; restorative, 53–54, 165; viable, 165
Freud, Sigmund: ambivalence, 81; compulsion to repeat, 20; and Hegel, 34; and Lacan, 14; on thanatos and eros, 20; *Totem and Taboo*, 17–18, 77; on uncanny, 20
Frye, Northrup: on epiphany of law, 169; on tragic hero, 162–63

Gaia, 13
Girard, René: on difference, 13, 17–18, 35, 49, 71, 144
Goldmann, Lucien, on tragic hero, 106

handclasp: in *Absalom, Absalom!*, 148; in bond/age, 14; in gothic fiction, 157; in *Hippolytus*, 38; in *Moby Dick*, 91–100; in *Paradise Lost*, 77–80, 156; in *Scarlet Letter*, 83–84, 89; in tragedy, 165
Hardy, Thomas: and George Eliot, 132; *Jude the Obscure*, 157–58; tragic bond/age in *The Mayor of Casterbridge*, 101–11, 158, *Tess of the d'Urbervilles*, 111–26, 158
Hawthorne, Nathaniel: and Milton, 84; tragic bond/age in *The Scarlet Letter*, 92–102, 157
Hegel, G. W. F.: on *Antigone*, 33, 36, 128, 150; on bond/age of woman, 149; on essence of tragedy, 161, 167, 169; on ethical one-sidedness, 38; on fragmentation of spirit, 18; *geist* in world, 160; on *Hamlet*, 42; on individuation, 149; on integrity, 165; on *Kriegstatt and Privatrecht*, 70; on master and bondsman, 19, 72, 109, 144; on Shakespearean tragedy, 42, 155; on tragic hero, 162, 165; on unreal self, 141
Heidegger, Martin, 157; on nothingness, 56; on uncanny man, 19–21
Henn, Thomas: on tragic plots and nets, 11–12, 98–99
Hephaestus, 13

hermeneutics, 159; failure of, 66, 158, 168; as liberation, 20
Holloway, John: on Henchard and animals, 107
Horae, 12

individuation, 100, 107; Apollonian, 21; impediments to, 14, 31; network of, 26; requirements of, 17; restriction of, 22
integrity, 163; of city, 35; of familial bond, 155; Jungian, 100; of kingdom, 46; Nietzchean, 100; religious, 152; Satan's, 82; social, 161; and tragedy, 63, 162, 165, 170; and tragic bondage, 161–63; unthought, 16; violation of, 165; of weave, 152; world of, 20, 171

James, Henry: and George Eliot, 114; realism in, 171; tragic bond/age in *The Portrait of a Lady*, 121–31, 158–59
James, Henry, Sr.: on individuality and identity, 122, 141, 147
Jaspers, Karl: on tragedy and transcendence, 172
Jung, Carl: on individuation, 100, 103; on mind of man, 135; on shadow, 137

King, Jeanette: on Henry James, 114; on realism and tragedy, 159 on tragic hero, 109
kinship: in Antigone, 33; claims of, 13, 105–6, 111–14, 116, 118, 156–58; conflicting threads of, 155; crime against, 28, 64, 103, 106, 109, 112, 154–55, 163–64, 166–68; and defilement, 39; delicate cadences of, 154; denial of, 104, 141, 143; distant, 137; in *King Lear*, 155–56; in *Moby Dick*, 91–93; new, 100; New England, 121; newly discovered, 114; Ophelia and, 48; patriarchal, 90; redefinition of, 91–92, 157, 165; remote, 137; restraints of, 44; as secret sharing, 137; in *Tess*, 111, 115, 120; tribal connections and, 111
knot(s): of bondage, 27; figurative, 16; in *Hamlet*, 48; inextricable, 39, 86–87; that inhibits, 19; of passion, 37; round neck, 37; that protect, 14; tragic, 162;

of tragic bond/age, 86
Kore, 118, 120
Krieger, Murray: on modern tragedy, 169–70

Lacan, Jacques: on *désir de la mère*, 15, 43, 54, 59, 109, 117; on desire, 118; on foreclosure and *Hamlet*, 52; on gaze, 126; on mirror stage, 15, 47, 152; on *le-nom-du-père*, 15, 43, 52, 54, 59, 109, 117; on *objet petit â,* 90; on phallus, 90; reappropriation of Freud, 14–15; on uncanny, 15
Lachesis, 12
language: and *aporia*, 23; as bondage, 24; bonds and binds, 21–23; carpet of, 22–23; dialectic on, 23; as fabric, 21; introduction to, 15; as loom, 22–23; prison house of, 23; snared in, 22; transcends chthonic, 22; weave of, 24
Leclaire, Anika: on repression and foreclosure, 52
Leech, Clifford: on justice in tragedy, 165–66
Leitmotifs, 150, 65, 94, 172; of babe, 64; of banquet, 27–29, 64, 66–72, 156, 165; of circle, 13, 33, 62, 71, 74, 86, 117, 134, 162, 172; of darkness, 37, 76, 130, 139, 166, 168; of discontent-(ment), 21, 38, 86,158; of fire, 25, 40, 162; of gaze, 83–84, 88, 126; of harness, 12–13, 154–55; of labyrinth, 14, 23, 47, 114, 123, 166; of loom, 22–23, 170–71; of mirror, 47–48, 72; of nothing(ness), 57–58, 61, 156, 171; of shadow, 60, 69, 94–95, 137, 138, 143, 147; of vegetation, 64
Lenson, David: on paradox of tragedy, 163; on silence and catharsis, 172; on tragic hero, 162
Lévi-Strauss, Claude: on chthonic, 21, 33; on familial, 49; on Oedipus, 18; on reading myth, 223
Lewis, C. S.: on hierarchy in *Paradise Lost*, 73
Lind, Ilse Dusoir: on chorus in *Absalom, Absalom!*, 150
Lukacs, Georg: on realism and tragedy, 171

matriarchy: in *Lear*, 58–59; in *Scarlet Letter*, 90; in *Tess*, 111, 119
Megaera, 12
Melville, Herman: and silence, 172; splitting of tragic hero, 157; tragic bond/age in *Moby Dick*, 91–100, 157
Meredith, George: on tragic life, 37
Merleau-Ponty, Maurice: on language as transformation, 22
Michelangelo, 25
Miller, Arthur: *Death of a Salesman*, 170–71
Milton, John: and Hawthorne, 84, 159; and hierarchy, 161; and Shakespeare, 172; and suffering, 166; and tragedy, 101; tragic poetry of, 159; tragic bond/age in *Paradise Lost*, 73–82, 101, 156–57
Morae, 12
Muller, John: on *Hamlet* and foreclosure, 52

Narcissus, 14–15, 38–39, 145
necessity, 27–28, 103, 154, 166–67; acceptance of, 169; of bond/age, 24, 168; calms soul, 169; Clytemaestra serves, 29; dark, 88; of death of fathers, 44; of deracination, 26; and fate, 74; fight, 36–37; and guilt, 167; in Hamlet, 46, 49; hostages to, 104; indifferent, 169; and intention, 41; in *Medea*, 41; in *Moby Dick*, 94; net of, 29; in *Paradise Lost*, 74; resisting, 106; rope of tragic, 119; and self-destruction, 103; separated by, 107; to serve, 29; social, 133; strings of, 44; tragic, 25, 94–97, 152; of tragic bond/age, 31, 155, 168; of tragic thought, 117; vulnerable to, 28; weaving of, 127; and woman, 30
Nemesis, 12; hero triggers, 165; of *Macbeth*, 66; net of, 85, 167;retribution of, 197; of tragedy, 270
net(s), 156–57; amorous, 79; Aphrodite's, 13; binding, 29, 84, 154; as bondage, 17, 27; of bond/age, 13, 110; chained, 13; of character and fate, 110; circling, 29; circular, 13; clap-, 115; of con-sciousness, 127; of death, 30; that destroys, 99; that ensnares, 45, 47, 160; as eros, 34; exacting, 166; on familial house, 166; fatalistic, 27, 29, 32; of

net(s) *(continued)*
  fate, 11–12, 27, 94–95, 109; figurative, 16; fishing, 29; imagery, 11, 101; of language, 133; malevolent, 29; as mesh, 36, 111; of necessity, 29, 94; of nemesis, 85, 107; purse, 11; of ruin, 26, 29–30; safety, 16; seine, 11, 110; static, 157; of tragic bond/age, 99, 112, 119; of tragic necessity,119; trammel, 11, 37, 40–41, 79, 85, 99, 110, 119, 146, 158; twisted, 36; of villanies, 47–48; and web, 165; woven, 94, 109, 167
network(s): of consciousness, 26; of counter claims, 155; intricate, 155, 159; of necessities, 16; of social order, 16–17, 122; of social unity, 17–18
Nietzsche, Friedrich: on Apollonian and Dionysian, 20–21, 72; *Birth of Tragedy*, 21; on language as prison, 21; on music and tragedy, 172; on Socratic hero, 99; on tragic mask, 150; *The Will to Power*, 20–21, 132
nomoi and *philoi*, 42–43, 54, 64, 70–71, 163–64, 167

Odin, 12
Oedipal complex: in *Absalom*, 144; Girard's reading of, 18; Lacan's reappropriation of, 14–16; and *Macbeth*, 71; in *Mayor*, 105; origins of, 17; tragic bond/age in, 108
O'Neill, Eugene: *Long Day's Journey into Night*, 170–71
orchestration: in *Absalom, Absalom!*, 150; in *King Lear*, 63; in *Moby Dick*, 94; and tragedy, 172; and tragic bond/age, 171–72; of via negativa, 67
order(s): collapse of, 43; cosmic, 163; cultural, 18, 24; and difference, 35; Foucault's, 16; of hours, 43; institutionalization of, 145; in natural cycle, 12; patriarchal, 71, 121; reaffirmation of, 28, 169; restoration of, 157; social, 56, 152; taboo and, 32; of things, 16; and transcendence, 161, 169; unthought, 18, 160
Orpheus, 117

past: bondage to, 32, 102, 120, 170; implacable, 118; intrusion of, 113, 141, 157–58; in *Mayor*, 102–4; in mind of man, 135; revelation of, 108; separation from, 118
patriarchy: ascendant, 119 in *Hamlet*, 53; in *Lear*, 58–59; in *Mayor*, 109; phallogocentric, 118; in *Tess*, 111, 119, 120; puritan, 86; purity of, 32
Penelope, 11
Persephone, 118, 120
Picasso, Pablo, 171
Pirithous, 13
Plato: and androgynous being, 117
Poe, Edgar Allan: and *Portrait*, 125
Pound, Ezra: on Henry James, 122
Prometheus, 84, 133

Racine, 37
Ricoeur, Paul: on defilement, 31; on scrupulous soul, 50; on self-seduction, 75; on symbols of evil, 86–87; on transference of bondage, 157; on veneration of order, 32
root(s), 28, 65; autochthonous, 18, 32, 138; and branch, 36; chthonic, 14, 24, 138, 166–67; establishment of, 127; insane, 67; remaining, 36; unfixed, 67
rootedness, 155; in *Antigone*, 36; in *Hippolytus*, 39; in *Macbeth*, 64–68
Rosenwieg, Franz: on silence and tragedy, 171–72
Rossiter, A. P.: on suffering and tragedy, 168

Scheler, Max: on guilt in tragedy, 168; on irony in tragedy, 162
Schopenhauer, William: on tragedy and existence, 160–61
separation: of Apollonian from Dionysian, 41; from Being, 168; as bondage, 32; from boundless, 25–26; chthonic, 27; from Eden, 26; from family, 35; of father and child, 106; from gods, 26; of living and dead, 43; from nature, 18, 26
Sewall, Richard: on *anagnorisis*, 168–69; on transcendence, 161
Shakespeare, William: and Aeschylus, 54, 64; disinheritance in, 166; hierarchy in, 161; and Milton, 172; suffering in, 168; and tragedy, 101; tragic poetry of, 159;

Index

tragic bond/age in *Hamlet*, 41–56; *King Lear*, 55–63, 155–56, *Macbeth*, 80–91, 155–56

silence: and catharsis, 171; as deliverance, 21; deliverance from, 166; ensuing, 53; essence of tragedy, 171–72; Hester's, 86; immense, 135; and music, 172; and order, 17; as punishment, 168; realm of, 67; terrible, 133; utter, 133

Sophocles: Heidegger on, 19; language in, 21; splitting of tragic hero, 157; tragic bond/age in *Antigone*, 33–37, 154–55, *Oedipus Rex*, 30–33, 154–56

sorority: in *Absalom, Absalom!*, 149, 53; in *Antigone*, 36; illicit, 49; in *Portrait*, 121, 29, 158; in *Tess*, 120; and tragic heroine, 165

Steiner, George: on *Antigone*, 19, 33; on death of tragedy, 169–70; on Hegel, 40; on recovery of tragedy, 171–72; on silence and tragedy, 171–72; on Sophoclean tragedy, 161; on tragic conflict, 19–21,

thanatos: in *Antigone*, 34; and eros, 20; in *Hamlet*, 52; in *Hippolytus*, 38
Themis, 12, 21, 27
Theseus, 13
Thomas, Dylan, 24, 51
Thoreau, Henry David: and Isabel Archer, 122, 125
thread(s): that bind, 94, 98, 146, 154; of bondage, 39; goddesses control, 12, 127, 139–40, 164; goddesses weave, 108; guiding, 23; of history, 16; of life, 91; of loom of time, 148; spun, 149; of tragic bond/age, 99; of webbed world, 53
Tisiphone, 12
tragedy: agons of, 19–20; ancient, 43; death of, 169; denouement of, 11; domestic, 163–64; essence of, 21, 171–72; Greek, 24, 42, 37, 56, 152, 157; modern 169; music and, 172; nemesis of, 170; paradox of, 163; plots of, 11–13; preferred, 12; realism and, 159; recognition and, 136, 143, 150; recovery of, 171; Shakespearean, 56, 151–52, 161, 168, 172; and silence, 171–72;

structure of, 12
tragic bond/age: in *Absalom, Absalom!*, 141–53, 159–60; *Agamemnon*, 27–30, 154–55; *Antigone*, 33–37, 154–55; *Hamlet*, 42–54, 155–56; *Heart of Darkness*, 60, 132–40, 158–59; *Hippolytus*, 37–39, 154–55; *King Lear*, 55–63, 155–56; *Macbeth*, 64–72, 156; *The Mayor of Casterbridge*, 101–11, 157–58; *Medea*, 40–41, 154–55; *Moby Dick*, 91–100, 156–57; *Oedipus Rex*, 30–33, 154–55; *Paradise Lost*, 73–82, 156–57; *The Portrait of a Lady*, 121–31, 158–59; *Prometheus Bound*, 25–27, 154–55; *The Scarlet Letter*, 83–90, 156–57; *Tess of the d'Urbervilles*, 111–21, 158; archetype of, 25; catharsis of, 110, 172; definition of, 11–24, 154–172; dialectical nature of, 89; in Greek drama, 25–41, 154–55; and integrity, 160–63; intersection of, 32; knot of, 36; mesh of, 85; and Narcissus, 145; necessity of, 31, 155;net of, 99; and Oedipal complex, 108; orchestration of, 172; paradoxical elements of, 83; and patrimony and matrimony, 111; psychological, 43; reflective examination of, 154–72; resolution of, 72; rope as symbol of, 97; and self-estrangement, 134; transcendence of, 172

uncanny: in childhood, 92–93; confrontation with, 62; feeling, 57; Freud on, 20; harbinger of, 152; in *Heart*, 138; in *Hippolytus*, 37; in Lacan, 15; in *Macbeth*, 72; in *Moby Dick*, 99
Uranus, 12

Van Ghent, Dorothy: on landscape in *Tess*, 112
Varuna, 12
Vernant, Jean-Pierre: anagnorisis and self-recognition, 168; on dike, 167; on hero, 162–63, 165; intelligence in Greek culture, 13; on *metis*, 162; on *nomoi* and *philoi*, 33
via negativa, 169; in *Heart of Darkness*, 136; in *King Lear*, 56–62, 155–56
Vidal-Naquet, Pierre: on fate in *Agamemnon*, 30; on unholy banquet, 28

Watts, Harold: on tragic hero, 162
weave(ing), 11, 96, 165; dynamic, 157; that ensnares, 29; as fate, 94; integrity of, 152; language as, 21, 24; in *Moby Dick*, 94–98, 100; of net, 127, 167; Penelopean, 11; that protects, 14; of social integrity, 161
web: of existence, 13; of fabrication, 17; fate, 12; of language, 92; into net, 165; of relationship, 24; semantic, 16; silver's worth of, 29; -like Wessex, 104; of world, 16; world's, 164

Wickens, Carl: on Demeter in *Tess*, 118
Wilde, Oscar: on nemesis and inheredity, 164
Williams, Raymond: on modern tragedy, 169–70; on social integrity, 161
Williams, Tennessee: *The Glass Menagerie*, 170–71
Woolf, Virginia: *A Room of One's Own* and the canon, 23

Zeus, 12, 25–26, 30